Publication Manual

of the American Psychological Association

Publication Manual

of the American Psychological Association

Fifth Edition

American Psychological Association • *Washington, DC*

First Printing July 2001
Second Printing August 2001

Published by
American Psychological Association
750 First Street, NE
Washington, DC 20002-4242
www.apa.org

To order
APA Order Department
P.O. Box 92984
Washington, DC 20090-2984
Tel: (800) 374-2721, Direct: (202) 336-5510
Fax: (202) 336-5502, TDD/TTY: (202) 336-6123
Online: www.apa.org/books/
Email: order@apa.org

In the U.K., Europe, Africa, and the Middle East, copies may be ordered from
American Psychological Association
3 Henrietta Street
Covent Garden, London
WC2E 8LU England

Typeset in Minion Display Regular and Memphis by EPS Group Inc., Easton, MD

Printer: Automated Graphic Systems, White Plains, MD
Cover Designer: Naylor Design, Washington, DC
Interior Designer: Anne Masters Design, Washington, DC
Technical/Production Editor: Catherine Hudson
Supervisor, Technical Editing and Design: Christina Davis
Copyeditor: Kathryn Hyde Loomis

Library of Congress Cataloging-in-Publication Data
Publication manual of the American Psychological Association.—5th ed.
     p. cm.
   Includes bibliographical references and index.
   ISBN 1-55798-790-4 (acid-free paper). — ISBN 1-55798-791-2 (pbk: acid-free paper). — ISBN 1-55798-810-2 (wir-o: acid-free paper)
     1. Psychology—Authorship—Handbooks, manuals, etc. 2. Social sciences—Authorship—Handbooks, manuals, etc. 3. Psychological literature—Publishing—Handbooks, manuals, etc. 4. Social science literature—Publishing—Handbooks, manuals, etc. I. American Psychological Association.
BF76.7 .P83 2001
808'.06615—dc21   2001022631

British Library Cataloguing-in-Publication Data
A CIP record is available from the British Library.

Printed in the United States of America

Contents

5 Manuscript Preparation and Sample Papers to Be Submitted for Publication **283**

List of Tables, Table Examples, Figures, and Figure Examples

Figures

Figure Examples

Preface

In 1928 editors and business managers of anthropological and psychological journals met to discuss the form of journal manuscripts and to write instructions for their preparation. The report of this meeting, which was chaired by Madison Bentley and sponsored by the National Research Council, is the forerunner of this book. The report was published as a seven-page article in the February 1929 issue of the *Psychological Bulletin*, a journal of the American Psychological Association (APA). The group agreed that it would not dictate to authors; instead, it recommended a "standard of procedures, to which exceptions would doubtless be necessary, but to which reference might be made in cases of doubt" ("Instructions," 1929, p. 57; see section 9.01 for references to the predecessors of this edition of the *Publication Manual*).

In the 70 years that followed, those "instructions" were revised and expanded a number of times. The first edition of the instructions under the title of *Publication Manual* was actually a 60-page supplement to the *Psychological Bulletin* published in 1952.

It was another 22 years before a new edition was published in 1974 with 136 pages. Publication of the 208-page third edition occurred in 1983, and the fourth edition of 368 pages rolled off the presses in 1994.

Seven years have elapsed since the last edition, during which time great changes have occurred in the publishing world and in the technology used by authors, editors, and publishers. The fourth edition stood the test of time well, but eventually there were more matters to be dealt with than could be easily accommodated on the APA Web site for updates. In

1999 the APA Publications and Communications Board authorized work to begin on this fifth edition of the *Publication Manual.*

Leslie Dodson ably served as the project leader for the revision, and many APA members and staff contributed their time, energy, and expertise to the preparation and editing of this volume. Mark Appelbaum and his colleagues on the Statistics Task Force (Leona S. Aiken, Joel R. Levin, Robert Rosenthal, and Howard Wainer) had a particularly difficult assignment. Although not always in agreement on the specifics, the task force did agree on the need to provide some additional assistance to authors in dealing with statistical representations in manuscripts. Lenore W. Harmon, the APA Chief Editorial Advisor, drew on her experience to work on the ethics and authorship sections and to chair the Task Force on the Publication of Case Material (with Janice Birk, Clara Hill, Ross Parke, and William Stiles). Kathleen Sheedy took aim at the moving target of electronic referencing and manuscript preparation. She will continue working with the APA Internet Services staff to keep the new APA Style Web site up to date with changes in this area as they occur. Susan Knapp and Demarie Jackson provided examples, text, and guidance along the way.

There is a section in the foreword to the fourth edition that aptly characterizes the *Publication Manual.*

> The *Publication Manual* presents explicit style requirements but acknowledges that alternatives are sometimes necessary; authors should balance the rules of the *Publication Manual* with good judgment. Because the written language of psychology changes more slowly than psychology itself, the *Publication Manual* does not offer solutions for all stylistic problems. In that sense, it is a transitional document: Its style requirements are based on the existing scientific literature rather than imposed on the literature.
>
> Every edition of the *Publication Manual* has been intended to aid authors in the preparation of manuscripts. The 1929 guide could gently advise authors on style, because there were then only about 200 authors who published in the 4 existing APA journals. Today,

the editors of APA's 24 primary journals consider close to 6,000 manuscript submissions per year (of which approximately 1,400 reach print). Without APA style conventions, the time and effort required to review and edit manuscripts would prohibit timely and cost-effective publication and would make clear communication harder to achieve.

The numbers are higher today, of course. There are now 27 APA primary journals. And at least a thousand other journals in psychology, the behavioral sciences, nursing, and personnel administration use the *Publication Manual* as their style guide. This standardization has greatly facilitated the communication of new ideas and research and simplified the tasks of publishers, editors, authors, and readers as well as enabled linkages of electronic files across articles and across publishers.

As noted in the foreword to the fourth edition, however, this "standard" is not static. Our APA Web site devoted to the *Publication Manual* will provide updates and the latest information on changes in APA style and in APA policies and procedures that will affect authors as they prepare their manuscripts.

What's new in APA Style?
Visit the APA *Publication Manual*
Web site:
www.apastyle.org

Introduction

Rules for the preparation of manuscripts should contribute to clear communication. Take, for example, the rule that some editors consider to be the most important: Double-space everything. A double-spaced manuscript allows each person in the publication process to function comfortably and efficiently. Authors and editors have space for handwritten notes; typists and typesetters can easily read all marks. Such mechanical rules, and most style rules, are usually the results of a confluence of established authorities and common usage. These rules introduce the uniformity necessary to convert manuscripts written in many styles to printed pages edited in one consistent style. They spare readers a distracting variety of forms throughout a work and permit readers to give full attention to content.

The rules provided in the *Publication Manual of the American Psychological Association* are drawn from an extensive body of psychological literature, from editors and authors experienced in psychological writing, and from recognized authorities on publication practices. Writers who conscientiously use the *Publication Manual* will express their ideas in a form and a style both accepted by and familiar to a broad, established readership in psychology.

Early versions of the *Publication Manual* were intended exclusively for American Psychological Association (APA) authors. Recognizing a need for commonly accepted guidelines in psychology as a whole, APA published the 1974 second edition for a much wider audience. The third edition, published in 1983, also was an extensive revision and achieved the goal of becoming a major guide for authors, editors, students, typists, and publishers; it has been used widely by members of graduate and undergraduate departments of psychology. The 1994 fourth edition was guided by two principles: specificity and sensitivity. With that in mind there were a number of revisions made to the *Publication Manual* on reporting results and statistics as well as on ethical principles in scientific publishing and on writing without bias.

This fifth edition builds on the fourth edition, updating and clarifying the formats for electronic and legal references, adding sections on the content of methodological and case study reports, outlining revisions to procedures (e.g., reporting of potential conflict of interest), and expanding on some of the issues involved in data sharing and verification. The statistics section has been largely rewritten to reflect emerging standards in the field (although there are still a number of disagreements on presentation). Instructions for manuscript preparation now take advantage of the nearly universal use of sophisticated word processors: the hanging indent is back, and authors can represent italicized and bold-faced entries as they will appear in print. The paragraphs that follow briefly describe each chapter and highlight the changes and additions in this new edition.

Organization of the Fifth Edition

Chapter 1, Content and Organization of a Manuscript, describes review, theoretical, methodological, and case study articles as well as empirical studies. There are guidelines on describing participants of a study and on reporting statistics, with the goal of enabling researchers to replicate published studies. Instructions on the preparation of abstracts have been updated.

Chapter 2, Expressing Ideas and Reducing Bias in Language, emphasizes the importance of organizing one's thinking and writing and of making every word contribute to clear and concise communication. Guidelines are included for reducing bias in language.

Chapter 3, APA Editorial Style, describes many of the mechanical aspects of editorial style in APA journals, including punctuation, spelling, capitalization, italics, abbreviations, quotations, mathematical copy, headings, tables, illustrations, footnotes, and citations in text.

Chapter 4, Reference List, is now a chapter in its own right and contains, in addition to a description of the components of common references, more examples, including updates on some forms for referencing electronic media.

Chapter 5, Manuscript Preparation and Sample Papers to be Submitted for Publication, provides instructions on preparing manuscripts with a word processor. The sample paper and outlines illustrate the format and application of APA style. Labels on the sample paper give more specific cross-references to relevant parts of the *Publication Manual.*

Chapter 6, Material Other Than Journal Articles, describes such manuscripts as theses, dissertations, student papers, material for oral presentations, and brief reports. Guidance is provided on how dissertations may be readied for publication as journal articles.

Chapter 7, Manuscript Acceptance and Production, provides instructions to authors on preparing the accepted manuscript for production. Ways to review copyedited manuscripts and typeset proofs of articles are also explained. A sample manuscript is provided to demonstrate how a manuscript should be coded for electronic processing.

Chapter 8, Journals Program of the American Psychological Association, discusses the general policies that govern all APA journals and includes discussion of the ethical principles of the APA that apply to authorship and publication. The chapter also explains the editorial review process and the management of submitted manuscripts.

Chapter 9, the **Bibliography,** lists works on the history of the *Publication Manual* and annotated references for further reading.

Appendixes A and **B** are checklists authors should review to ensure that they have met the criteria for submitting manuscripts for publication and for transmitting accepted manuscripts for electronic production, respectively. **Appendix C** is an extract from the APA Ethical Principles containing all of the sections that may have relevance to authorship and to publication. **Appendix D** contains reference examples for legal materials using the *Blue Book.* Finally, **Appendix E** is a sample cover letter illustrating the kinds of information an author might include when submitting a manuscript for consideration to a journal editor.

The **Index** has been expanded and includes section numbers as well as page numbers. Finding your way around this new edition should be a great deal easier.

Specific Style Changes in the Fifth Edition

Readers who are familiar with the fourth edition of the *Publication Manual* will find, besides the revisions and additions outlined in the previous section, a detailed listing of specific changes in style requirements introduced with the fifth edition at the APA Web site for the *Publication Manual.*

Changes in requirements for manuscript preparation may initially be inconvenient and frustrating to authors submitting papers. Such changes arise because of changes in APA policy, in production technology, in the economy, or in the state of science. Should future changes in requirements occur before the preparation of another edition of the *Publication Manual,* they will be published on the APA Web site and keyed to this edition.

Although the *Publication Manual* provides some specific rules of usage and grammar, it does not address general problems of writing and language, which are adequately dealt with elsewhere. The *Publication Manual* does not cover exceptional writing situations in psychology in which style precedents may need to be set. When you are without a rule or a reference and the answer to a question can be narrowed to several reasonable choices, aim for simplicity, plain language, and direct statements.

How to Use the *Publication Manual*

The *Publication Manual* describes requirements for the preparation and submission of manuscripts for publication. Chapters in the *Publication Manual* provide substantively different kinds of information and are arranged in the sequence in which one considers the elements of manuscript preparation, from initial concept through publication. Although each chapter is autonomous, each chapter also develops from the preceding chapter. For example, chapter 1 explains how to organize the parts of a manuscript, and chapter 2 describes how to express specific ideas within the manuscript. Chapters 3 and 4 describe APA style and bibliographic reference format. Chapters 5, 6, and 7, which concern preparing a manuscript, provide information you will use only after you have reviewed the first four chapters; that is, you will not prepare your manuscript until you have organized and written it. To use the *Publication Manual* most effectively, you should be familiar with the contents of all its chapters before you begin writing.

The design of the fifth edition provides specific aids that allow you to locate information quickly. Format aids, such as changes in typeface, will help you easily locate and identify the answers to questions on style and format. Organizational aids, such as checklists and cross-references to other sections, will help you organize and write the manuscript and check major points of style and format when you have finished. Do not use these aids independently of the explanatory text; they highlight important information, but they do not include everything you need to know to prepare your manuscript. Lists of some of these format and organizational aids follow.

Format Aids

- The examples of points of style or format that appear in chapters 3 and 4 are in a typeface that looks like that produced on a word processor. This typeface not only helps you locate the examples quickly but shows how material appears when typed:

  This is an example of the word processor typeface.

  (Note that manuscript examples are not fully double-spaced. Authors should, however, follow the instructions in chapter 5 for manuscript preparation.)
- A detailed table of contents, which lists the sections for each chapter, helps you locate categories of information quickly.
- A list of tables and a list of figures, which appear in the table of contents, help you locate specific tables and figures.

- Sample tables and figures give you guidance on preparing your own tables and figures in what the APA considers ideal forms.
- An improved and comprehensive index helps you locate section and page numbers for specific topics quickly.
- The tabs and key (see inside back cover) help you easily locate frequently used sections.

Organizational Aids

- A section on evaluating content (section 1.02) lists questions you can use—before you begin writing—to decide whether the research is likely to merit publication.
- A section at the end of chapter 1 on the quality of presentation lists questions you can use to evaluate the organization and presentation of information in the manuscript.
- Table Examples 1–12 show how tables should be prepared. A table checklist (section 3.74) provides a final review of major points of table style and format.
- Figure Examples 1–10 show how figures should be prepared. A figure checklist (section 3.86) provides a final review of major points of figure style and format.
- Sample papers and outlines (Figures 5.1–5.3) are provided: The sample one-experiment paper shows how a typical manuscript looks as prepared with a word-processing program (Figure 5.1). The outlines for a sample two-experiment and a sample review paper (Figures 5.2 and 5.3) show the typical organization of these kinds of papers.
- Section 9.03 of the Bibliography lists publications that provide more information on topics discussed in the *Publication Manual.*

Publication

Manual

of the American Psychological Association

CHAPTER ONE

Content and Organization of a Manuscript

Research is complete only when the results are shared with the scientific community. Although such sharing is accomplished in various ways, both formal and informal, the traditional medium for communicating research results is the scientific journal.

The scientific journal is the repository of the accumulated knowledge of a field. In the literature are distilled the successes and failures, the information, and the perspectives contributed by many investigators over many years. Familiarity with the literature allows an individual investigator to avoid needlessly repeating work that has been done before, to build on existing work, and in turn to contribute something new. A literature built of meticulously prepared, carefully reviewed contributions thus fosters the growth of a field.

Although writing for publication is sometimes tedious, the rewards of publication are many for the writer, the reader, and the science. The writing process initially requires a thorough review and evaluation of previous work in the literature, which helps acquaint one with the field as a whole and establishes whether one's idea is truly new and significant. Authors beginning the writing process will find that there is no better way to clarify and organize their ideas than by trying to explain them to someone else. In fact, scientists "will get to really know a field only if [they] become sufficiently involved to contribute to it" (Orne, 1981, p. 4; see section 9.02 for references cited in the *Publication Manual*). Thus, the content and the organization of a scientific manuscript reflect the logical thinking in scientific investigation, and the preparation of a manuscript for journal publication is an integral part of the individual research effort.

Just as each investigator benefits from the publication process, so the body of scientific literature depends for its vitality on the active participation of individual investigators. Authors of individual scientific articles contribute most to the literature when they communicate clearly and concisely.

This chapter discusses several considerations authors should weigh before writing for publication—considerations both about their own research and about the scientific publishing tradition in which they are to take part. First, the answers to questions about the quality of the research will determine whether the article is worth writing or is publishable. Second, consideration of contributions to the research will suggest who will take credit and responsibility as an author. Third, a survey of the typical kinds of articles will suggest which basic organization of the article would be most effective. Fourth, the parts of a manuscript are described. Consistency of presentation and format within and across journal articles is an aspect of the scientific publishing tradition that enables authors to present material easily. Finally, questions that address the quality of presentation will help writers to judge the thoroughness, originality, and clarity of their work and to facilitate communication with others within the same tradition.

Quality of Content

No amount of skill in writing can disguise research that is poorly designed or managed. Indeed, such defects are a major cause for the rejection of manuscripts. Before committing a report to manuscript form, you as a potential author should critically review the quality of research and ask if the research is sufficiently important and free from flaws to justify publication. If the report came from another researcher, would you read it? Would it influence your work? Most researchers have in the back of a drawer one or more studies that failed to meet this test. No matter how well written, a paper that reflects poor methods is unacceptable.

1.01 *Designing and Reporting Research*

You, as an author, should familiarize yourself with the criteria and standards that editors and reviewers use to evaluate manuscripts. (See sections 8.12–8.14 for a discussion of the review process.) Editors find in submitted papers the following kinds of defects in the design and reporting of research:

- piecemeal publication, that is, the separation of a single substantial report into a series of overlapping papers;
- the reporting of only a single correlation—even a significant correlation between two variables rarely has any interpretable value;
- the reporting of negative results without attention to a power analysis (see section 1.10);
- lack of congruence between a study's specific operations (including those related to the design and analysis) and the author's interpretation and discussion of the study's outcomes (e.g., failure to report the statistical test at the level being claimed);
- failure to report effect sizes;
- failure to build in needed controls, often for a subtle but important aspect of the study; and
- exhaustion of a problem—there is a difference between ongoing research that explores the limits of the generality of a research finding and the endless production of papers that report trivial changes in previous research.

1.02 *Evaluating Content*

Before preparing a manuscript, you should evaluate the research and judge that it is an important contribution to the field. An editorial by Brendan A. Maher (1974) will be helpful in making that judgment, and a humorous account by Robert R. Holt (1959, "Researchmanship or How to Write a Dissertation in Clinical Psychology Without Really Trying") makes some sharp but pertinent points about research design. The following checklist (based on Bartol, 1981) may also help in assessing the quality of content and in deciding whether the research is likely to merit publication:

- Is the research question significant, and is the work original and important?
- Have the instruments been demonstrated to have satisfactory reliability and validity?
- Are the outcome measures clearly related to the variables with which the investigation is concerned?
- Does the research design fully and unambiguously test the hypothesis?
- Are the participants representative of the population to which generalizations are made?
- Did the researcher observe ethical standards in the treatment of participants—for example, if deception was used for humans?
- Is the research at an advanced enough stage to make the publication of results meaningful?

Characteristics of Articles

1.03 *Authorship*

Authorship is reserved for people who make a primary contribution to and hold primary responsibility for the data, concepts, and interpretation of results for a published work (Huth, 1987). Authorship encompasses not only those who do the actual writing but also those who have made substantial scientific contributions to a study. This concept of authorship is discussed in the "Ethical Principles of Psychologists and Code of Conduct" (APA, 1992a), Principle 6.23, which is reprinted in Appendix C and discussed in section 8.05.

To prevent misunderstanding and to preserve professional reputations and relationships, it is best to establish as early as possible in a research project who will be listed as an author, what the order of authorship will be, and who will receive an alternative form of recognition (see sections 1.15, 7.01, and 8.05).

1.04 *Types of Articles*

Journal articles are usually reports of empirical studies, review articles, theoretical articles, methodological articles, and case studies. They are primary publications (for a discussion of duplicate publication, see section 8.05).

Reports of empirical studies are reports of original research. They typically consist of distinct sections that reflect the stages in the research process and that appear in the sequence of these stages:

- **introduction:** development of the problem under investigation and statement of the purpose of the investigation,
- **method:** description of the method used to conduct the investigation,
- **results:** report of the results that were found, and
- **discussion:** interpretation and discussion of the implications of the results.

(See Figures 5.1 and 5.2 in chapter 5 for a sample one-experiment paper and an outline of a sample two-experiment paper, respectively.)

Review articles, including meta-analyses, are critical evaluations of material that has already been published. By organizing, integrating, and evaluating previously published material, the author of a review article considers the progress of current research toward clarifying a problem. In a sense, a review article is tutorial in that the author

- defines and clarifies the problem;
- summarizes previous investigations in order to inform the reader of the state of current research;
- identifies relations, contradictions, gaps, and inconsistencies in the literature; and
- suggests the next step or steps in solving the problem.

The components of review articles, unlike the sections of reports of empirical studies, are arranged by relationship rather than by chronology. (See Figure 5.3 for an outline of a sample review paper.)

Theoretical articles are papers in which the author draws on existing research literature to advance theory in any area of psychology. Review and theoretical articles are often similar in structure, but theoretical articles present empirical information only when it affects theoretical issues. The author traces the development of theory to expand and refine theoretical constructs. Ordinarily, the author presents a new theory. Alternatively, the author may analyze existing theory, pointing out flaws or demonstrating the superiority of one theory over another. In this type of theoretical analysis, the author customarily examines a theory's internal and external consistency, that is, whether a theory is self-contradictory and whether the theory and empirical observation contradict each other. The sections of a theoretical article, like those of a review article, are usually ordered by relationship rather than by chronology. (See Figure 5.3 in chapter 5 for an outline of a sample review paper.)

Methodological articles are papers in which new methodological approaches, modifications of existing methods, and discussions of quantitative and data analytic approaches are presented to the community of researchers. These papers should focus on the methodological or data analytic approach at hand and should introduce empirical data only as an illustration of the approach. Methodological articles should be presented at a level that makes them accessible to the well-read researcher and should present sufficient detail that researchers can assess the applicability of the methodology to their research problem. Further, the article should allow the reader to reasonably compare the proposed approach to currently used alternative approaches and to execute the approach. In methodological articles, highly technical materials (e.g., derivations, proofs, details of simulations) should be presented in appendixes to improve the overall readability of the article.

Case studies are papers in which the author describes case material obtained while working with an individual or organization to illustrate a problem, to indicate a means for solving a problem, or to shed light on needed research or theoretical matters. In writing case studies, authors carefully consider the balance between providing important illustrative material and using confidential case material responsibly. (See Appendix C, Ethical Principle 5.08, Use of Confidential Information for Didactic or Other Purposes.) Confidentiality is generally handled by one of two means. One option is to prepare the descriptive case material, present it to the subject of the case report, and obtain written consent for its publication from the subject. The other option is to disguise some aspects of the case material so that neither the subject nor those who know the subject would be identifiable. Such disguising of cases is a delicate issue, because it is essential not to change variables related to the phenomena being described. Three main strategies have emerged for achieving this: (a) altering specific characteristics, (b) limiting the description of specific characteristics, and (c) obfuscating case detail by adding extraneous material. For additional information on the presentation of case material, see VandenBos (2001).

Other, less frequently published types of articles in APA journals include brief reports, comments and replies on previously published articles, and monographs. Although the contents of these articles are dissimilar, the manuscripts should still be logically and coherently organized according to the guidelines described in the previous paragraphs. Authors should refer to the journal to which they are submitting the manuscript for specific information regarding these kinds of articles.

> For more information on how to protect
> confidentiality in case reports, see
> www.apastyle.org

1.05 *Length, Headings, and Tone*

Before beginning to write, you should consider the following major characteristics of a journal article: length, headings, and tone.

Length. Determine the typical length of an article in the journal for which you are writing, and do not exceed that length unless you are writing a monograph or some other exceptional material. To estimate how long your manuscript might run in printed pages for most APA journals, count every manuscript page (including the title and abstract pages, tables, and figures) and divide the number of manuscript pages by 4 (i.e., 1 printed page = 4 manuscript pages).

Discursive writing often obscures an author's main points, and long manuscripts are frequently improved by condensing. If a paper is too long, shorten it by stating points clearly and directly, confining the discussion to the specific problem under investigation, deleting or combining tabular material, eliminating repetition across sections, and writing in the active voice.

Headings. Carefully outline the hierarchy of the ideas you wish to present, and use headings to convey the sequence and levels of importance. Headings help a reader grasp the article's organization and the relative importance of the parts of the article (see section 3.30).

Tone. Although scientific writing differs in form from literary writing, it need not and should not lack style or be dull. In describing your research, present the ideas and findings directly, but aim for an interesting and compelling manner that reflects your involvement with the problem (see chapter 2 on expression of ideas).

Scientific writing often contrasts the positions of different researchers. Differences should be presented in a professional, noncombative manner: For example, "Fong and Nisbett did not consider . . ." is acceptable, whereas "Fong and Nisbett completely overlooked . . ." is not.

Parts of a Manuscript

Most journal articles published in psychology are reports of empirical studies, and therefore this section emphasizes their preparation.

1.06 *Title Page*

Title. A title should summarize the main idea of the paper simply and, if possible, with style. It should be a concise statement of the main topic and should identify the actual variables or theoretical issues under investigation and the relationship between them. An example of a good title is "Effect of Transformed Letters on Reading Speed."

A title should be fully explanatory when standing alone. Although its principal function is to inform readers about the study, a title is also used as a statement of article content for abstracting and information services, such as APA's *Psychological Abstracts* and PsycINFO database. A good title easily compresses to the short title used for editorial purposes and to the running head used with the published article (see end of this section and section 5.15).

Titles are commonly indexed and compiled in numerous reference works. Therefore, avoid words that serve no useful purpose; they increase length and can mislead indexers. For example, the words *method* and *results* do not normally appear in a title, nor should such redundancies as "A Study of" or "An Experimental Investigation of" begin a title. Avoid using abbreviations in a title: Spelling out all terms will help ensure accurate, complete indexing of the article. The recommended length for a title is 10 to 12 words.

Author's name (byline) and institutional affiliation. Every manuscript includes a byline consisting of two parts: the name of the author and the institution where the investigation was conducted (without the words *by* or *from the*).

- *Author's name (byline).* The preferred form of an author's name is first name, middle initial(s), and last name; this form reduces the likelihood of mistaken identity. To assist researchers as well as librarians, use the same form for publication throughout your career; that is, do not use initials on one manuscript and the full name on a later one. Determining whether Juanita A. Smith is the same person as J. A. Smith, J. Smith, or A. Smith can be difficult, particularly when citations span several years and institutional affiliations change. Omit all titles (e.g., Dr., Professor) and degrees (e.g., PhD, PsyD, EdD).
- *Institutional affiliation.* The affiliation identifies the location where the author or authors conducted the investigation, which is usually

an institution. Include a dual affiliation only if two institutions con-tributed substantial financial support to the study. Include no more than two affiliations. When an author has no institutional affiliation, list the city and state of residence below the author's name. If the institutional affiliation has changed since the work was completed, give the current affiliation in the author identification notes. (See sections 3.89 and 5.15 for format instructions.)

Running head for publication. The running head is an abbreviated title that is printed at the top of the pages of a published article to identify the article for readers. The head should be a maximum of 50 characters, counting letters, punctuation, and spaces between words.

1.07 *Abstract*

An abstract is a brief, comprehensive summary of the contents of the article; it allows readers to survey the contents of an article quickly, and, like a title, it enables abstracting and information services to index and retrieve articles. All APA journals except *Contemporary Psychology: APA Review of Books* require an abstract.

A well-prepared abstract can be the most important paragraph in your article. "Once printed in the journal, your abstract is just beginning an active and frequently very long life as part of collections of abstracts" in printed and electronic forms (APA, 1984). Most people will have their first contact with an article by seeing just the abstract, usually on a computer screen with several other abstracts, as they are doing a literature search through an electronic abstract-retrieval system. Readers frequently decide on the basis of the abstract whether to read the entire article; this is true whether the reader is at a computer or is thumbing through a journal. The abstract needs to be dense with information but also read-able, well organized, brief, and self-contained. Also, embedding many key words in your abstract will enhance the user's ability to find it. A good abstract is

■ **accurate:** Ensure that the abstract correctly reflects the purpose and content of the manuscript. Do not include information that does not appear in the body of the paper. If the study extends or replicates previous research, note this in the abstract, and cite the author (initials and surname) and year. Comparing an abstract with an outline of the paper's headings is a useful way to verify its accuracy.

- **self-contained:** Define all abbreviations (except units of measurement) and acronyms. Spell out names of tests and drugs (use generic names for drugs). Define unique terms. Paraphrase rather than quote. Include names of authors (initials and surnames) and dates of publication in citations of other publications (and give a full bibliographic citation in the article's reference list).
- **concise and specific:** Make each sentence maximally informative, especially the lead sentence. Be as brief as possible. Abstracts should not exceed 120 words. Begin the abstract with the most important information (but do not waste space by repeating the title). This may be the purpose or thesis or perhaps the results and conclusions. Include in the abstract only the four or five most important concepts, findings, or implications.

Ways to improve conciseness:

- Use digits for all numbers, except those that begin a sentence (consider recasting a sentence that begins with a number).
- Abbreviate liberally (e.g., use *vs.* for *versus*), although all abbreviations that need to be explained in the text (see sections 3.21–3.26, 3.29) must also be explained on first use in the abstract.
- Use the active voice (but without the personal pronouns *I* or *we*, see section 2.04).

- **nonevaluative:** Report rather than evaluate; do not add to or comment on what is in the body of the manuscript.
- **coherent and readable:** Write in clear and vigorous prose. Use verbs rather than their noun equivalents and the active rather than the

passive voice. Use the present tense to describe results with continuing applicability or conclusions drawn; use the past tense to describe specific variables manipulated or tests applied. Use the third person rather than the first person. Avoid boilerplate sentences and phrases that contain no real information (e.g., "Policy implications are discussed" or "It is concluded that").

An abstract of a *report of an empirical study* should describe

- the problem under investigation, in one sentence if possible;
- the participants or subjects, specifying pertinent characteristics, such as number, type, age, sex, and genus and species;
- the experimental method, including the apparatus, data-gathering procedures, complete test names, and complete generic names and the dosage and routes of administration of any drugs (particularly if the drugs are novel or important to the study);
- the findings, including statistical significance levels; and
- the conclusions and the implications or applications.

An abstract for a *review or theoretical article* should describe

- the topic, in one sentence;
- the purpose, thesis, or organizing construct and the scope (comprehensive or selective) of the article;
- the sources used (e.g., personal observation, published literature); and
- the conclusions.

An abstract for a *methodological paper* should describe

- the general class of method being proposed or discussed;
- the essential features of the proposed method;

- the range of application of the proposed method; and
- the behavior of the method, including its power and robustness to violations of assumptions.

An abstract for a *case study* should describe

- the subject and relevant characteristics of the individual or organization presented;
- the nature of or solution to a problem illustrated by the case example; and
- the questions raised for additional research or theory.

An abstract that is accurate, succinct, quickly comprehensible, and informative will increase the audience and the future retrievability of your article. You may submit only one version of the abstract. If it exceeds the 120-word limit, the abstractors in some secondary services may truncate your abstract to fit their databases, and this could impair retrievability. For information on how abstracts are used to retrieve articles, consult the *PsycINFO User Reference Manual* (APA, 1992b).

Note to authors of book chapters: Book chapters do not usually require an abstract. However, the early inclusion of a specific purpose statement will benefit the reader as well as help abstracting and indexing services to construct appropriate content representations that will assist users in retrieving your chapter. Providing up front a clear statement of the purpose and content of your chapter increases the probability of accurate representation in secondary electronic databases. For chapters that report empirical research, either the introductory sentences or the purpose statement could include a summary of the study, sample description, and findings.

1.08 *Introduction*

Introduce the problem. The body of a paper opens with an introduction that presents the specific problem under study and describes the research strategy. Because the introduction is clearly identified by its position in the article, it is not labeled. Before writing the introduction, consider

- Why is this problem important?
- How do the hypothesis and the experimental design relate to the problem?
- What are the theoretical implications of the study, and how does the study relate to previous work in the area?
- What theoretical propositions are tested, and how were they derived?

A good introduction answers these questions in a paragraph or two and, by summarizing the relevant arguments and the data, gives the reader a firm sense of what was done and why.

Develop the background. Discuss the literature, but do not include an exhaustive historical review. Assume that the reader is knowledgeable about the field for which you are writing and does not require a complete digest. A scholarly review of earlier work provides an appropriate history and recognizes the priority of the work of others. Citation of and specific credit to relevant earlier works are part of the author's scientific and scholarly responsibility and are essential for the growth of a cumulative science. At the same time, cite and reference only works pertinent to the specific issue and not works of only tangential or general significance. If you summarize earlier works, avoid nonessential details; instead, emphasize pertinent findings, relevant methodological issues, and major conclusions. Refer the reader to general surveys or reviews of the topic if they are available.

Demonstrate the logical continuity between previous and present work. Develop the problem with enough breadth and clarity to make it generally understood by as wide a professional audience as possible. Do not let the goal of brevity mislead you into writing a statement intelligible only to the specialist.

Controversial issues, when relevant, should be treated fairly. A simple statement that certain studies support one conclusion and others support another conclusion is better than an extensive and inconclusive discussion. Whatever your personal opinion, avoid animosity and ad hominem arguments in presenting the controversy. Do not support your position or justify your research by citing established authorities out of context.

State the purpose and rationale. After you have introduced the problem and developed the background material, you are in a position to explain your approach to solving the problem. Make this statement in the closing paragraphs of the introduction. At this point, a definition of the variables and a formal statement of your hypotheses give clarity to the paper. Bear in mind the following questions in closing the introduction: What variables did I plan to manipulate? What results did I expect, and why did I expect them? The logic behind "Why did I expect them?" should be made explicit. Clearly develop the rationale for each hypothesis.

1.09 *Method*

The Method section describes in detail how the study was conducted. Such a description enables the reader to evaluate the appropriateness of your methods and the reliability and the validity of your results. It also permits experienced investigators to replicate the study if they so desire.

If your paper is an update of an ongoing or earlier study and the method has been published in detail elsewhere, you may refer the reader to that source and simply give a brief synopsis of the method in this section.

> We present cross-sectional and 3-year longitudinal data from a study of adults aged 55 to 84. . . . The memory tasks were those used in our previous research (Zelinski et al., 1990; Zelinski, Gilewski, & Thompson, 1980).

(See section 1.12 for treatment of multiple experiments.)

Identify subsections. It is both conventional and expedient to divide the Method section into labeled subsections. These usually include descriptions of the participants or subjects, the apparatus (or materials), and the procedure. If the design of the experiment is complex or the stimuli require detailed description, additional subsections or subheadings to divide the subsections may be warranted to help readers find specific information. Your own judgment is the best guide on what number and type of subheadings to use (see section 3.32 for guidelines.)

Include in these subsections only the information essential to comprehend and replicate the study. Insufficient detail leaves the reader with questions; too much detail burdens the reader with irrelevant information.

Participants or subjects. Appropriate identification of research subjects and clientele is critical to the science and practice of psychology, particularly for assessing the results (making comparisons across groups); generalizing the findings; and making comparisons in replications, literature reviews, or secondary data analyses. The sample should be adequately described, and it should be representative (if it is not, give the underlying reasons). Conclusions and interpretations should not go beyond what the sample would warrant.

When humans participated as the subjects of the study, report the procedures for selecting and assigning them and the agreements and payments made. (If case studies are included, see Appendix C, Ethical Principle 5.08, on informed consent and confidentiality issues.) Report major demographic characteristics such as sex, age, and race/ethnicity, and, where possible and appropriate, characteristics such as socioeconomic status, disability status, and sexual orientation. When a particular demographic characteristic is an experimental variable or is important for the interpretation of results, describe the group specifically—for example, in terms of national origin, level of education, health status, and language preference and use:

> The second group included 40 Central American women between the ages of 20 and 30 years, all of whom had emigrated from El Salvador, had at least 12 years of education, had been permanent residents of the United States for at least 10 years, and lived in Washington, DC.

To determine how far the data can be generalized, it may be useful to identify subgroups:

> The Asian sample included 30 Chinese and 45 Vietnamese persons

or

> Among the Latino and Hispanic American men, 20 were Mexican American and 20 were Puerto Rican.

Even when a characteristic is not an analytic variable, reporting it may give readers a more complete understanding of the sample and often proves useful in meta-analytic studies that incorporate the article's results.

When animals are the subjects, report the genus, species, and strain number or other specific identification, such as the name and location of the supplier and the stock designation. Give the number of animals and the animals' sex, age, weight, and physiological condition. In addition, specify all essential details of their treatment and handling so that the investigation can be successfully replicated.

Give the total number of subjects and the number assigned to each experimental condition. If any did not complete the experiment, state how many and explain why they did not continue.

When you submit your manuscript, indicate to the journal editor that the treatment of subjects (people or animals) was in accordance with the ethical standards of the APA (see Principles 6.1–6.20 in the "Ethical Principles of Psychologists and Code of Conduct," APA, 1992a).

Apparatus. The subsection on apparatus briefly describes the apparatus or materials used and their function in the experiment. Standard laboratory equipment, such as furniture, stopwatches, or screens, can usually be mentioned without detail. Identify specialized equipment obtained from a commercial supplier by the model number of the equipment and the supplier's name and location. Complex or custom-made equipment may be illustrated by a drawing or photograph. A detailed description of complex equipment may be included in an appendix.

Procedure. The subsection on procedure summarizes each step in the execution of the research. Include the instructions to the participants, the formation of the groups, and the specific experimental manipulations. Describe randomization, counterbalancing, and other control features in the design. Summarize or paraphrase instructions, unless they are unusual or compose an experimental manipulation, in which case they may be presented verbatim. Most readers are familiar with standard testing procedures; unless new or unique procedures are used, do not describe them in detail.

If a language other than English is used in the collection of information, the language should be specified. When an instrument is translated into another language, the specific method of translation should be described (e.g., back translation, in which a text is translated into another language and then back into the first to ensure that it is equivalent enough that results can be compared).

Remember that the Method section should tell the reader *what* you did and *how* you did it in sufficient detail so that a reader could reasonably replicate your study. Methodological articles may defer highly detailed accounts of approaches (e.g., derivations and details of data simulation approaches) to an appendix.

1.10 *Results*

The Results section summarizes the data collected and the statistical or data analytic treatment used. Report the data in sufficient detail to justify the conclusions. Mention all relevant results, including those that run counter to the hypothesis. Do not include individual scores or raw data, with the exception, for example, of single-case designs or illustrative samples. Discussing the implications of the results is not appropriate here.

Tables and figures. To report the data, choose the medium that presents them most clearly and economically. Tables commonly provide exact values and, if well prepared, can present complex data and analyses in a format that is familiar to the reader (e.g., ANOVA tables). Figures of professional quality attract the reader's eye, provide a quick visual impression, and best illustrate complex relationships and general comparisons but are not intended to be as precise as tables. Always be aware that the scale and form of figures can have a great influence on the resulting interpretation of the data, and be scrupulous in presenting the data in as fair a manner as possible. Figures are more expensive than tables to reproduce, and both formats are more expensive than text to compose, so reserve them for your most important data and situations where their use enhances your ability to communicate your findings.

Summarizing the results and the analysis in tables or figures instead of text may be helpful; for example, a table may enhance the readability of complex sets of analysis of variance results. Avoid repeating the same data in several places and using tables for data that can be easily presented in a few sentences in the text.

When you use tables or figures, be certain to mention all of them in the text. Refer to all tables as *tables* and to all graphs, pictures, or drawings as *figures*. Tables and figures supplement the text; they cannot do the entire job of communication. Always tell the reader what to look for in tables and figures, and provide sufficient explanation to make them readily intelligible (see sections 3.62–3.86 for detailed information on tables and figures).

Statistical presentation. The field of psychology is not of a single mind on a number of issues surrounding the conduct and reporting of what is commonly known as *null hypothesis significance testing*. These issues include, but are not limited to, the reporting and interpretation of results of hypothesis tests, the selection of effect size indicators, the role of hypothesis-generating versus hypothesis-testing studies, and the relative merits of multiple degree-of-freedom tests. A discussion of these and other issues can be found in Wilkinson and the Task Force on Statistical

Inference (1999). It is not the role of the *Publication Manual* to resolve these issues. The inclusion of a particular approach should not be interpreted as an endorsement of that approach or as a lack of endorsement of some alternative approach. This edition attempts only to reflect the current views on the best practices with regard to data analytic approaches, reporting, and display. It must be recognized, however, that the needs of individual studies will, at times, differ from these generalizations. In all cases, the accurate and responsible reporting of the results of research studies must guide the research scientist and journal editor.

When reporting inferential statistics (e.g., t tests, F tests, and chi-square), include information about the obtained magnitude or value of the test statistic, the degrees of freedom, the probability of obtaining a value as extreme as or more extreme than the one obtained, and the direction of the effect. Be sure to include sufficient descriptive statistics (e.g., per-cell sample size, means, correlations, standard deviations) so that the nature of the effect being reported can be understood by the reader and for future meta-analyses. This information is important, even if no significant effect is being reported. When point estimates are provided, always include an associated measure of variability (precision), specifying its nature (e.g., the standard error). (See sections 3.57 and 3.58 for information on style of statistics.)

The reporting of confidence intervals (for estimates of parameters, for functions of parameters such as differences in means, and for effect sizes) can be an extremely effective way of reporting results. Because confidence intervals combine information on location and precision and can often be directly used to infer significance levels, they are, in general, the best reporting strategy. The use of confidence intervals is therefore strongly recommended. As a rule, it is best to use a single confidence interval size (e.g., a 95% or 99% confidence interval) throughout the course of the paper.

Assume that your reader has a professional knowledge of statistics. Basic assumptions should not be reviewed. If there is, however, a question about the appropriateness of a particular test or approach, be sure to justify its use.

Informationally adequate statistics. When reporting inferential statistics, include sufficient information to help the reader fully understand the analyses conducted and possible alternative explanations for the outcomes of these analyses. Because each analytic technique depends on different aspects of the data, it is impossible to specify what constitutes a set of minimally adequate statistics for every analysis. However, a minimally adequate set usually includes at least the following: the per-cell sample size, the observed cell means (or frequencies of cases in each category for a categorical variable), the cell standard deviations, and an estimate of the pooled within-cell variance. In the case of multivariable analytic systems such as multivariate analyses, regression analyses, and structural equation modeling analyses, the mean(s), sample size(s), and the variance–covariance (or correlation) matrix or matrices are a part of a minimally adequate statistics set.

- **For parametric tests of location** (e.g., single-group, multiple-group, or multiple-factor tests of means), a set of sufficient statistics consists of cell means, cell sample sizes, and some measure of variability (such as cell standard deviations or variances). Alternatively, a set of sufficient statistics consists of cell means, along with the mean square error and degrees of freedom associated with the effect being tested.
- **For randomized-block layouts, repeated measures designs, and multivariate analyses of variance,** vectors of cell means and cell sample sizes, along with the pooled within-cell variance–covariance matrix, constitute a set of sufficient statistics.
- **For correlational analyses** (e.g., multiple regression analysis, factor analysis, and structural equation modeling), the sample size and variance–covariance (or correlation) matrix are needed, accompanied by other information specific to the procedure used (e.g., variable means, reliabilities, hypothesized structural models, and other parameters (e.g., see Raykov, Tomer, & Nesselroade, 1991).
- **For nonparametric analyses** (e.g., chi-square analyses of contingency tables, order statistics), various summaries of the raw data

(e.g., number of cases in each category, sum of the ranks, sample sizes in each cell) are sufficient statistics.

- **For analyses based on very small samples** (including single-case investigations), consider providing the complete data in a table or figure.

Statistical power. Take seriously the statistical power considerations associated with your tests of hypotheses. Such considerations relate to the likelihood of correctly rejecting the tested hypotheses, given a particular alpha level, effect size, and sample size. In that regard, you should routinely provide evidence that your study has sufficient power to detect effects of substantive interest (e.g., see Cohen, 1988). You should be similarly aware of the role played by sample size in cases in which not rejecting the null hypothesis is desirable (i.e., when you wish to argue that there are no differences), when testing various assumptions underlying the statistical model adopted (e.g., normality, homogeneity of variance, homogeneity of regression), and in model fitting (e.g., see Serlin & Lapsley, 1985).

Statistical significance. Two types of probabilities are generally associated with the reporting of significance levels in inferential statistics. One refers to the a priori probability you have selected as an acceptable level of falsely rejecting a given null hypothesis. This probability, called the "alpha level" (or "significance level"), is the probability of a Type I error in hypothesis testing and is commonly set at .05 or .01. The other kind of probability, the p value (or significance probability), refers to the a posteriori likelihood of obtaining a result that is as extreme as or more extreme than the observed value you obtained, assuming that the null hypothesis is true.

The APA is neutral on which interpretation is to be preferred in psychological research (although individual journal editors may hold decided opinions on the issue). Because most statistical packages now report the p value (given the null and alternative hypotheses provided) and because this probability can be interpreted according to either mode of thinking, in general it is the exact probability (p value) that should be reported. There will be cases—for example, large tables of correlations or complex tables of path coefficients—where the reporting of exact probabilities could be awkward. In these cases, you may prefer to identify or highlight a subset of values in the table that reach some prespecified level of statistical significance. To do so, follow those values with a single asterisk (*) or double asterisk (**) to indicate $p < .05$ or $p < .01$, respectively. When using prespecified significance levels, you should routinely state the particular alpha level you selected for the statistical tests you conducted:

> An alpha level of .05 was used for all statistical tests.

Two common approaches for reporting statistical results using the exact probability formulation are as follows:

> With an alpha level of .05, the effect of age was statistically significant, $F(1, 123) = 7.27$, $p < .01$.

> The effect of age was not statistically significant, $F(1, 123) = 2.45$, $p = .12$.

The second example should be used only if you have included a statement of significance level earlier in your article.

Effect size and strength of relationship. Neither of the two types of probability value directly reflects the magnitude of an effect or the strength of a relationship. For the reader to fully understand the importance of your findings, it is almost always necessary to include some index of effect size or strength of relationship in your Results section. You can estimate the magnitude of the effect or the strength of the relationship with a number of common effect size estimates, including (but not limited to) r^2, η^2, ω^2, R^2, ϕ^2, Cramérs V, Kendall's W, Cohen's d and κ, Goodman–Kruskal's λ and γ, Jacobson and Truax's (1991) and

Kendall's (1999) proposed measures of clinical significance, and the multivariate Roy's Θ and the Pillai–Bartlett V.

As a general rule, multiple degree-of-freedom effect indicators tend to be less useful than effect indicators that decompose multiple degree-of-freedom tests into meaningful one degree-of-freedom effects—particularly when these are the results that inform the discussion. The general principle to be followed, however, is to provide the reader not only with information about statistical significance but also with enough information to assess the magnitude of the observed effect or relationship.

1.11 *Discussion*

After presenting the results, you are in a position to evaluate and interpret their implications, especially with respect to your original hypothesis. You are free to examine, interpret, and qualify the results, as well as to draw inferences from them. Emphasize any theoretical consequences of the results and the validity of your conclusions. (When the discussion is relatively brief and straightforward, some authors prefer to combine it with the previous Results section, yielding Results and Discussion or Results and Conclusions.)

Open the Discussion section with a clear statement of the support or nonsupport for your original hypothesis. Similarities and differences between your results and the work of others should clarify and confirm your conclusions. Do not, however, simply reformulate and repeat points already made; each new statement should contribute to your position and to the reader's understanding of the problem. Acknowledge limitations, and address alternative explanations of results.

You are encouraged, when appropriate and justified, to end the Discussion section with commentary on the importance of your findings. This concluding section may be brief or extensive, provided that it is tightly reasoned and self-contained. In this section you might address the following sorts of issues:

■   **Problem choice:** Why is this problem important? What larger issues, those that transcend the particulars of the subfield, hinge on the findings? What propositions are confirmed or disconfirmed by the extrapolation of these findings to such overarching issues?

- **Levels of analysis:** How can the findings be linked to phenomena at more complex and less complex levels of analysis? What needs to be known for such links to be forged?
- **Application and synthesis:** If the findings are valid and replicable, what real-life psychological phenomena might be explained or modeled by the results? Are applications warranted on the basis of this research?

The responses to these questions are the core of your contribution and justify why readers outside your own specialty should attend to your findings. These readers should receive clear, unambiguous, and direct answers.

1.12 *Multiple Experiments*

If you are integrating several experiments in one paper, describe the method and results of each experiment separately. If appropriate, include for each experiment a short discussion of the results, or combine the discussion with the description of results (e.g., Results and Discussion). Always make the logic and rationale of each new experiment clear to the reader. Always include a comprehensive general discussion of all the work after the last experiment.

The arrangement of sections reflects the structure previously described. Label the experiments *Experiment 1*, *Experiment 2*, and so forth. These labels are centered main headings (see section 3.31 on levels of headings). They organize the subsections and make referring to a specific experiment convenient for the reader. The Method and Results sections (and the Discussion section, if a short discussion accompanies each experiment) appear under each experiment heading. (Refer to Figure 5.2 for the form of a two-experiment paper.)

1.13 *References*

Just as data in the paper support interpretations and conclusions, so reference citations document statements made about the literature. All citations in the manuscript must appear in the reference list, and all references must be cited in text. The reference list should be succinct, not exhaustive; simply provide sufficient references to support your research. Choose references judiciously and cite them accurately. For example, if you retrieve an abstract but do not also retrieve and read the full article, your reference should be identified as an abstract. The standard procedures for citation ensure that references are accurate, complete, and useful to investigators and readers (see sections 3.94–3.103, chapter 4, and Appendix D on citations and references).

Whenever possible, support your statements by citing empirical work, such as method and results of an empirical study or a review of empirical studies (Lalumière, 1993). When you cite nonempirical work, make this clear in your narrative:

> Cho (1991) theorized that
>
> Audeh (in press) argued that
>
> (see discussion in Ginsburg, 1993).

Similarly, when you want to direct the reader to background information, signal the reader with phrases such as "for a review, see" and "(e.g., see [author, year])."

1.14 *Appendix*

An appendix is helpful if the detailed description of certain material is distracting in, or inappropriate to, the body of the paper. Some examples of material suitable for an appendix are (a) a new computer program specifically designed for your research and unavailable elsewhere, (b) an unpublished test and its validation, (c) a complicated mathematical proof, (d) a list of stimulus materials (e.g., those used in psycholinguistic research), and (e) a detailed description of a complex piece of equipment.

Include an appendix only if it helps readers to understand, evaluate, or replicate the study.

1.15 *Author Note*

The author note (a) identifies the departmental affiliation of each author, (b) identifies sources of financial support, (c) provides a forum for authors to acknowledge colleagues' professional contributions to the study and personal assistance, and (d) tells whom the interested reader may contact for further information concerning the article.

In addition, the author note is the place for disclosure: for example, mentioning the bases of a study, such as a dissertation or whether the study is part of a large-scale multidisciplinary project; indicating that the results have been presented at a meeting; and explaining relevant interests or relationships that raise the possibility of being perceived as a conflict of interest. (APA authors are required to complete a conflict of interest form; see the journal's instructions to authors.) Authors of book chapters that present a revised, condensed, or expanded version of a previously published journal article should also disclose this information in a note of this type. (See sections 3.89 and 5.20 for details on the arrangement and format of the author note.)

Quality of Presentation

A manuscript that is important enough to write deserves thoughtful preparation. You should evaluate the content and organization of the manuscript just as you evaluated the investigation itself. The following questions (based on Bartol, 1981) may help you assess the quality of your presentation:

- Is the topic appropriate for the journal to which the manuscript is submitted?
- Is the introduction clear and complete?
- Are the techniques of data analysis clearly enough presented so that an individual with a copy of the data set and the coding system could reproduce your analyses?

- Does the statement of purpose adequately and logically orient the reader?
- Is the literature adequately reviewed?
- Are the citations appropriate and complete?
- Is the research question clearly identified, and is the hypothesis explicit?
- Are the conceptualization and rationale perfectly clear?
- Is the method clearly and adequately described? In other words, can the study be replicated from the description provided in the paper?
- If observers were used to assess variables, is the interobserver reliability reported?
- Are the techniques of data analysis appropriate, and is the analysis clear? Are the assumptions underlying the statistical procedures clearly met by the data to which they are applied?
- Are the results and conclusions unambiguous, valid, and meaningful?
- Is the discussion thorough? Does it stick to the point and confine itself to what can be concluded from the significant findings of the study?
- Is the paper concise?
- Is the manuscript prepared according to the Checklist for Manuscript Submission? (See Appendix A to this volume.)

CHAPTER TWO

Expressing Ideas and Reducing Bias in Language

Good writing is an art and a craft, and instructing in its mastery is beyond the scope of the *Publication Manual*. Instead, this chapter provides some general principles of expository writing, demonstrates how correct grammar can facilitate clear communication, and suggests ways to assess and improve writing style. Just as a disciplined scientific investigation contributes to the growth and development of a field, so too does carefully crafted writing contribute to the value of scientific literature. Thoughtful concern for the language can yield clear and orderly writing that sharpens and strengthens your personal style and allows for individuality of expression and purpose.

You can achieve clear communication, which is the prime objective of scientific reporting, by presenting ideas in an orderly manner and by expressing yourself smoothly and precisely. By developing ideas clearly and logically and leading readers smoothly from thought to thought, you make the task of reading an agreeable one. The references on writing style listed in section 9.03 elaborate on these objectives.

Writing Style

The style requirements in the *Publication Manual* are intended to facilitate clear communication. The requirements are explicit, but alternatives to prescribed forms are permissible if they ensure clearer communication. In all cases, the use of rules should be balanced with good judgment.

2.01 *Orderly Presentation of Ideas*

Thought units—whether a single word, a sentence or paragraph, or a longer sequence—must be orderly. So that readers will understand what you are presenting, you must aim for continuity in words, concepts, and thematic development from the opening statement to the conclusion. Readers will be confused if you misplace words or phrases in sentences, abandon familiar syntax, shift the criterion for items in a series, or clutter the sequence of ideas with wordiness or irrelevancies.

Continuity can be achieved in several ways. For instance, punctuation marks contribute to continuity by showing relationships between ideas. They cue the reader to the pauses, inflections, subordination, and pacing normally heard in speech. Use the full range of punctuation aids available: Neither overuse nor underuse one type of punctuation, such as commas or dashes. Overuse may annoy the reader; underuse may confuse. Instead, use punctuation to support meaning. (See sections 3.01– 3.09 for details on the use of punctuation.)

Another way to achieve continuity is through the use of transitional words. These words help maintain the flow of thought, especially when the material is complex or abstract. A pronoun that refers to a noun in the preceding sentence not only serves as a transition but also avoids repetition. Be sure the referent is obvious. Other transition devices are time links (*then, next, after, while, since*), cause–effect links (*therefore, consequently, as a result*), addition links (*in addition, moreover, furthermore, similarly*), and contrast links (*but, conversely, nevertheless, however, although, whereas*).

Some transitional words (e.g., *while, since*) create confusion because they have been adopted in informal writing style and in conversation for transitions other than time links. For example, *since* is often used when *because* is meant. Scientific writing, however, must be precise; therefore, limiting the use of these transitional words to their temporal meanings is preferred (see section 2.10 for examples).

2.02 *Smoothness of Expression*

Scientific prose and creative writing serve different purposes. Devices that are often found in creative writing—for example, setting up ambiguity, inserting the unexpected, omitting the expected, and suddenly shifting the topic, tense, or person—can confuse or disturb readers of scientific prose. Therefore, try to avoid these devices and aim for clear and logical communication.

Because you have spent so much time close to your material and thus may have lost some objectivity, you may not immediately see certain problems, especially contradictions the reader may infer. A reading by a colleague may uncover such problems. You can usually catch omissions, irrelevancies, and abruptness by putting the manuscript aside and re-reading it later. If you also read the paper aloud, you have an even better chance of finding problems such as abruptness.

If, on later reading, you do find that your writing is abrupt, more transition from one topic to another may be helpful. Possibly you have abandoned an argument or theme prematurely; if so, you need to amplify the discussion.

Abruptness may result from sudden, unnecessary shifts in verb tense within the same paragraph or in adjacent paragraphs. By being consistent in the use of verb tenses, you can help ensure smooth expression. Past tense (e.g., "Smith *showed*") or present perfect tense (e.g., "researchers *have shown*") is appropriate for the literature review and the description of the procedure if the discussion is of past events. Stay within the chosen tense. Use past tense (e.g., "anxiety *decreased* significantly") to describe the results. Use the present tense (e.g., "the results of Experiment 2 *indicate*") to discuss the results and to present the conclusions. By reporting conclusions in the present tense, you allow readers to join you in deliberating the matter at hand. (See section 2.06 for details on the use of tense.)

Noun strings, meaning several nouns used one after another to modify a final noun, create another form of abruptness. The reader is sometimes forced to stop to determine how the words relate to each other. Skillful hyphenation can clarify the relationships between words, but often the best approach is to untangle the string. For example, consider the following string:

> commonly used investigative expanded issue control question technique

This is dense prose to the reader knowledgeable about studies on lie detection—and gibberish to a reader unfamiliar with such studies. Possible ways to untangle the string are as follows:

- a control-question technique that is commonly used to expand issues in investigations
- an expanded-issue control-question technique that is commonly used in investigations
- a common technique of using control questions to investigate expanded issues
- a common investigative technique of using expanded issues in control questions

One approach to untangling noun strings is to move the last word to the beginning of the string and fill in with verbs and prepositions. For example, "early childhood thought disorder misdiagnosis" might be rearranged to read "misdiagnosis of thought disorders in early childhood."

Many writers strive to achieve smooth expression by using synonyms or near-synonyms to avoid repeating a term. The intention is commendable, but by using synonyms you may unintentionally suggest a subtle difference. Therefore, choose synonyms with care. The discreet use of pronouns can often relieve the monotonous repetition of a term without introducing ambiguity.

2.03 *Economy of Expression*

Say only what needs to be said. The author who is frugal with words not only writes a more readable manuscript but also increases the chances that the manuscript will be accepted for publication. The number of printed pages a journal can publish is limited, and editors therefore often request authors to shorten submitted papers. You can tighten long papers by eliminating redundancy, wordiness, jargon, evasiveness, overuse of the passive voice, circumlocution, and clumsy prose. Weed out overly detailed descriptions of apparatus, participants, or procedures (particularly if methods were published elsewhere, in which case you should simply cite the original study); gratuitous embellishments; elaborations of the obvious; and irrelevant observations or asides.

Short words and short sentences are easier to comprehend than are long ones. A long technical term, however, may be more precise than several short words, and technical terms are inseparable from scientific reporting. Yet the technical terminology in a paper should be understood by psychologists throughout the discipline. An article that depends on terminology familiar to only a few specialists does not sufficiently contribute to the literature. The main causes of uneconomical writing are jargon and wordiness.

Jargon. *Jargon* is the continuous use of a technical vocabulary even in places where that vocabulary is not relevant. Jargon is also the substitution of a euphemistic phrase for a familiar term (e.g., *monetarily felt scarcity* for *poverty*), and you should scrupulously avoid using such jargon. Federal bureaucratic jargon has had the greatest publicity, but scientific jargon also grates on the reader, encumbers the communication of information, and wastes space.

Wordiness. Wordiness is every bit as irritating and uneconomical as jargon and can impede the ready grasp of ideas. Change *based on the fact that* to *because, at the present time* to *now,* and *for the purpose of* to simply *for* or *to.* Use *this study* instead of *the present study* when the context is clear. Change *there were several students who completed* to *several students completed. Reason* and *because* often appear in the same sentence; however, they have the same meaning, and therefore they should not be used together. Unconstrained wordiness lapses into embellishment and flowery writing, which are clearly inappropriate in scientific style. Mullins (1977) comprehensively discussed examples of wordiness found in the social sciences literature.

Redundancy. Writers often become redundant in an effort to be emphatic. Use no more words than are necessary to convey your meaning.

In the following examples, the italicized words are redundant and should be omitted:

They were *both* alike	one *and* the same
a *total* of 68 participants	in *close* proximity
Four *different* groups saw	*completely* unanimous
instructions, which were *exactly* the same as those used	*just* exactly
	very close to significance
absolutely essential	*period* of time
has been *previously* found	summarize *briefly*
small *in size*	the reason is *because*

Unit length. Although writing only in short, simple sentences produces choppy and boring prose, writing exclusively in long, involved sentences creates difficult, sometimes incomprehensible material. Varied sentence length helps readers maintain interest and comprehension. When involved concepts require long sentences, the components should proceed logically, not randomly dodge about. Direct, declarative sentences with simple, common words are usually best.

Similar cautions apply to paragraph length. Single-sentence paragraphs are abrupt. Paragraphs that are too long are likely to lose the reader's attention. New paragraphs provide a pause for the reader—a chance to assimilate one step in the conceptual development before beginning another. If a paragraph runs longer than one double-spaced manuscript page, you may lose your readers in the dense forest of typeset words. Look for a logical place to break a long paragraph, or reorganize the material. Unity, cohesiveness, and continuity should characterize all paragraphs.

2.04 *Precision and Clarity*

Word choice. Make certain that every word means exactly what you intend it to mean. Sooner or later most authors discover a discrepancy between the meaning they attribute to a term and its dictionary definition. In informal style, for example, *feel* broadly substitutes for *think* or *believe*, but in scientific style such latitude is not acceptable.

Colloquial expressions. Likewise, avoid colloquial expressions (e.g., *write up* for *report*), which diffuse meaning. Approximations of quantity (e.g., *quite a large part, practically all,* or *very few*) are interpreted differently by different readers or in different contexts. Approximations weaken statements, especially those describing empirical observations.

Pronouns. Pronouns confuse readers unless the referent for each pronoun is obvious; readers should not have to search previous text to determine the meaning of the term. Simple pronouns are the most troublesome, especially *this, that, these,* and *those* when they refer to a previous sentence. Eliminate ambiguity by writing, for example, *this test, that trial, these participants,* and *those reports.* (See also section 2.08.)

Comparisons. Ambiguous or illogical comparisons result from omission of key verbs or from nonparallel structure. Consider, for example, "Ten-year-olds were more likely to play with age peers than 8-year-olds." Does this sentence mean that 10-year-olds were more likely than 8-year-olds to play with age peers? Or does it mean that 10-year-olds were more likely to play with age peers and less likely to play with 8-year-olds? An illogical comparison occurs when parallelism is overlooked for the sake of brevity, as in "Her salary was lower than a convenience store clerk." Thoughtful attention to good sentence structure and word choice reduces the chance of this kind of ambiguity.

Attribution. Inappropriately or illogically attributing action in an effort to be objective can be misleading. Examples of undesirable attribution include use of the third person, anthropomorphism, and use of the editorial *we.*

- **third person:** Writing "The experimenters instructed the participants" when "the experimenters" refers to yourself is ambiguous and may give the impression that you did not take part in your own study. Instead, use a personal pronoun: "We instructed the participants."

■   **anthropomorphism:** In addition, do not attribute human characteristics to animals or to inanimate sources.

Anthropomorphism:

Ancestral horses probably traveled as wild horses do today, either in bands of bachelor males or in harems of mares headed by a single stallion.

Solution:

Ancestral horses probably traveled as wild horses do today, either in bands of males or in groups of several mares and a stallion.

Anthropomorphism:

The community program was persuaded to allow five of the observers to become tutors.

Solution:

The staff for the community program was persuaded to allow five of the observers to become tutors.

An experiment cannot *attempt to demonstrate, control unwanted variables,* or *interpret findings,* nor can tables or figures *compare* (all of these can, however, *show* or *indicate*). Use a pronoun or an appropriate noun as the subject of these verbs. *I* or *we* (meaning the author or authors) can replace *the experiment* (but do not use *we* in the editorial sense; see next paragraph); *the reader may compare* or *comparisons of* can solve the latter problem.

■ **editorial *we*:** For clarity, restrict your use of *we* to refer only to yourself and your coauthors (use *I* if you are the sole author of the paper). Broader uses of *we* leave your readers to determine to whom you are referring; instead, substitute an appropriate noun or clarify your usage:

Poor:

We usually classify bird song on the basis of frequency and temporal structure of the elements.

Better:

Researchers usually classify bird song on the basis of frequency and temporal structure of the elements.

Some alternatives to *we* to consider are *people, humans, researchers, psychologists, cognitive psychologists,* and so on.

We is an appropriate and useful referent:

Acceptable:

Humans are passionate about health and pleasure. We yearn for a tasty, fat-free chocolate cookie.

Unacceptable:

We are passionate and yearn . . .

Acceptable:

As behaviorists, we tend to dispute . . .

Unacceptable:

We tend to dispute . . .

2.05 *Strategies to Improve Writing Style*

Authors use various strategies in putting their thoughts on paper. The fit between author and strategy is more important than the particular strategy used. Three approaches to achieving professional and effective communication are (a) writing from an outline; (b) putting aside the first draft, then rereading it after a delay; and (c) asking a colleague to critique the draft for you.

Writing from an outline helps preserve the logic of the research itself. An outline identifies main ideas, defines subordinate ideas, helps you discipline your writing and avoid tangential excursions, and helps you notice omissions.

Rereading your own copy after setting it aside for a few days permits a fresh approach. Reading the paper aloud enables you not only to see faults that you overlooked on the previous reading, but to hear them as well. When these problems are corrected, give a polished copy to a colleague—preferably a person who has published but who is not too familiar with your own work—for a critical review. Even better, get critiques from two colleagues, and you have a trial run of a journal's review process.

These strategies, particularly the latter, may require you to invest more time in a manuscript than you had anticipated. The results of these strategies, however, may be greater accuracy and thoroughness and clearer communication.

Grammar

Incorrect grammar and careless construction of sentences distract the reader, introduce ambiguity, and generally obstruct communication. For example, the sentence "We scheduled a 10-min break between each test" suggests that each test was interrupted by a break. The sentence should read, "We scheduled 10-min breaks between the tests" or "We scheduled a 10-min break after each test." Correct grammar and thoughtful construction of sentences ease the reader's task and facilitate unambiguous communication.

The examples in the next section of this chapter represent the kinds of problems of grammar and usage that occur frequently in manuscripts submitted to APA journals. These examples should help authors steer clear of the most common errors. For discussions of problems not addressed in this section and for more comprehensive discussions of grammar and usage in general, consult appropriate authoritative manuals (e.g., the sources on writing style in section 9.03).

2.06 *Verbs*

Verbs are vigorous, direct communicators. Use the active rather than the passive voice, and select tense or mood carefully.

Prefer the active voice.

Poor:

The survey was conducted in a controlled setting.

Better:

We conducted the survey in a controlled setting.

Poor:

The experiment was designed by Simpson (2001).

Better:

Simpson (2001) designed the experiment.

Poor:

The participants were seated in comfortable chairs equipped with speakers that delivered the tone stimuli.

Better:

Participants sat in comfortable chairs. . . .

The passive voice is acceptable in expository writing and when you want to focus on the object or recipient of the action rather than on the actor. For example, "The speakers were attached to either side of the chair" emphasizes the placement of speakers, not who placed them—the more appropriate focus in the Method section. "The President was shot" emphasizes the importance of the person shot.

Use the past tense to express an action or a condition that occurred at a specific, definite time in the past, as when discussing another researcher's work and when reporting your results. (See also section 2.02 for guidelines on using verb tense in various sections of a manuscript.)

Incorrect:

Sanchez (2000) presents the same results.

Correct:

Sanchez (2000) presented the same results.

Results section:

In Experiment 2, response varied (see Figure 4).

Discussion section:

As demonstrated in Experiment 2, response varies. . . .

Use the present perfect tense to express a past action or condition that did not occur at a specific, definite time or to describe an action beginning in the past and continuing to the present.

Incorrect:

Since that time, investigators from several studies used this method.

Correct:

Since that time, investigators from several studies have used this method.

Use the subjunctive to describe only conditions that are contrary to fact or improbable; do not use the subjunctive to describe simple conditions or contingencies.

Incorrect:

If the experiment was not designed this way, the participants' performances would suffer.

Correct:

If the experiment were not designed this way, the participants' performances would suffer.

Incorrect:

If the participant were finished answering the questions, the data are complete.

Correct:

If the participant is finished answering the questions, the data
are complete.

Use *would* with care. *Would* can correctly be used to mean *habitually,*
as "The child would walk about the classroom," or to express a conditional action, as "We would sign the letter if we could." Do not use *would*
to hedge; for example, change *it would appear that* to *it appears that.*

2.07 *Agreement of Subject and Verb*

A verb must agree in number (i.e., singular or plural) with its subject,
regardless of intervening phrases that begin with such words as *together
with, including, plus,* and *as well as.*

Incorrect:

The percentage of correct responses as well as the speed of the
responses increase with practice.

Correct:

The percentage of correct responses as well as the speed of the
responses increases with practice.

The plural form of some nouns of foreign origin, particularly those
that end in the letter *a,* may appear to be singular and can cause authors
to select a verb that does not agree in number with the noun:

Incorrect:

The data indicates that Terrence was correct.

Correct:

The data indicate that Terrence was correct.

Incorrect:

The phenomena occurs every 100 years.

Correct:

The phenomena occur every 100 years.

Consult section 3.10 and a dictionary (APA prefers *Merriam-Webster's Collegiate Dictionary*) when in doubt about the plural form of nouns of foreign origin.

Collective nouns (e.g., *series, set, faculty,* or *pair*) can refer either to several individuals or to a single unit. If the action of the verb is on the group as a whole, treat the noun as a singular noun. If the action of the verb is on members of the group as individuals, treat the noun as a plural noun. The context (i.e., your emphasis) determines whether the action is on the group or on individuals.

Singular in context:

The number of people in the state is growing.
A pair of animals was in each cage.
The couple is surrounded.

Plural in context:

A number of people are watching.
A pair of animals were then yoked.
The couple are separated.

The pronoun *none* can also be singular or plural. When the noun that follows it is singular, use a singular verb; when the noun is plural, use a plural verb. If you mean "not one," use *not one* instead of *none* and use a singular verb.

Singular in context:

None of the information was correct.

Plural in context:

None of the children were finished in the time allotted.

but

Not one of the children was finished in the time allotted.

When the subject is composed of a singular and a plural noun joined by *or* or *nor*, the verb agrees with the noun that is closer.

Incorrect:

Neither the participants nor the confederate were in the room.

Correct:

Neither the participants nor the confederate was in the room.

or

Neither the confederate nor the participants were in the room.

If the number of the subject changes, retain the verb in each clause.

Incorrect:

The positions in the sequence were changed, and the test rerun.

Correct:

The positions in the sequence were changed, and the test was rerun.

2.08 *Pronouns*

Pronouns replace nouns. Each pronoun should refer clearly to its antecedent and should agree with the antecedent in number and gender.

A pronoun must agree in number (i.e., singular or plural) with the noun it replaces.

Incorrect:

It is unlikely that any sexualized transference will be resolved successfully if the patient does not feel that their interactions with their therapist are confidential.

Correct:

It is unlikely that any sexualized transference will be resolved successfully if the patient does not feel that interactions with his or her therapist are confidential.

Incorrect:

Neither the highest scorer nor the lowest scorer in the group had any doubt about their competence.

Correct:

Neither the highest scorer nor the lowest scorer in the group had any doubt about his or her competence.

A pronoun must agree in gender (i.e., masculine, feminine, or neuter) with the noun it replaces. This rule extends to relative pronouns (pronouns that link subordinate clauses to nouns). Use *who* for human beings; use *that* or *which* for animals and for things.

Incorrect:

The rats who completed the task successfully were rewarded.

Correct:

The rats that completed the task successfully were rewarded.

Use neuter pronouns to refer to animals (e.g., "the dog . . . it") unless the animals have been named:

The chimps were tested daily. . . . Sheba was tested unrestrained in an open testing area, which was her usual context for training and testing.

(See section 2.10 for further discussion of the use of relative pronouns.)

Pronouns can be subjects or objects of verbs or prepositions. Use *who* as the subject of a verb and *whom* as the object of a verb or a preposition. You can determine whether a relative pronoun is the subject or object of a verb by turning the subordinate clause around and substituting a personal pronoun. If you can substitute *he* or *she*, *who* is correct; if you can substitute *him* or *her*, *whom* is the correct pronoun.

Incorrect:

Name the participant whom you found achieved scores above the median. [You found *him* or *her* achieved scores above the median.]

Correct:

Name the participant who you found achieved scores above the median. [You found *he* or *she* achieved scores above the median.]

Incorrect:

The participant who I identified as the youngest dropped out. [I identified *he* or *she* as the youngest.]

Correct:

The participant whom I identified as the youngest dropped out. [I identified *him* or *her* as the youngest.]

In a phrase consisting of a pronoun or noun plus a present participle (e.g., *running, flying*) that is used as an object of a preposition, the participle can be either a noun or a modifier of a noun, depending on the intended meaning. When you use a participle as a noun, make the other pronoun or noun possessive.

Incorrect:

We had nothing to do with them being the winners.

Correct:

We had nothing to do with their being the winners.

Incorrect:

The significance is questionable because of one participant performing at incredible speed.

Correct:

The significance is questionable because of one participant's performing at incredible speed. [The significance is questionable because of the performance, not because of the participant.]

but

We spoke to the person sitting at the table. [The person, not the sitting, is the object of the preposition.]

2.09 *Misplaced and Dangling Modifiers and Use of Adverbs*

An adjective or an adverb, whether a single word or a phrase, must clearly refer to the word it modifies.

Misplaced modifiers, because of their placement in a sentence, ambiguously or illogically modify a word. You can eliminate these by placing an adjective or an adverb as close as possible to the word it modifies.

Unclear:

The investigator tested the participants using this procedure. [The sentence is unclear about whether the investigator or the participants used this procedure.]

Clear:

Using this procedure, the investigator tested the participants.

Clear:

The investigator tested the participants who were using the procedure.

Incorrect:

Based on this assumption, we developed a model. . . . [This construction says, "we are based on an assumption."]

Correct:

On the basis of this assumption, we developed a model. . . .

Correct:

Based on this assumption, the model. . . .

Many writers have trouble with the word *only*. Place *only* next to the
word or phrase it modifies.

Incorrect:

These data only provide a partial answer.

Correct:

These data provide only a partial answer.

Incorrect:

We found a mean of 7.9 errors on the first trial and only a mean
of 1.3 errors on the second trial.

Correct:

We found a mean of 7.9 errors on the first trial and a mean of
only 1.3 errors on the second trial.

Dangling modifiers have no referent in the sentence. Many of these result from the use of passive voice. By writing in the active voice, you can avoid many dangling modifiers.

Incorrect:

After separating the participants into groups, Group A was tested.

Correct:

After separating the participants into groups, I tested Group A. [I, not Group A, separated the participants into groups.]

Incorrect:

The participants were tested using this procedure.

Correct:

Using this procedure, I tested the participants. [I, not the participants, used the procedure.]

Incorrect:

To test this hypothesis, the participants were divided into two groups.

Correct:

To test this hypothesis, we divided the participants into two groups. [We, not the participants, tested the hypothesis.]

Incorrect:

Congruent with other studies, Mulholland and Williams (2000) found that this group performed better.

Correct:

Mulholland and Williams (2000) found that this group performed better, results that are congruent with those of other studies. [The results, not Mulholland and Williams, are congruent.]

Adverbs can be used as introductory or transitional words. Adverbs modify verbs, adjectives, and other adverbs and express manner or quality. Some adverbs, however—such as *fortunately, similarly, certainly, consequently, conversely,* and *regrettably*—can also be used as introductory or transitional words as long as the sense is confined to, for example, "it is fortunate that" or "in a similar manner." Use adverbs judiciously as introductory or transitional words. Ask yourself whether the introduction or transition is needed and whether the adverb is being used correctly.

Some of the more common introductory adverbial phrases are *importantly, more importantly,* and *interestingly.* Although *importantly* is used widely, whether its adverbial usage is proper is debatable. Both *importantly* and *interestingly* can often be recast to enhance the message of a sentence or simply be omitted without a loss of meaning.

Problematic:

More importantly, the total amount of available long-term memory activation, and not the rate of spreading activation, drives the rate and probability of retrieval.

Preferred:

More important, the total amount of available long-term memory activation, and not the rate of spreading activation, drives the rate and probability of retrieval.

Correct adverbial usage:

Expressive behavior and autonomic nervous system activity also have figured importantly. . . .

Problematic:

Interestingly, the total amount of available long-term memory activation, and not the rate of spreading activation, drives the rate and probability of retrieval.

Preferred:

We were surprised to learn that the total. . . .
We find it interesting that the total. . . .
An interesting finding was that. . . .

Another adverb often misused as an introductory or transitional word is *hopefully. Hopefully* means "in a hopeful manner" or "full of hope"; *hopefully* should not be used to mean "I hope" or "it is hoped."

Incorrect:

Hopefully, this is not the case.

Correct:

I hope this is not the case.

2.10 *Relative Pronouns and Subordinate Conjunctions*

Relative pronouns (*who, whom, that, which*) and subordinate conjunctions (e.g., *since, while, although*) introduce an element that is subordinate to the main clause of the sentence and reflect the relationship of the subordinate element to the main clause. Therefore, select these pronouns and conjunctions with care; interchanging them may reduce the precision of your meaning. (See section 2.08 for further discussion of relative pronouns.)

Relative pronouns

That **versus** *which.* *That* clauses (called *restrictive*) are essential to the meaning of the sentence:

> The animals that performed well in the first experiment were used in the second experiment.

Which clauses can merely add further information (nonrestrictive) or can be essential to the meaning (restrictive) of the sentence. APA prefers to reserve *which* for nonrestrictive clauses and use *that* in restrictive clauses.

Nonrestrictive:

> The animals, which performed well in the first experiment, were not proficient in the second experiment. [The second experiment was more difficult for all of the animals.]

Restrictive:

> The animals which performed well in the first experiment were not proficient in the second experiment. [Only those animals that performed well in the first experiment were not proficient in the second; prefer *that.*]

Consistent use of *that* for restrictive clauses and *which* for nonrestrictive clauses, which are set off with commas, will help make your writing clear and precise.

Subordinate conjunctions

***While* and *since*.** Some style authorities accept the use of *while* and *since* when they do not refer strictly to time; however, words like these, with more than one meaning, can cause confusion. Because precision and clarity are the standards in scientific writing, restricting your use of *while* and *since* to their temporal meanings is helpful. (See also section 2.04 on precision and clarity.)

> Bragg (1965) found that participants performed well while listening to music.

> Several versions of the test have been developed since the test was first introduced.

***While* versus *although*.** Use *while* to link events occurring simultaneously; use *although, whereas, and,* or *but* in place of *while*.

Imprecise:

> Bragg (1965) found that participants performed well, while Bohr (1969) found that participants did poorly.

Precise:

> Bragg (1965) found that participants performed well, whereas Bohr (1969) found that participants did poorly.

Imprecise:

> While these findings are unusual, they are not unique.

Precise:

> Although these findings are unusual, they are not unique.

or

These findings are unusual, but they are not unique.

Since versus **because.** *Since* is more precise when it is used to refer only to time (to mean "after that"); otherwise, replace with *because.*

Imprecise:

Data for 2 participants were incomplete since these participants did not report for follow-up testing.

Precise:

Data for 2 participants were incomplete because these participants did not report for follow-up testing.

2.11 *Parallel Construction*

To enhance the reader's understanding, present parallel ideas in parallel or coordinate form. Make certain that all elements of the parallelism are present before and after the coordinating conjunction (i.e., *and, but, or, nor*).

Incorrect:

The results show that such changes could be made without affecting error rate and latencies continued to decrease over time.

Correct:

The results show that such changes could be made without affecting error rate and that latencies continued to decrease over time.

With coordinating conjunctions used in pairs (*between ... and, both ... and, neither ... nor, either ... or, not only ... but also*), place the first conjunction immediately before the first part of the parallelism.

Between and *and*

Incorrect:

We recorded the difference between the performance of subjects that completed the first task and the second task.

Correct:

We recorded the difference between the performance of subjects that completed the first task and the performance of those that completed the second task. [The difference is between the subjects' performances, not between the performance and the task.]

Incorrect:

between 2.5–4.0 years of age

Correct:

between 2.5 and 4.0 years of age

Both and *and*

Incorrect:

The names were both difficult to pronounce and spell.

Correct:

The names were difficult both to pronounce and to spell.

Never use *both* with *as well as*: The resulting construction is redundant.

Incorrect:

The names were difficult both to pronounce as well as to spell.

Correct:

The names were difficult to pronounce as well as to spell.

Neither and *nor* and *either* and *or*

Incorrect:

Neither the responses to the auditory stimuli nor to the tactile stimuli were repeated.

Correct:

Neither the responses to the auditory stimuli nor the responses to the tactile stimuli were repeated.

Incorrect:

The respondents either gave the worst answer or the best answer.

Correct:

The respondents either gave the worst answer or gave the best answer.

or

> The respondents gave either the worst answer or the best answer.

Not only and *but* (*also*)

Incorrect:

> It is not only surprising that pencil-and-paper scores predicted this result but that all other predictors were less accurate.

Correct:

> It is surprising not only that pencil-and-paper scores predicted this result but (also) that all other predictors were less accurate.

Elements in a series should also be parallel in form.

Incorrect:

> The participants were told to make themselves comfortable, to read the instructions, and that they should ask about anything they did not understand.

Correct:

> The participants were told to make themselves comfortable, to read the instructions, and to ask about anything they did not understand.

Take care to use parallel structure in lists and in table stubs (see section 3.33 and 3.67).

When you develop a clear writing style and use correct grammar, you show concern not only for accurately presenting your knowledge and ideas but also for easing the reader's task. Another consideration in writing is that of maintaining the reader's focus of attention. Such a concern demands the thoughtful use of language. The next section is a discussion of the importance of choosing words that are appropriate to your subject and free from bias, which is another way to achieve disciplined writing and precise, unambiguous communication.

2.12 *Linguistic Devices*

Devices that attract attention to words, sounds, or other embellishments instead of to ideas are inappropriate in scientific writing. Avoid heavy alliteration, rhyming, poetic expressions, and clichés. Use metaphors sparingly; although they can help simplify complicated ideas, metaphors can be distracting. Avoid mixed metaphors (e.g., *a theory representing one branch of a growing body of evidence*) and words with surplus or unintended meaning (e.g., *cop* for *police officer*), which may distract if not actually mislead the reader. Use figurative expressions with restraint and colorful expressions with care; these expressions can sound strained or forced.

Guidelines to Reduce Bias in Language

As a publisher, APA accepts authors' word choices unless those choices are inaccurate, unclear, or ungrammatical. As an organization, APA is committed both to science and to the fair treatment of individuals and groups, and this policy requires authors of APA publications to avoid perpetuating demeaning attitudes and biased assumptions about people in their writing. Constructions that might imply bias against persons on the basis of gender, sexual orientation, racial or ethnic group, disability, or age should be avoided. Scientific writing should be free of implied or irrelevant evaluation of the group or groups being studied.

Long-standing cultural practice can exert a powerful influence over even the most conscientious author. Just as you have learned to check what you write for spelling, grammar, and wordiness, practice reading over your work for bias. You can test your writing for implied evaluation by reading it while (a) substituting your own group for the group or groups you are discussing or (b) imagining you are a member of the group you are discussing (Maggio, 1991). If you feel excluded or offended, your material needs further revision. Another suggestion is to ask people from that group to read your material and give you candid feedback.

What follows is a set of guidelines, followed in turn by discussions of specific issues that affect particular groups. These are not rigid rules. You may find that some attempts to follow the guidelines result in wordiness or clumsy prose. As always, good judgment is required. If your writing reflects respect for your participants and your readers, and if you write with appropriate specificity and precision, you will be contributing to the goal of accurate, unbiased communication. Specific examples for each guideline are given in Table 2.1 at the end of this chapter.

Guideline 1: Describe at the appropriate level of specificity

Precision is a necessity in scientific writing; when you refer to a person or persons, choose words that are accurate, clear, and free from bias. The appropriate degree of specificity depends on the research question and the present state of knowledge in the field of study. When in doubt, it is better to be more specific rather than less, because it is easier to aggregate published data than to disaggregate them. For example, using *man* to refer to all human beings is simply not as accurate as the phrase *men and women*. To describe age groups, it is better to give a specific age range ("ages 65–83") instead of a broad category ("over 65"; see Schaie, 1993). When describing racial and ethnic groups, be appropriately specific and sensitive to issues of labeling. For example, instead of describing participants as Asian American or Hispanic American, it may be helpful to describe them by their nation or region of origin (e.g., Chinese Americans, Mexican Americans). If you are discussing sexual orientation, realize that some people interpret *gay* as referring to men and women, whereas others interpret the term as including only men (for clarity, *gay men* and *lesbians* currently are preferred).

Broad clinical terms such as *borderline* and people at *risk* are loaded with innuendo unless properly explained. Specify the diagnosis that is borderline (e.g., "people with borderline personality disorder"). Identify the risk and the people it involves (e.g., "children at risk for early school dropout").

Gender is cultural and is the term to use when referring to men and women as social groups. *Sex* is biological; use it when the biological distinction is predominant. Note that the word *sex* can be confused with *sexual behavior*. *Gender* helps keep meaning unambiguous, as in the following example: "In accounting for attitudes toward the bill, sexual orientation rather than gender accounted for most of the variance. Most gay men and lesbians were for the proposal; most heterosexual men and women were against it."

Part of writing without bias is recognizing that differences should be mentioned only when relevant. Marital status, sexual orientation, racial and ethnic identity, or the fact that a person has a disability should not be mentioned gratuitously.

Guideline 2: Be sensitive to labels

Respect people's preferences; call people what they prefer to be called (Maggio, 1991). Accept that preferences will change with time and that individuals within groups often disagree about the designations they prefer (see Raspberry, 1989). Make an effort to determine what is appropriate for your situation; you may need to ask your participants which designations they prefer, particularly when preferred designations are being debated within groups.

Avoid labeling people when possible. A common occurrence in scientific writing is that participants in a study tend to lose their individuality; they are broadly categorized as objects (noun forms such as *the gays* and *the elderly*) or, particularly in descriptions of people with disabilities, are equated with their conditions—*the amnesiacs, the depressives, the schizophrenics, the LDs*, for example. One solution is to use adjectival forms (e.g., "gay *men*," "elderly *people*," "amnesic *patients*"). Another is to "put the person first," followed by a descriptive phrase (e.g., "people diagnosed with schizophrenia"). Note that the latter solution currently is preferred when describing people with disabilities.

When you need to mention several groups in a sentence or paragraph, such as when reporting results, do your best to balance sensitivity, clarity, and parsimony. For example, it may be cumbersome to repeat phrases such as "person with _____." If you provide operational definitions of groups early in your paper (e.g., "Participants scoring a minimum of X on the X scale constituted the high verbal group, and those scoring below X constituted the low verbal group"), it is scientifically informative and concise to describe participants thereafter in terms of the measures used to classify them (e.g., "... was significant: high verbal group, $p < .05$"), *provided the terms are inoffensive.* A label should not be used in any form that is perceived as pejorative; if such a perception is possible, you need to find more neutral terms. For example, *the demented* is not repaired by changing it to *demented group*, but *dementia group* would be acceptable. Abbreviations or series labels for groups usually sacrifice clarity and may offend: *LDs* or *LD group* to describe people with specific learning difficulties is offensive; *HVAs* for "high verbal ability group" is difficult to decipher. *Group A* is not offensive, but neither is it descriptive.

Recognize the difference between *case*, which is an occurrence of a disorder or illness, and *patient*, which is a person affected by the disorder or illness and receiving a doctor's care (Huth, 1987). "Manic–depressive cases were treated" is problematic; revise to "The patients with bipolar disorders were treated."

Bias may be promoted when the writer uses one group (usually the writer's own group) as the standard against which others are judged. In some contexts, the term *culturally deprived* may imply that one culture is the universally accepted standard. The unparallel nouns in the phrase *man and wife* may inappropriately prompt the reader to evaluate the roles of the individuals (i.e., the woman is defined only in terms of her relationship to the man) and the motives of the author. The phrase *husband and wife* or *man and woman* is parallel and undistracting. Usage of *normal* may prompt the reader to make the comparison of *abnormal*, thus stigmatizing individuals with differences. For example, contrasting lesbians with "the general public" or with "normal women" portrays lesbians as marginal to society. More appropriate comparison groups might be "heterosexual women," "heterosexual women and men," or "gay men."

Guideline 3: Acknowledge participation

Write about the people in your study in a way that acknowledges their participation. Replace the impersonal term *subjects* with a more descriptive term when possible and appropriate—*participants, individuals, college students, children,* or *respondents,* for example. *Subjects* and *sample* are appropriate when discussing statistics, and *subjects* may also be appropriate when there has been no direct consent by the individual involved in the study (e.g., infants or some individuals with severe brain damage or dementia). The passive voice suggests individuals are *acted on* instead of being actors ("the students *completed* the survey" is preferable to "the students *were given* the survey" or "the survey was *administered* to the students"). "Participants completed the trial" or "we collected data from the participants" is preferable to "the participants *were run.*" Although not grammatically passive, "presented with symptoms" suggests passiveness; "reported symptoms" or "described symptoms" is preferred (Knatterud, 1991). Similarly, consider avoiding terms such as *patient management* and *patient placement* when appropriate. In most cases, it is treatment, not patients, that is managed; some alternatives are "coordination of care," "supportive services," and "assistance." If patients are able to discuss their living arrangements, describe them as such. *Failed,* as in "8 participants failed to complete the Rorschach and the MMPI," can imply a personal shortcoming instead of a research result; *did not* is a more neutral choice (Knatterud, 1991).

As you read the rest of this chapter, consult Table 2.1 for examples of problematic and preferred language. Section 9.03 lists references for further information about nondiscriminatory language and for the guidelines that the APA Publications and Communications Board received as working papers for the additions to this section; the full texts of these papers are available in updated form on an ongoing basis.

2.13 *Gender*

Avoid ambiguity in sex identity or sex role by choosing nouns, pronouns, and adjectives that specifically describe your participants. Sexist bias can occur when pronouns are used carelessly, as when the masculine pronoun *he* is used to refer to both sexes or when the masculine or feminine pronoun is used exclusively to define roles by sex (e.g., "the nurse . . . *she*"). The use of *man* as a generic noun or as an ending for an occupational title (e.g., *policeman*) can be ambiguous and may imply incorrectly that all persons in the group are male. Be clear about whether you mean one sex or both sexes.

To avoid stereotypes, use caution when providing examples:

> To illustrate this idea, **an American boy's** potential for becoming a football player might be an aggregate of strength, running speed, balance, fearlessness, and resistance to injury. [The manuscript was revised to *a child's.*]

There are many alternatives to the generic *he* (see Table 2.1), including rephrasing (e.g., from "When an individual conducts this kind of self-appraisal, *he* is a much stronger person" to "When an individual conducts this kind of self-appraisal, that person is much stronger" or "This kind of self-appraisal makes an individual much stronger"), using plural nouns or plural pronouns (e.g., from "A therapist who is too much like his client can lose *his* objectivity" to "Therapists who are too much like their clients can lose *their* objectivity"), replacing the pronoun with an article (e.g., from "A researcher must apply for *his* grant by September 1" to "A researcher must apply for *the* grant by September 1"), and dropping the pronoun (e.g., from "The researcher must avoid letting *his* own biases and expectations" to "The researcher must avoid letting biases and expectations"). Replacing *he* with *he or she* or *she or he* should be done sparingly because the repetition can become tiresome. Combination forms such as *he/she* or *(s)he* are awkward and distracting. Alternating between *he* and *she* also may be distracting and is not ideal; doing so implies that *he* or *she* can in fact be generic, which is not the case. Use of either pronoun unavoidably suggests that specific gender to the reader.

2.14 *Sexual Orientation*

Sexual orientation is not the same as *sexual preference*. In keeping with Guideline 2, *sexual orientation* currently is the preferred term and is to be used unless the implication of choice is intentional.

The terms *lesbians* and *gay men* are preferable to *homosexual* when referring to specific groups. *Lesbian* and *gay* refer primarily to identities and to the culture and communities that have developed among people who share those identities. Furthermore, *homosexuality* has been associated in the past with negative stereotypes. Also, the term *homosexual* is ambiguous because some believe it refers only to men. *Gay* can be interpreted broadly, to include men and women, or more narrowly, to include only men. Therefore, if the meaning is not clear in the context of your usage, specify gender when using this term (e.g., *gay men*). The clearest way to refer inclusively to people whose orientation is not heterosexual is to write *lesbians, gay men,* and *bisexual women or men*—although somewhat long, the phrase is accurate.

Sexual behavior should be distinguished from sexual orientation; some men and women engage in sexual activities with others of their own sex but do not consider themselves to be gay or lesbian. In contrast, the terms *heterosexual* and *bisexual* currently are used to describe both identity and behavior; adjectives are preferred to nouns. *Same-gender, male–male, female–female,* and *male–female sexual behavior* are appropriate terms for specific instances of sexual behavior in which people engage, regardless of their sexual orientation (e.g., a married heterosexual man who once had a same-gender sexual encounter).

2.15 *Racial and Ethnic Identity*

Preferences for terms referring to racial and ethnic groups change often. One reason for this is simply personal preference; preferred designations are as varied as the people they name. Another reason is that over time, designations can become dated and sometimes negative (see Raspberry, 1989). Authors are reminded of the two basic guidelines of specificity and sensitivity. In keeping with Guideline 2, authors are encouraged to ask their participants about preferred designations and are expected to avoid terms perceived as negative. For example, some people of African ancestry prefer *Black* and others prefer *African American*; both terms currently are acceptable. On the other hand, *Negro* and *Afro-American* have become dated; therefore, usage generally is inappropriate. In keeping with Guideline 1, precision is important in the description of your sample (see section 1.09); in general, use the more specific rather than the less specific term.

Racial and ethnic groups are designated by proper nouns and are capitalized. Therefore, use *Black* and *White* instead of *black* and *white* (colors to refer to other human groups currently are considered pejorative and should not be used). For modifiers, do not use hyphens in multiword names, even if the names act as unit modifiers (e.g., *Asian American* participants).

Designations for some ethnic groups are described next. These groups frequently are included in studies published in APA journals. The list is far from exhaustive but serves to illustrate some of the complexities of naming (see Table 2.1).

Depending on where a person is from, individuals may prefer to be called *Hispanic, Latino, Chicano,* or some other designation; *Hispanic* is not necessarily an all-encompassing term, and authors should consult with their participants. In general, naming a nation or region of origin is generally helpful (e.g., *Cuban* or *Central American* is more specific than *Hispanic*).

American Indian and *Native American* are both accepted terms for referring to indigenous peoples of North America, although *Native Americans* is a broader designation because the U.S. government includes Hawaiians and Samoans in this category. There are close to 450 Native groups, and authors are encouraged to name the participants' specific groups.

The term *Asian* or *Asian American* is preferred to the older term *Oriental.* It is generally useful to specify the name of the Asian subgroup: Chinese, Vietnamese, Korean, Pakistani, and so on.

2.16 *Disabilities*

The guiding principle for "nonhandicapping" language is to maintain the integrity of individuals as human beings. Avoid language that equates persons with their condition (e.g., *neurotics, the disabled*); that has superfluous, negative overtones (e.g., stroke *victim*); or that is regarded as a slur (e.g., *cripple*).

Use *disability* to refer to an attribute of a person and *handicap* to refer to the source of limitations, which may include attitudinal, legal, and architectural barriers as well as the disability itself (e.g., steps and curbs handicap people who require the use of a ramp). *Challenged* and *special* are often considered euphemistic and should be used only if the people in your study prefer those terms (Boston, 1992). As a general rule, "person with _____," "person living with _____," and "person who has _____" are neutral and preferred forms of description (see Table 2.1).

2.17 *Age*

Age should be defined in the description of participants in the Method section (see section 1.09). Be specific in providing age ranges; avoid open-ended definitions such as "under 18" or "over 65" (Schaie, 1993). *Boy* and *girl* are correct terms for referring to people of high school age and younger. *Young man* and *young woman* and *male adolescent* and *female adolescent* may be used as appropriate. For persons 18 and older (or of college age and older), use *men* and *women. Elderly* is not acceptable as a noun and is considered pejorative by some as an adjective. *Older person* is preferred. Age groups may also be described with adjectives; gerontologists may prefer to use combination terms for older age groups (*young-old, old-old, very old,* and *oldest old*), which should be used only as adjectives. *Dementia* is preferred to *senility; senile dementia of the Alzheimer's type* is an accepted term.

Table 2.1. *Guidelines for Unbiased Language*

Problematic	Preferred
Guideline 1: Use an appropriate level of specificity	
The client's behavior was typically female.	The client's behavior was [specify].
Comment: Being specific avoids stereotypic bias.	
Guideline 2: Be sensitive to labels	
Participants were 300 Orientals.	There were 300 Asian participants [perhaps adding "150 from Southeast Asia (Thailand, Laos, and Vietnam) and 150 from East Asia (North and South Korea)"].
Comment: Orientals is considered pejorative; use *Asian,* or be more specific.	
the elderly	older people
Comment: Use adjectives as adjectives instead of as nouns.	
girls and men	women and men
Comment: Use parallel terms; *girls* is correct if females of high school age or younger are meant.	
Guideline 3: Acknowledge participation	
Our study included 60 subjects.	Sixty people participated in our study.
Comment: Participants is preferred to *subjects.*	
Gender	
1. The client is usually the best judge of the value of his counseling.	The client is usually the best judge of the value of counseling.
	The client is usually the best judge of his or her counseling.
	Clients are usually the best judges of the value of the counseling they receive.

Table 2.1. (*continued*)

Problematic	Preferred
	The best judge of the value of counseling is usually the client.
2. man, mankind	people, humanity, human beings, humankind, human species
man a project	staff a project, hire personnel, employ staff
man–machine interface	user–system interface, person–system interface, human–computer interface
manpower	workforce, personnel, workers, human resources
man's search for knowledge	the search for knowledge
3. males, females	men, women, boys, girls, adults, children, adolescents

Comment: Specific nouns reduce the possibility of stereotypic bias and often clarify discussion. Use *male* and *female* as adjectives where appropriate and relevant (*female experimenter, male participant*). *Males* and *females* may be appropriate when the age range is quite broad or ambiguous. Avoid unparallel usage such as 10 *men* and 16 *females*.

4. Research scientists often neglect their wives and children.	Research scientists often neglect their spouses and children.

Comment: Alternative wording acknowledges that women as well as men are research scientists.

5. woman doctor, lady lawyer, male nurse, woman driver	doctor or physician, lawyer, nurse, driver

Comment: Specify sex only if it is a variable or if sex designation is necessary to the discussion ("13 female doctors and 22 male doctors"). *Woman* and *lady* are nouns; *female* is the adjective counterpart to *male.*

(*table continues*)

Table 2.1. (*continued*)

Problematic	*Preferred*
6. mothering	parenting, nurturing [or specify exact behavior]
7. chairman (of an academic department)	chairperson, chair [use *chairman* only if it is known that the institution has established that form as an official title]

Comment: Department head may be appropriate; however, the term is not synonymous with *chair* and *chairperson* at all institutions.

chairman (presiding officer of a committee or meeting)	chairperson, chair, moderator, discussion leader

Comment: In parliamentary usage, *chairman* is the official term and should not be changed. Alternatives are acceptable in most writing.

8. foreman, mailman, salesmanship	supervisor or superintendent, postal worker or letter carrier, selling ability

Comment: Substitute preferred noun.

9. The authors acknowledge the assistance of Mrs. John Smith.	The authors acknowledge the assistance of Jane Smith.

Comment: Use given names.

10. cautious men and timid women	cautious women and men, cautious people
	timid men and women, timid people

Comment: Some adjectives, depending on whether the person described is a man or a woman, connote bias. The examples illustrate some common usages that may not always convey exact meaning, especially when paired, as in the first column.

11. Participants were 16 men and 4 women. The women were housewives.	The men were [specify], and the women were [specify].

Table 2.1. (*continued*)

Problematic	Preferred

Comment: Describe women and men in parallel terms, or omit description of both. Do not use *housewife* to identify occupation, a term that indicates sex and marital status and excludes men. Use *homemaker*, which can denote a man.

Sexual orientation

Problematic	Preferred
1. The sample consisted of 200 adolescent homosexuals.	The sample consisted of 200 gay male adolescents.
	The sample consisted of 100 gay male and 100 lesbian adolescents.

Comment: Avoid use of *homosexual*, and specify gender of participants.

Problematic	Preferred
2. Manuscript title: "Gay Relationships in the 1990s"	"Gay Male Relationships in the 1990s"
	"Lesbian and Gay Male Relationships in the 1990s"

Comment: Specify gender equitably.

Problematic	Preferred
3. Participants were asked about their homosexuality.	Participants were asked about the experience of being a lesbian or a gay man.

Comment: Avoid the label *homosexuality.*

Problematic	Preferred
4. The women reported lesbian sexual fantasies.	The women reported female–female sexual fantasies.

Comment: Avoid confusing lesbian orientation with specific sexual behaviors.

Problematic	Preferred
5. It was the participants' sex, not their sexual orientation, that affected number of friendships.	It was the participants' gender, not their sexual orientation, that affected number of friendships.

Comment: Avoid confusing gender with sexual activity.

(*table continues*)

Table 2.1. (**continued**)

Problematic	Preferred
6. participants who had engaged in sexual intercourse	participants who had engaged in penile–vaginal intercourse
	participants who had engaged in sexual intercourse or had sex with another person

Comment: The first preferred example specifies kind of sexual activity, if penile–vaginal intercourse is what is meant. The second avoids the assumption of heterosexual orientation if sexual experiences with others is what is meant.

7. Ten participants were married, and 5 were single.	Ten participants were married, 4 were unmarried and living with partners, and 1 was unmarried and living alone.

Comment: The preferred example increases specificity and acknowledges that legal marriage is only one form of committed relationship. Marital status is sometimes not a reliable indicator of cohabitation (e.g., married couples may be separated), sexual activity, or sexual orientation.

Racial and ethnic identity

1. The sample included 400 undergraduate participants.	The sample of 400 under-graduates included 250 White students (125 men and 125 women) and 150 Black students (75 men and 75 women).

Comment: Human samples should be fully described with respect to gender, age, and, when relevant to the study, race or ethnicity. Where appropriate, additional information should be presented (generation, linguistic background, socioeconomic status, national origin, sexual orientation, special interest group membership, etc.). Note that *African American* currently may be preferred.

2. The 50 American Indians represented. . . .	The 50 American Indians (25 Choctaw, 15 Hopi, and 10 Seminole) represented. . . .

Table 2.1. (*continued*)

Problematic	Preferred

Comment: When appropriate, authors should identify American Indian groups by specific group or nation; when the broader designation is appropriate, note that *Native American* may be preferred to *American Indian.* In general, American Indian, African, and other groups prefer *people* or *nation* to *tribe.*

3. We studied Eskimos

We studied Inuit from Canada and Aleuts

Comment: Native peoples of northern Canada, Alaska, eastern Siberia, and Greenland may prefer *Inuk* (*Inuit* for plural) to *Eskimo.* Alaska Natives include many groups in addition to Eskimos.

4. Table entries:

Race			Race		
White	21	15	White	21	15
Non-White	15	4	African American	10	1
			Asian	5	3

Comment: Non-White implies a standard of comparison and is imprecise.

5. the articulate Mexican American professor

the Mexican American professor

Comment: Qualifying adjectives may imply that the "articulate" Mexican American professor is an exception to the norm (for Mexican American professors). Depending on the context of the sentence, ethnic identity may not be relevant and therefore should not be mentioned.

Disabilities

1. *Put people first, not their disability*

disabled person

person with (who has) a disability

defective child

child with a congenital disability

child with a birth impairment

(table continues)

Table 2.1. (*continued*)

Problematic	Preferred
mentally ill person	person with mental illness

Comment: Preferred expressions avoid the implication that the person as a whole is disabled.

2. *Do not label people by their disability or overextend its severity*

depressives	people who are depressed
epileptics	individuals with epilepsy
borderlines	people diagnosed with borderline personality disorder
neurotic patients	patients with a neurosis (or neuroses)
the learning disabled	children with [specify the learning characteristics]
retarded adult	adult with mental retardation

Comment: Because the person is *not* the disability, the two concepts should be separate.

3. *Use emotionally neutral expressions*

stroke victim	individual who had a stroke
person afflicted with cerebral palsy	person with cerebral palsy
population suffering from multiple sclerosis	people who have multiple sclerosis
individual confined to a wheelchair	individual who uses a wheelchair

Comment: Problematic expressions have excessive, negative overtones and suggest continued helplessness.

CHAPTER THREE

APA Editorial Style

When editors or typesetters refer to *style*, they usually do not mean writing style; they mean editorial style—the rules or guidelines a publisher observes to ensure clear, consistent presentation of the printed word. Editorial style concerns uniform use of punctuation and abbreviations, construction of tables, selection of headings, and citation of references, as well as many other elements that are part of every manuscript.

An author writing for a publication must follow the style rules established by the publisher to avoid inconsistencies among journal articles or book chapters. For example, without rules of style, three different manuscripts might use *sub-test, subtest,* and *Subtest* in one issue of a journal or one book. Although the meaning of the word is the same and the choice of one style over the other may seem arbitrary (in this case, *subtest* is APA style), such variations in style may distract or confuse the reader.

This chapter describes the style for APA journals. It omits general rules explained in widely available style books and examples of usage with little relevance to APA journals. Among the most helpful general guides to editorial style are *Words into Type* (Skillin & Gay, 1974) and the *Chicago Manual of Style* (University of Chicago Press, 1993), both of which were used in developing this section. Style manuals agree more often than they disagree; where they disagree, the *Publication Manual,* because it is based on the special requirements of psychology, takes precedence for APA publications.

Punctuation

Punctuation establishes the cadence of a sentence, telling the reader where to pause (comma, semicolon, and colon), stop (period and question mark), or take a detour (dash, parentheses, and brackets; Nurnberg, 1972). Punctuation of a sentence usually denotes a pause in thought; different kinds of punctuation indicate different kinds and lengths of pauses.

3.01 *Period*

Use a period to end a complete sentence. For other uses of periods, see the following sections: Abbreviations (section 3.27), Quotations (sections 3.36–3.39), Numbers (section 3.46), and References (chapter 4).

3.02 *Comma*

Use a comma

- between elements (including before *and* and *or*) in a series of three or more items. (See section 3.33 for use of commas in numbered or lettered series.)

  the height, width, or depth

  in a study by Stacy, Newcomb, and Bentler (1991)

- to set off a nonessential or nonrestrictive clause, that is, a clause that embellishes a sentence but if removed would leave the grammatical structure and meaning of the sentence intact.

  Switch A, which was on a panel, controlled the recording device.

  Significant differences were found for both ratings of controllability by self, $F(3, 132) = 19.58$, $p \leq .01$, est $\eta^2 = .31$, and ratings of controllability by others, $F(3, 96) = 3.21$, $p = .03$, est $\eta^2 = .09$.

- to separate two independent clauses joined by a conjunction.

  Cedar shavings covered the floor, and paper was available for shredding and nest building.

- to set off the year in exact dates.

  April 18, 1992, was the correct date.

  but

  April 1992 was the correct month.

- to set off the year in parenthetical reference citations.

  (Patrick, 1993)

  (Kelsey, 1993, discovered . . .)

- to separate groups of three digits in most numbers of 1,000 or more (see section 3.48 for exceptions).

Do not use a comma

- before an essential or restrictive clause, that is, a clause that limits or defines the material it modifies. Removal of such a clause from the sentence would alter the intended meaning.

  The switch that stops the recording device also controls the light.

- between the two parts of a compound predicate.

  The results contradicted Smith's hypothesis and indicated that the effect was nonsignificant.

- to separate parts of measurement.

  8 years 2 months   3 min 40 s

3.03 *Semicolon*
Use a semicolon

- to separate two independent clauses that are not joined by a conjunction.

  The participants in the first study were paid; those in the second were unpaid.

- to separate elements in a series that already contain commas. (See section 3.33 for the use of semicolons in numbered or lettered series.)

  The color order was red, yellow, blue; blue, yellow, red; or yellow, red, blue.

  (Davis & Hueter, 1994; Pettigrew, 1993)

  main effects of age, $F(1, 76) = 7.86$, $p < .01$, $d = .09$ ($MSE = .019$); condition, $F(1, 76) = 4.11$, $p = .05$, $d = .06$; and the Age × Condition interaction, $F(1, 76) = 4.96$, $p = .03$, $d = .07$

3.04 *Colon*
Use a colon

- between a grammatically complete introductory clause (one that could stand as a sentence) and a final phrase or clause that illustrates, extends, or amplifies the preceding thought. If the clause following the colon is a complete sentence, it begins with a capital letter.

For example, Freud (1930/1961) wrote of two urges: an urge toward union with others and an egoistic urge toward happiness.

They have agreed on the outcome: Informed participants perform better than do uninformed participants.

■ in ratios and proportions.

The proportion (salt:water) was 1:8.

■ in references between place of publication and publisher.

New York: Wiley.   St. Louis, MO: Mosby.

Do not use a colon

■ after an introduction that is not a complete sentence.

The formula is $r_i = e + a$

The instructions for the task were

> Your group's task is to rank the 15 items in terms of their importance for the crew's survival. When your group has come to an agreement, indicate your group's ranking in the space below. Put a number 1 by the most important item, a number 2 by the second most important item, and so on through number 15, the least important item. Do not give the same ranking to more than 1 item; that is, no ties are allowed. You have 20 minutes to complete the rankings.

3.05 *Dash*

Use the dash to indicate only a sudden interruption in the continuity of a sentence. Overuse weakens the flow of material. (See also section 3.13 for capitalization following dashes in titles.)

These 2 participants—1 from the first group, 1 from the second —were tested separately.

3.06 *Quotation Marks*

Observe the following guidelines for uses of double quotation marks other than in material quoted directly from a source. See section 3.36 for a discussion of double and single quotation marks in quoted material.

Use double quotation marks

■ to introduce a word or phrase used as an ironic comment, as slang, or as an invented or coined expression. Use quotation marks the first time the word or phrase is used; thereafter, do not use quotation marks.

considered "normal" behavior

the "good-outcome" variable . . . the good-outcome variable [no quotation marks after the initial usage]

but

Subjects in the *small* group [*Small* is italicized to prevent mis-reading—here it means a group designation, not the size of the group. See also section 3.19 for other uses of italics.]

■ to set off the title of an article or chapter in a periodical or book when the title is mentioned in text. (Titles in the reference list are not enclosed in quotation marks; see section 4.10.)

Riger's (1992) article, "Epistemological Debates, Feminist Voices: Science, Social Values, and the Study of Women"

■ to reproduce material from a test item or verbatim instructions to participants.

The first fill-in item was "could be expected to _____."

If instructions are long, set them off from text in a block format without quotation marks. (See sections 3.34, 3.36, and 5.13 for discussion of block format.)

Do not use double quotation marks

■ to identify the anchors of a scale. Instead, italicize them.

   We ranked the items on a scale ranging from 1 (*all of the time*) to 5 (*never*).

■ to cite a letter, word, phrase, or sentence as a linguistic example. Instead, italicize the term.

   He clarified the distinction between *farther* and *further*.

■ to introduce a technical or key term. Instead, italicize the term.

   The term *zero-base budgeting* appeared frequently in the speech.

   She compared it with *meta-analysis*, which is described in the next section.

■ to hedge. Do not use any punctuation with such expressions.

   Incorrect:
   The teacher "rewarded" the class with tokens.

   Correct:
   The teacher rewarded the class with tokens.

3.07 *Parentheses*
Use parentheses

■ to set off structurally independent elements.

The patterns were significant (see Figure 5).

(When a complete sentence is enclosed in parentheses, place punctuation in the sentence inside the parentheses, like this.) If only part of a sentence is enclosed in parentheses (like this), place punctuation outside the parentheses (like this).

■ to set off reference citations in text (see sections 3.94–3.103 and Appendix D for further discussion of reference citations in text).

Dumas and Doré (1991) reported

is fully described elsewhere (Hong & O'Neil, 1992)

■ to introduce an abbreviation.

effect on the galvanic skin response (GSR)

■ to set off letters that identify items in a series within a sentence or paragraph (see also section 3.33 on seriation).

The subject areas included (a) synonyms associated with cultural interactions, (b) descriptors for ethnic group membership, and (c) psychological symptoms and outcomes associated with bicultural adaptation.

■ to group mathematical expressions (see also sections 3.09 and 3.60).

$(k - 1)/(g - 2)$

- to enclose the citation or page number of a direct quotation (see also section 3.39).

  The author stated, "The effect disappeared within minutes" (Lopez, 1993, p. 311), but she did not say which effect.

  Lopez (1993) found that "the effect disappeared within minutes" (p. 311).

- to enclose numbers that identify displayed formulas and equations.

$$M_j = \alpha M_{j-1} + f_j + g_j * g_{j'} \tag{1}$$

- to enclose statistical values.

  was significant ($p < .05$)

- to enclose degrees of freedom.

  $t(75) = 2.19$

  $F(2, 116) = 3.71$

Do not use parentheses

- to enclose material within other parentheses.

  (the Beck Depression Inventory [BDI]) [the use of brackets avoids nested parentheses]

  was significant, $F(4, 132) = 13.62$, $p < .01$.

- back to back.

  (e.g., defensive pessimism; Norem & Cantor, 1986)

3.08 *Brackets*
Use brackets

■ to enclose parenthetical material that is already within parentheses.

(The results for the control group [n = 8] are also presented in Figure 2.)

Exception 1: Do not use brackets if the material can be set off easily with commas without confounding meaning:

Unnecessary:

(as Imai [1990] later concluded)

Better:

(as Imai, 1990, later concluded)

Exception 2: In mathematical material, the placement of brackets and parentheses is reversed; that is, parentheses appear within brackets. (See section 3.60 for further discussion of brackets in equations.)

■ to enclose material inserted in a quotation by some person other than the original writer.

"when [his own and others'] behaviors were studied" (Hanisch, 1992, p. 24)

Do not use brackets

■ to set off statistics that already include parentheses.

was significant, $F(1, 32) = 4.37$, $p < .05$.

not

was significant, $(F[1, 32] = 4.37, p < .05)$.

was significant, $[F(1, 32) = 4.37, p < .05]$.

3.09 *Slash*

Use a slash (also called a *virgule, solidus,* or *shill*)

■   to clarify a relationship in which a hyphenated compound is used.

the classification/similarity-judgment condition

hits/false-alarms comparison

■   to separate numerator from denominator.

X/Y

■   to indicate *per* to separate units of measurement accompanied by a numerical value.

0.5 deg/s   7.4 mg/kg

but

luminance is measured in candelas per square meter

■   to set off English phonemes.

/o/

■   to cite a republished work in text.

Freud (1923/1961)

Do not use a slash

■ when a phrase would be clearer.

Each child handed the ball to her mother or guardian.

not

Each child handed the ball to her mother/guardian.

■ for simple comparisons. Use a hyphen or short dash (en dash) instead.

test–retest reliability

not

test/retest reliability

■ more than once to express compound units. Use centered dots and parentheses as needed to prevent ambiguity.

$nmol \cdot hr^{-1} \cdot mg^{-1}$

not

nmol/hr/mg

Spelling

3.10 *Preferred Spelling*

Merriam-Webster's Collegiate Dictionary is the standard spelling reference for APA journals and books.[1] If a word is not in *Webster's Collegiate*, consult the more comprehensive *Webster's Third New International Dictionary*. If the dictionary gives a choice, use the first spelling listed; for example, use *aging* and *canceled* rather than *ageing* and *cancelled*.

> Consult www.apastyle.org
> for the latest information.

Plural forms of some words of Latin or Greek origin can be troublesome; a list of proper and preferred spellings of some of the more common ones follows. Authors are reminded that plural nouns take plural verbs.

Singular	Plural	Singular	Plural
appendix	appendixes	matrix	matrices
cannula	cannulas	phenomenon	phenomena
datum	data	schema	schemas

3.11 *Hyphenation*

Compound words take many forms; that is, two words may be written as (a) two separate words, (b) a hyphenated word, or (c) one unbroken, "solid" word. Choosing the proper form is sometimes frustrating. For example, is *follow up*, *follow-up*, or *followup* the form to be used? The dictionary is an excellent guide for such decisions, especially for non-scientific words (the term is *follow-up* when functioning as a noun or adjective but *follow up* when functioning as a verb). When a compound can be found in the dictionary, its usage is established and it is known

---

[1]Dictionaries are not a good guide to the rapidly proliferating vocabulary of the Internet and the World Wide Web. The 10th edition of *Merriam-Webster's Collegiate*, for example, lists *E-mail* as the preferred spelling, but the term is now so common that it is usually spelled *e-mail* or even *email* (APA currently uses *e-mail*).

as a *permanent compound* (e.g., *high school, caregiver,* and *self-esteem*). Dictionaries do not always agree on the way a compound should be written (open, solid, or hyphenated); APA follows *Webster's Collegiate* in most cases. Compound terms are often introduced into the language as separate or hyphenated words, and as they become more commonplace, they tend to fuse into a solid word. For example, the hyphen was dropped from *life-style* in the 10th edition of *Webster's Collegiate,* and *data base* is now *database.*

There is another kind of compound—the *temporary compound,* which is made up of two or more words that occur together, perhaps only in a particular paper, to express a thought. Because language is constantly expanding, especially in science, temporary compounds develop that are not yet listed in the dictionary. If a temporary compound modifies another word, it may or may not be hyphenated, depending on (a) its position in the sentence and (b) whether the pairing of a compound with another word can cause the reader to misinterpret meaning. The main rule to remember is that if a temporary compound *precedes* what it modifies, it may need to be hyphenated, and if it *follows* what it modifies, it usually does not. If a compound is not in the dictionary, follow the general principles of hyphenation given here and in Table 3.1. When you are still in doubt, use hyphens for clarity rather than omit them. (See also Tables 3.2 and 3.3 for treatment of prefixes.)

General Principle 1

Do not use a hyphen unless it serves a purpose. If a compound adjective cannot be misread or, as with many psychological terms, its meaning is established, a hyphen is not necessary.

least squares solution	sex role differences
semantic differential technique	constant stimulus method
covert learning conditions	rank order correlation
day treatment program	repeated measures design
health care reform	heart rate scores
grade point average	

Table 3.1. *Guide to Hyphenating Terms*

Rule	Example
Hyphenate	
1. A compound with a participle when it precedes the term it modifies	■ role-playing technique ■ anxiety-arousing condition ■ water-deprived animals
2. A phrase used as an adjective when it precedes the term it modifies	■ trial-by-trial analysis ■ to-be-recalled items ■ all-or-none questionnaire
3. An adjective-and-noun compound when it precedes the term it modifies	■ high-anxiety group ■ middle-class families ■ low-frequency words
4. A compound with a number as the first element when the compound precedes the term it modifies	■ two-way analysis of variance ■ six-trial problem ■ 12th-grade students ■ 16-s interval
Do not hyphenate	
1. A compound including an adverb ending in *-ly*	■ widely used text ■ relatively homogeneous sample ■ randomly assigned participants
2. A compound including a comparative or superlative adjective	■ better written paper ■ less informed interviewers ■ higher scoring students ■ higher order learning
3. Chemical terms	■ sodium chloride solution ■ amino acid compound
4. Foreign phrases used as adjectives or adverbs	■ a posteriori test ■ post hoc comparisons ■ fed ad lib [but hyphenate the adjectival form: ad-lib feeding; see *Webster's Collegiate*]
5. A modifier including a letter or numeral as the second element	■ Group B participants ■ Type II error ■ Trial 1 performance
6. Common fractions used as nouns	■ one third of the participants

Table 3.2. *Prefixes That Do Not Require Hyphens*

Prefix	Example	Prefix	Example
after	aftereffect	multi	multiphase
anti	antisocial	non	nonsignificant
bi	bilingual	over	overaggressive
co	coworker	post	posttest
counter	counterbalance	pre	preexperimental
equi	equimax	pro	prowar
extra	extracurricular	pseudo	pseudoscience
infra	infrared	re	reevaluate
inter	interstimulus	semi	semidarkness
intra	intraspecific	socio	socioeconomic
macro	macrocosm	sub	subtest
mega	megawatt	super	superordinate
meta[a]	metacognitive	supra	supraliminal
micro	microcosm	ultra	ultrahigh
mid	midterm	un	unbiased
mini	minisession	under	underdeveloped

[a]But *meta-analysis*.

General Principle 2

In a temporary compound that is used as an adjective before a noun, use a hyphen if the term can be misread or if the term expresses a single thought (i.e., all words together modify the noun). For example, are *different word lists* (a) word lists that are different from other word lists (if so, *different* modifies *word lists*; thus, write *different word lists*) or (b) lists that present different words (if so, the first word modifies the second, and together they modify *lists*, thus, *different-word lists*). Likewise, "the adolescents resided in two parent homes" means that two homes served as residences, whereas if the adolescents resided in "two-parent homes,"

Table 3.3. Prefixed Words That Require Hyphens

Occurrence	Example
Compounds in which the base word is	
capitalized	■ pro-Freudian
a number	■ post-1970
an abbreviation	■ pre-UCS trial
more than one word	■ non-achievement-oriented students
All *self-* compounds, whether they are adjectives or nouns[a]	■ self-report technique ■ the test was self-paced ■ self-esteem
Words that could be misunderstood	■ re-pair [pair again] ■ re-form [form again] ■ un-ionized
Words in which the prefix ends and the base word begins with the same vowel[b]	■ meta-analysis ■ anti-intellectual ■ co-occur

[a]But *self psychology.*
[b]*Pre* and *re* compounds are usually set solid to base words beginning with *e.*

they each would live in a household headed by two parents. A properly placed hyphen helps the reader understand the intended meaning.

General Principle 3

Most compound adjective rules are applicable only when the compound adjective *precedes* the term it modifies. If a compound adjective *follows* the term, do not use a hyphen, because relationships are sufficiently clear without one.

client-centered counseling

but

the counseling was client centered

t-test results

but

results from *t* tests

same-sex children

but

children of the same sex

General Principle 4
Write most words formed with prefixes as one word (see Table 3.2). Some exceptions, as in Table 3.3, require hyphens.

General Principle 5
When two or more compound modifiers have a common base, this base is sometimes omitted in all except the last modifier, but the hyphens are retained.

long- and short-term memory

2-, 3-, and 10-min trials

See section 5.11 for use of hyphens and dashes in mathematical copy.

Capitalization
Capitalize words, that is, use an uppercase letter for the first letter of a word, according to the guidelines in the following sections.

3.12 *Words Beginning a Sentence*
Capitalize

■ the first word in a complete sentence.
■ the first word after a colon that begins a complete sentence.

The author made one main point: No explanation that has been suggested so far answers all questions.

3.13 *Major Words in Titles and Headings*
Capitalize

■ major words in titles of books and articles within the body of the paper. Conjunctions, articles, and short prepositions are not considered major words; however, capitalize all words of four letters or more. Capitalize all verbs (including linking verbs), nouns, adjectives, adverbs, and pronouns. When a capitalized word is a hyphenated compound, capitalize both words. Also, capitalize the first word after a colon or a dash in a title.

In her book, *History of Pathology*

The criticism of the article, "Attitudes Toward Mental Health Workers"

"Ultrasonic Vocalizations Are Elicited From Rat Pups"

"Memory in Hearing-Impaired Children: Implications for Vocabulary Development"

Exception: In titles of books and articles in reference lists, capitalize only the first word, the first word after a colon or a dash, and proper nouns. Do not capitalize the second word of a hyphenated compound. (See chapter 4 for further discussion of reference style.)

Hanson, R. K., Steffy, R. A., & Gauthier, R. (1993). Long-term recidivism of child molesters.

Kalichman, S. C., Kelly, J. A., Hunter, T. L., Murphy, D. A., & Tyler, R. (1993). Culturally tailored HIV-AIDS risk-reduction messages targeted to African-American urban women: Impact on risk sensitization and risk reduction.

- major words in article headings and subheadings.

Exception: In indented paragraph (Level 4) headings, capitalize only the first word and proper nouns (see section 3.31).

- major words in table titles and figure legends. In table *headings* and figure *captions*, capitalize only the first word and proper nouns (see sections 3.67 for table headings and 3.84 for captions).
- references to titles of sections within the same article.

as explained in the Method section

which is discussed in the *Data Analyses* subsection

3.14 *Proper Nouns and Trade Names*
Capitalize

- proper nouns and adjectives and words used as proper nouns. Proper adjectives that have acquired a common meaning are not capitalized; consult *Webster's Collegiate* for guidance.

Freudian slip

Wilks's lambda

Greco-Latin square

but

eustachian tube

cesarean section

- names of university departments if they refer to a specific department within a specific university and complete names of academic courses if they refer to a specific course.

Department of Sociology, University of Washington

Psychology 101

Developmental Psychopathology

but

a sociology department

an introductory psychology course

■ trade and brand names of drugs, equipment, and food.

Elavil [*but* amitriptyline hydrochloride]

Hunter Klockounter

Plexiglas

Purina Monkey Chow

Xerox

Do not capitalize names of laws, theories, models, or hypotheses.

the empirical law of effect

parallel distributed processing model

associative learning model

but

Gregory's theory of illusions [Retain uppercase in personal names.]

3.15 *Nouns Followed by Numerals or Letters*

Capitalize nouns followed by numerals or letters that denote a specific place in a numbered series.

On Day 2 of Experiment 4

during Trial 5, the no-delay group performed

as shown in Table 2 and Figure 3B

Grant AG02726 from the National Institute on Aging

Exception: **Do not capitalize** nouns that denote common parts of books or tables followed by numerals or letters.

chapter 4   page iv

row 3   column 5

Do not capitalize nouns that precede a variable.

trial n and item x

but

Trial 3 and Item b [The number and letter are not variables.]

3.16 *Titles of Tests*

Capitalize exact, complete titles of published and unpublished tests. Words such as *test* or *scale* are not capitalized if they refer to subscales of tests.

Advanced Vocabulary Test

Minnesota Multiphasic Personality Inventory

Stroop Color–Word Interference Test

the authors' Mood Adjective Checklist

but

MMPI Depression scale

Do not capitalize shortened, inexact, or generic titles of tests.

   a vocabulary test   Stroop color test

3.17 *Names of Conditions or Groups in an Experiment*
Do not capitalize names of conditions or groups in an experiment.

   experimental and control groups

   participants were divided into information and no-information
   conditions

   but

   Conditions A and B [See section 3.15.]

3.18 *Names of Factors, Variables, and Effects*
Capitalize names of derived factors within a factor analysis. The word *factor* is not capitalized unless it is followed by a number (see section 3.15).

   Mealtime Behavior (Factor 4)

   Factors 6 and 7

   Big Five personality factors

   Do not capitalize effects or variables unless they appear with multiplication signs. (Take care that you do not use the term *factor* when you mean *effect* or *variable*, for example, in an interaction or analysis of variance.)

   a significant age effect

   the sex, age, and weight variables

but

the Sex × Age × Weight interaction

a 3 × 3 × 2 (Group × Trial × Response) design

a 2 (methods) × 2 (item type)

Italics

3.19 *Italicizing Words*

For specific use of italics in APA journals, see the guidelines listed below. In general, use italics infrequently. (If you are using a typewriter instead of a word-processing program with an italics function, underline the text to be italicized.)

Use italics for

■ titles of books, periodicals, and microfilm publications

    The Elements of Style

    American Psychologist

■ genera, species, and varieties

    Macaca mulatta

■ introduction of a new, technical, or key term or label (after a term has been used once, do not italicize it)

    The term *backward masking*

    box labeled *empty*

■ letter, word, or phrase cited as a linguistic example

words such as *big* and *little*

the letter *a*

the meaning of *to fit tightly together*

a row of *X*s

■ words that could be misread

the *small* group [meaning a designation, not group size]

■ letters used as statistical symbols or algebraic variables

$F(1, 53) = 10.03$

t test

trial *n*

$a/b = c/d$

SEM

■ some test scores and scales

Rorschach scores: $F + \%$, *Z*

MMPI scales: *Hs, Pd*

■ periodical volume numbers in reference lists

26, 46–67

■ anchors of a scale

health ratings ranged from 1 (poor) to 5 (*excellent*)

Do not use italics for

- foreign phrases and abbreviations common in English (i.e., phrases found as main entries in *Webster's Collegiate Dictionary*)

a posteriori	et al.
a priori	per se
ad lib	vis-à-vis

- chemical terms

  NaCl, LSD

- trigonometric terms

  sin, tan, log

- nonstatistical subscripts to statistical symbols or mathematical expressions

  F_{max}

  $S_A + S_B$, where S_A represents Group A's score and S_B represents Group B's score

- Greek letters

  β

- mere emphasis (Italics are acceptable if emphasis might otherwise be lost; in general, however, use syntax to provide emphasis.)

  it is *important* to bear in mind that *this* process is *not* proposed as a *stage* theory of developments. [italics are not necessary]

■   letters used as abbreviations

intertrial interval (ITI)

Abbreviations

3.20 *Use of Abbreviations*

To maximize clarity, APA prefers that authors use abbreviations sparingly. Although abbreviations are sometimes useful for long, technical terms in scientific writing, communication is usually garbled rather than clarified if, for example, an abbreviation is unfamiliar to the reader.

Overuse. Consider whether the space saved by abbreviations in the following sentence justifies the time necessary to master the meaning:

> The advantage of the LH was clear from the RT data, which reflected high FP and FN rates for the RH.

Without abbreviations the passage reads as follows:

> The advantage of the left hand was clear from the reaction time data, which reflected high false-positive and false-negative rates for the right hand.

Underuse. Excessive use of abbreviations, whether standard or unique to one manuscript, can hinder reading comprehension. Conversely, abbreviations introduced on first mention of a term and used fewer than three times thereafter, particularly in a long paper, may be difficult for a reader to remember, and you probably serve the reader best if you write them out each time. In the following example, however, a standard abbreviation for a long, familiar term eases the reader's task:

> Patients at seven hospitals completed the MMPI-2.

Deciding whether to abbreviate. In all circumstances other than in the reference list (see section 4.03) and in the abstract, you must decide (a) whether to spell out a given expression every time it is used in an article or (b) whether to spell it out initially and abbreviate it thereafter. For example, the abbreviations *L* for large and *S* for small in a paper discussing different sequences of reward (*LLSS* or *LSLS*) would be an effective and readily understood shortcut. In another paper, however, writing about the *L reward* and the *S reward* would be both unnecessary and confusing. In most instances, abbreviating experimental group names is ineffective because the abbreviations are not adequately informative or easily recognizable and may even be more cumbersome than the full name. In general, use an abbreviation only (a) if it is conventional and if the reader is more familiar with the abbreviation than with the complete form or (b) if considerable space can be saved and cumbersome repetition avoided (Reisman, 1962). In short, use only those abbreviations that will help you communicate with your readers. Remember, they have not had the same experience with your abbreviations as you have.

3.21 *Explanation of Abbreviations*

Because the abbreviations that psychologists use in their daily writing may not be familiar to students or to readers in other disciplines or other countries, a term to be abbreviated must, on its first appearance, be written out completely and followed immediately by its abbreviation in parentheses. Thereafter, the abbreviation is used in text without further explanation (do not switch between the abbreviated and written-out forms of a term).

> The results of studies of simple reaction time (RT) to a visual target have shown a strong negative relation between RT and luminance.

Abbreviations in a figure must be explained in the caption or legend. Those in a table must also be explained either in the table title (if it includes words that are abbreviated in the body of the table; see section

3.66) or in the table note (see section 3.70). An abbreviation that is used in several figures or tables must be explained in each figure or table in which the abbreviation is used. Avoid introducing abbreviations into figure captions or table notes if they do not appear in the figure or table. Standard abbreviations for units of measurement do not need to be written out on first use (see section 3.25).

3.22 *Abbreviations Accepted as Words*

APA style permits the use of abbreviations that appear as word entries (i.e., that are not labeled *abbr*) in *Webster's Collegiate.* Such abbreviations do not need explanation in text. Examples:

IQ   REM   ESP   AIDS   HIV   NADP   ACTH

3.23 *Abbreviations Used Often in APA Journals*

Some abbreviations are not in the dictionary but appear frequently in the journal for which you are writing. Although probably well understood by many readers, these abbreviations should still be explained when first used. Examples:

Minnesota Multiphasic Personality Inventory (MMPI)

conditioned stimulus (CS)

conditioned avoidance (CA)

intertrial interval (ITI)

consonant–vowel–consonant (CVC)

short-term memory (STM)

reaction time (RT)

Do not use the abbreviations *S, E,* or *O* for subject, experimenter, and observer.

3.24 *Latin Abbreviations*

Use the following standard Latin abbreviations only in parenthetical material; in nonparenthetical material, use the English translation of the Latin terms:

cf.	compare	i.e.,	that is,
e.g.,	for example,	viz.,	namely,
, etc.	, and so forth	vs.	versus, against

Exception: Use the abbreviation *v.* (for *versus*) in references and text citations to court cases, whether parenthetical or not (see Appendix D, section D.03).

Exception: In the reference list and in text, use the Latin abbreviation et al., which means "and others," in nonparenthetical as well as parenthetical material.

3.25 *Scientific Abbreviations*

Units of measurement. Use abbreviations and symbols for metric and nonmetric units of measurement that are accompanied by numeric values (e.g., 4 cm, 30 s, 12 min, 18 hr, 5 lb, 45°).

Units of time: To prevent misreading, do not abbreviate the following units of time, even when they are accompanied by numeric values:

day   week   month   year

A list of some common abbreviations for units of measurement follows.

A, ampere
Å, angstrom
AC, alternating current
a.m., ante meridiem

°C, degree Celsius

Ci, curie

cm, centimeter

cps, cycles per second

dB, decibel (specify scale)

DC, direct current

deg/s, degrees per second

dl, deciliter

°F, degree Fahrenheit

g, gram

g, gravity

hr, hour

Hz, hertz

in., inch (include metric equivalent in parentheses)

IQ, intelligence quotient

IU, international unit

kg, kilogram

km, kilometer

kph, kilometers per hour

kW, kilowatt

L, liter

m, meter

mA, milliampere

mEq, milliequivalent

meV, million electron volts

mg, milligram

min, minute

ml, milliliter

mm, millimeter

mM, millimolar

mmHg, millimeters of mercury

mmol, millimole

mol wt, molecular weight

mph, miles per hour (include metric equivalent in parentheses) ms, millisecond

MΩ, megohm

N, newton

ns, nanosecond

p.m., post meridiem

ppm, parts per million

psi, pounds per square inch (include metric equivalent in
parentheses)

rpm, revolutions per minute

s, second

S, siemens

V, volt

W, watt

m, micrometer

Abbreviated units of measure need not be repeated when expressing multiple amounts:

16–30 kHz   0.3, 1.5, and 3.0 mg/dl

Write out abbreviations for metric and nonmetric units that are not accompanied by numeric values (e.g., measured in centimeters, several pounds).

Chemical compounds. Chemical compounds may be expressed by common name or by chemical name. If you prefer to use the common name, provide the chemical name in parentheses on first mention in the Method section. Avoid expressing compounds with chemical formulas, as these are usually less informative to the reader and have a high likelihood of being typed or typeset incorrectly. If names of compounds include Greek letters, retain the letters as symbols and do not write them out (e.g., aspirin or salicylic acid, *not* $C_9H_8O_4$).

Long names of organic compounds are often abbreviated; if the abbreviation is listed as a word entry in *Webster's Collegiate Dictionary* (e.g.,

NADP for *nicotinamide adenine dinucleotide phosphate*), you may use it freely, without writing it out on first use.

Concentrations. If you express a solution as a percentage concentration instead of as a molar concentration, be sure to specify the percentage as a weight-per-volume ratio (wt/vol), a volume ratio (vol/vol), or a weight ratio (wt/wt) of solute to solvent (Pfaffman, Young, Dethier, Richter, & Stellar, 1954). The higher the concentration is, the more ambiguous the expression as a percentage. Specifying the ratio is especially necessary for concentrations of alcohol, glucose, and sucrose. Specifying the salt form is also essential for precise reporting: *d*-amphetamine HCl or *d*-amphetamine SO_4 (note that expression of chemical name in combination with a formula is acceptable in this case).

12% (vol/vol) ethyl alcohol solution

1% (wt/vol) saccharin solution

Routes of administration. You may abbreviate a route of administration when it is paired with a number-and-unit combination. Preferred style for APA is no periods: icv = intracerebral ventricular, im = intramuscular, ip = intraperitoneal, iv = intravenous, sc = subcutaneous, and so on.

anesthetized with sodium pentobarbital (90 mg/kg ip)

but

the first of two subcutaneous injections (*not* sc injections)

3.26 *Other Abbreviations*
Use abbreviations for statistics as described in section 3.58. For information on the International System of Units (SI), see sections 3.50–3.52.

3.27 *Use of Periods With Abbreviations*

Use the following guide for the use of periods with abbreviations.

Use periods with

- initials of names (J. R. Smith).
- abbreviation for United States when used as an adjective (U.S. Navy).
- identity-concealing labels for study participants (F.I.M.).
- Latin abbreviations (a.m., cf., i.e., vs.).
- reference abbreviations (Vol. 1, 2nd ed., p. 6, F. Supp.).

Do not use periods with

- abbreviations of state names (NY; OH; Washington, DC) in reference list entries or in vendor locations (e.g., for drugs and apparatus described in the Method section). See section 4.03 for the official abbreviations.
- capital letter abbreviations and acronyms (APA, NDA, NIMH, IQ).
- metric and nonmetric measurement abbreviations (cd, cm, ft, hr, kg, lb, min, ml, s).

Exception: The abbreviation for inch (in.) takes a period because without the period it could be misread.

- abbreviations for routes of administration (icv, im, ip, iv, sc).

3.28 *Plurals of Abbreviations*

To form the plural of most abbreviations and statistical symbols, add *s* alone, but not italicized, without an apostrophe.

IQs Eds. vols. *M*s *p*s *n*s

Exception: Do not add an *s* to make abbreviations of units of measurement plural (see section 3.51).

Exception: To form the plural of the reference abbreviation p. (page), write pp.; do not add an *s.*

3.29 *Abbreviations Beginning a Sentence*

Never begin a sentence with a lowercase abbreviation (e.g., lb) or a symbol that stands alone (e.g., α). Begin a sentence with a capitalized abbreviation or acronym (e.g., U.S. or APA) or with a symbol connected to a word (e.g., β-Endorphins) only when necessary to avoid indirect and awkward writing. In the case of chemical compounds, capitalize the first letter of the word to which the symbol is connected; keep the locant, descriptor, or positional prefix (i.e., Greek, small capital, and italic letters and numerals) intact.

In running text:	*At beginning of sentence:*
L-methionine	L-Methionine
N,N'-dimethylurea	*N,N'*-Dimethylurea
γ-hydroxy-β-aminobutyric acid	γ-Hydroxy-β-aminobutyric acid

Headings and Series

3.30 *Organizing a Manuscript With Headings*

Levels of heading establish via format or appearance the hierarchy of sections to orient the reader. All topics of equal importance have the same level of heading throughout a manuscript. For example, in a multiexperiment paper, the headings for the Method and Results sections in Experiment 1 should be the same level as the headings for the Method and Results sections in Experiment 2.

In manuscripts submitted to APA journals, headings function as an outline to reveal a manuscript's organization. Avoid having only one subsection heading and subsection within a section, just as you would avoid in an outline. Use at least two subsection headings within any given section, or use none (e.g., in an outline, you could divide a section numbered I into a minimum of A and B sections; just an A section could not stand alone).

Regardless of the number of levels of subheading within a section, the heading structure for all sections follows the same top-down progression. Each section starts with the highest level of heading, even if one section may have fewer levels of subheading than another section. For example, the Method and Results sections of a paper may each have two levels of subheading, and the Discussion section may have only one level of sub-heading. There would then be three levels of heading for the paper over-all: the section headings (Method, Results, and Discussion) and the two levels of subheading, as follows:

Method

Sample and Procedures

Measures

    Perceived control.

    Autonomy.

    Behavior and emotion.

Results

Initial Analyses

    Descriptive statistics.

    Intraconstruct correlations.

    Interconstruct correlations.

Unique Effects of Perceived Control and Autonomy on Behavior and Emotion

Motivational Profiles

Discussion

Limitations of the Study

Implications for Intervention

Conclusions

APA's heading style consists of five possible formatting arrangements, according to the number of levels of subordination. Each heading level is numbered (Level 1, Level 2, and so forth), but the specific levels used are not necessarily consecutive. Follow the guidelines in section 3.32 to select the proper heading style according to the levels of subordination within your paper.

If your paper has a complex organization, or if you find it difficult to follow APA heading style, you may submit an outline with your accepted manuscript for the copy editor to follow to ensure that your paper is organized as you envision.

The introduction to a manuscript does not carry a heading labeling it the introduction (the first part of a manuscript is assumed to be the introduction). Therefore, if the introduction contains headings, the first heading and later equivalent headings within the section are assigned the highest level of heading (Level 1 for all but five-level papers).

Do not label headings with numbers or letters. The sections and headings in the *Publication Manual* are numbered only to permit indexing and cross-referencing.

3.31 *Levels of Heading*

The five levels of headings in APA journals are formatted as follows:

CENTERED UPPERCASE HEADING ◄— Level 5

Centered Uppercase and Lowercase Heading ◄— Level 1

Centered, Italicized, Uppercase and Lowercase Heading ◄— Level 2

Flush Left, Italicized, Uppercase and Lowercase Side Heading ◄— Level 3

    Indented, italicized, lowercase paragraph heading ending ◄— Level 4
with a period.

The headings for an article using all five levels of heading would be formatted as follows:

EXPERIMENT 1: AN INTERVIEW VALIDATION STUDY

External Validation

Method

Participants

Sleep-deprived group.

3.32 *Selecting the Levels of Heading*

Find the section of your paper that breaks into the finest level of sub-ordinate categories. Then use the guidelines that follow to determine the level, position, and arrangement of headings. Few articles require all levels of heading. Note that each subheading must have at least one counterpart at the same level within a section (see section 3.30); for brevity, the examples that follow do not include counterparts.

One level. For a short article, one level of heading may be sufficient. In such cases, use only centered uppercase and lowercase headings (Level 1).

Two levels. For many articles in APA journals, two levels of heading meet the requirements. Use Level 1 and Level 3 headings:

Method ◄── (Level 1)

Procedure ◄── (Level 3)

If the material subordinate to the Level 1 headings is short or if many Level 3 headings are necessary, indented, italicized lowercase paragraph headings (Level 4) may be more appropriate than Level 3 headings. (A Level 4 heading should apply to all text between it and the next heading, regardless of the heading level of the next heading.)

Three levels. For many articles, three levels of heading are needed. Use Level 1, Level 3, and Level 4 headings.

In a *single-experiment study*, these three levels of heading may look like this:

Method ◄——(Level 1)

Apparatus and Procedure ◄——(Level 3)

   Pretraining period. ◄——(Level 4)

In a *multiexperiment study*, these three levels of heading may look like this:

Experiment 2 ◄——(Level 1)

Method ◄——(Level 3)

   Participants. ◄——(Level 4)

(See section 3.30 for a full outline of a three-level paper.)

Four levels. For some articles, particularly multiexperiment studies, monographs, and lengthy literature reviews, four levels of heading are needed. Use heading Levels 1 through 4:

Experiment 2 ◄——(Level 1)

Method ◄——(Level 2)

Stimulus Materials ◄——(Level 3)

   Auditory stimuli. ◄——(Level 4)

Five levels. Occasionally, an article requires five levels of heading. In such cases, subordinate all four levels above by introducing a Level 5 heading—a centered uppercase heading—above the other four (as shown in section 3.31).

3.33 *Seriation*

Enumerate elements in a series to prevent misreading or to clarify the sequence or relationship between elements, particularly when they are lengthy or complex. Identify the elements by a letter (within a paragraph or sentence) or by a number (at the start of each paragraph in a series).

Within a paragraph or sentence, identify elements in a series by lowercase letters (not italicized) in parentheses.

> The participant's three choices were (a) working with another participant, (b) working with a team, and (c) working alone.

Within a sentence, use commas to separate three or more elements that do not have internal commas; use semicolons to separate three or more elements that have internal commas.

> We tested three groups: (a) low scorers, who scored fewer than 20 points; (b) moderate scorers, who scored between 20 and 50 points; and (c) high scorers, who scored more than 50 points.

If the elements of a series within a paragraph constitute a compound sentence and are preceded by a colon, capitalize the first word of the first item (see section 3.04 on the use of the colon).

> The experiments on which we report were designed to address two such findings: (a) Only a limited class of patterned stimuli, when paired with color, subsequently contingently elicit aftereffects, and (b) decreasing the correlation between grid and color does not degrade the McCollough effect.

Separate paragraphs in a series, such as itemized conclusions or steps in a procedure, are identified by an arabic numeral followed by a period but not enclosed in or followed by parentheses.

> Using the learned helplessness theory, we predicted that the depressed and nondepressed participants would make the following judgments of control:

1. Individuals who . . . [paragraph continues].

2. Nondepressed persons exposed to . . . [paragraph continues].

3. Depressed persons exposed to . . . [paragraph continues].

4. Depressed and nondepressed participants in the no-noise groups . . . [paragraph continues].

In any series, with or without enumeration, any item should be syntactically and conceptually parallel to the other items in the series (see section 2.11).

Quotations

3.34 *Quotation of Sources*

Material directly quoted from another author's work or from one's own previously published work, material duplicated from a test item, and verbatim instructions to participants should be reproduced word for word. Incorporate a short quotation (fewer than 40 words) into text, and enclose the quotation with double quotation marks. (See section 3.06 for other uses of double quotation marks.)

Display a quotation of 40 or more words in a freestanding block of typewritten lines, and omit the quotation marks. Start such a *block quotation* on a new line, and indent the block about $\frac{1}{2}$ in. (1.3 cm, or five spaces) from the left margin (in the same position as a new paragraph). If there are additional paragraphs within the quotation, indent the first line of each an additional $\frac{1}{2}$ in. The entire quotation should be double-spaced.

The following examples illustrate the application of APA style to direct quotation of a source. When quoting, always provide the author, year, and specific page citation in the text, and include a complete reference in the reference list. (See section 5.13 for formatting instructions.)

Quotation 1:

She stated, "The 'placebo effect' . . . disappeared when behaviors were studied in this manner" (Miele, 1993, p. 276), but she did not clarify which behaviors were studied.

Quotation 2:

Miele (1993) found that "the 'placebo effect,' which had been verified in previous studies, disappeared when [only the first group's] behaviors were studied in this manner" (p. 276).

Quotation 3:

Miele (1993) found the following:

> The "placebo effect," which had been verified in previous studies, disappeared when behaviors were studied in this manner. Furthermore, the behaviors were *never exhibited again* [italics added], even when reel [*sic*] drugs were administered. Earlier studies (e.g., Abdullah, 1984; Fox, 1979) were clearly premature in attributing the results to a placebo effect. (p. 276)

3.35 *Accuracy*

Direct quotations must be accurate. Except as noted in sections 3.37 and 3.38, the quotation must follow the wording, spelling, and interior punctuation of the original source, even if the source is incorrect.

If any incorrect spelling, punctuation, or grammar in the source might confuse readers, insert the word *sic*, italicized and bracketed, immediately after the error in the quotation. (See Quotation 3 in section 3.34, and see section 3.38 for the use of brackets.) Always check the manuscript copy against the source to ensure that there are no discrepancies.

3.36 *Double or Single Quotation Marks*

In text. Use double quotation marks to enclose quotations in text. Use single quotation marks within double quotation marks to set off material that in the original source was enclosed in double quotation marks (see section 3.34, Quotation 2).

In block quotations (any quotations of 40 or more words). Do not use quotation marks to enclose block quotations. Do use double quotation marks to enclose any quoted material within a block quotation (see section 3.34, Quotation 3).

With other punctuation. Place periods and commas within closing single or double quotation marks. Place other punctuation marks inside quotation marks only when they are part of the quoted material.

3.37 *Changes From the Source Requiring No Explanation*

The first letter of the first word in a quotation may be changed to an uppercase or a lowercase letter. The punctuation mark at the end of a sentence may be changed to fit the syntax. Single quotation marks may be changed to double quotation marks and vice versa (see section 3.36). Any other changes (e.g., italicizing words for emphasis or omitting words) must be explicitly indicated (see section 3.38).

3.38 *Changes From the Source Requiring Explanation*

Omitting material. Use three spaced ellipsis points (. . .) within a sentence to indicate that you have omitted material from the original source (see section 3.34, Quotation 1). Use four points to indicate any omission between two sentences. The first point indicates the period at the end of the first sentence quoted, and the three spaced ellipsis points follow. Do not use ellipsis points at the beginning or end of any quotation unless, to prevent misinterpretation, you need to emphasize that the quotation begins or ends in midsentence.

Inserting material. Use brackets, not parentheses, to enclose material (additions or explanations) inserted in a quotation by some person other than the original author (see section 3.34, Quotation 2).

Adding emphasis. If you want to emphasize a word or words in a quotation, italicize the word or words. Immediately after the italicized words, insert within brackets the words *italics added*, that is, [italics added] (see section 3.34, Quotation 3).

3.39 *Citation of Sources*

Whether paraphrasing or quoting an author directly, you must credit the source (see the subsection in section 8.05 on plagiarism and section 3.41 on permission to quote). For a direct quotation in the text, the information provided will vary depending on whether your source was in print or electronic form. When citing print sources, give the author, year, and page number in parentheses.

Many electronic sources do not provide page numbers (unless they are PDF reproductions of printed material). If paragraph numbers are visible, use them in place of page numbers. Use the ¶ symbol or the abbreviation para.

> As Myers (2000, ¶ 5) aptly phrased it, "positive emotions are both an end—better to live fulfilled, with joy [and other positive emotions]—and a means to a more caring and healthy society."

If there are headings in the document and neither paragraph nor page numbers are visible, cite the heading and the number of the ¶ following it to direct the reader to the location of the quoted material.

> "The current system of managed care and the current approach to defining empirically supported treatments are shortsighted" (Beutler, 2000, Conclusion section, ¶ 1)

In some cases, it may be necessary to omit a location reference altogether, such as when no page or paragraph numbers are visible and headings either are not provided or their use would prove unwieldy or confusing. In documents accessed with a Web browser, readers will be able to search for the quoted material.

When paraphrasing or referring to an idea contained in another work, authors are not required to provide a location reference (e.g., a page or paragraph number). Nevertheless, authors are encouraged to do so, especially when it would help an interested reader locate the relevant passage in a long or complex text.

Punctuation around source citations will differ depending on where the quotation or paraphrased material falls within a sentence or the text.

In midsentence. End the passage with quotation marks, cite the source in parentheses immediately after the quotation marks, and continue the sentence. Use no other punctuation unless the meaning of the sentence requires such punctuation (see section 3.34, Quotation 1).

At the end of a sentence. Close the quoted passage with quotation marks, cite the source in parentheses immediately after the quotation marks, and end with the period or other punctuation outside the final parenthesis (see section 3.34, Quotation 2).

At the end of a block quote. Cite the quoted source in parentheses after the final punctuation mark (see section 3.34, Quotation 3).

3.40 *Citations Within Quotations*

Do not omit citations embedded within the original material you are quoting. The works cited need not be included in the list of references (unless you happen to cite them elsewhere in your paper).

3.41 *Permission to Quote*

Any direct quotation, regardless of length, must be accompanied by a reference citation that, if at all possible, includes a page number. (For the form of the citation of a source, see sections 3.94–3.103.) If you quote at length from a copyrighted work in material you intend to publish, you usually also need written permission from the owner of the copyright. Requirements for obtaining permission to quote copyrighted material vary from one copyright owner to another; for example, APA policy permits use of up to 500 words of APA-copyrighted journal text without explicit permission. It is the author's responsibility to determine whether permission is required from the copyright owner and to obtain it for both print and electronic reuse when required. APA cannot publish previously copyrighted material that exceeds the copyright holder's determination of "fair use" without permission.

If you must obtain written permission from the copyright owner, append a footnote to the quoted material with a superscript number, and in the footnote, acknowledge permission from the owner of the copyright. Format the footnote like the permission footnotes used for tables and figures (see section 3.73), but substitute the indented superscript number for the word *Note.* Place the footnote number at the end of the quotation, after any punctuation. Enclose a copy of the letter of permission with the final version of the manuscript.

Numbers

The general rule governing APA style on the use of numbers is to use figures to express numbers 10 and above and words to express numbers below 10. Sections 3.42–3.44 expand on this rule and state exceptions and special usages.

3.42 *Numbers Expressed in Figures*
Use figures to express

    a. all numbers 10 and above. (*Exceptions:* See sections 3.43–3.44.)

12 cm wide	the 15th trial
the remaining 10%	13 lists
25 years old	105 stimulus words
10th-grade students	

b. all numbers below 10 that are grouped for comparison with numbers 10 and above (and that appear in the same paragraph). (*Exceptions:* See sections 3.43–3.44.)

3 of 21 analyses

of 10 conditions . . . the 5th condition

5 and 13 lines

in the 2nd and 11th grades . . . the 2nd-grade students

on 2 trials . . . on the remaining 18 trials

4 of the 40 stimulus words

in 7 blocks . . . in 12 blocks

the 6th group . . . 12 groups

the 1st and 12th items of all 15 lists

2 of the 20 responses

toys included 14 balloons, 3 stuffed animals, and 5 balls

25 words . . . 8 verbs, 12 nouns, and 5 adjectives

but

15 traits on each of four checklists [Traits and checklists are not being compared; they are different categories of items.]

c. numbers that immediately precede a unit of measurement.

a 5-mg dose

with 10.54 cm of

d. numbers that represent statistical or mathematical functions, fractional or decimal quantities, percentages, ratios, and percentiles and quartiles.

multiplied by 5

3 times as many [proportion; cf. 3.43a]

0.33 of the

more than 5% of the sample

a ratio of 16:1

the 1st quartile

the 5th percentile

e. numbers that represent time; dates; ages; sample, subsample, or population size; specific numbers of subjects or participants in an experiment; scores and points on a scale; exact sums of money; and numerals as numerals.

in about 3 years

2 weeks ago

1 hr 34 min

at 12:30 a.m.

March 30, 1994

2-year-olds

3 participants [*but* two raters, seven observers]

9 rats

scored 4 on a 7-point scale

were paid $5 each

the numerals on the scorecard were 0–6

f. numbers that denote a specific place in a numbered series, parts of books and tables, and each number in a list of four or more numbers.

Grade 8 [*but* the eighth grade; see section 3.45]

Trial 3

Table 3

page 71

chapter 5

row 5

1, 3, 4, and 7 words, respectively

g. all numbers in the abstract of a paper.

3.43 *Numbers Expressed in Words*
Use words to express

a. numbers below 10 that do not represent precise measurements and that are grouped for comparison with numbers below 10.

repeated the task three times [cf. 3.42d]

the only one who

two words that mean

five trials . . . the remaining seven trials

three conditions

seven lists

one-tailed *t* test

nine words each

three-dimensional blocklike figures

eight items

four responses

six sessions

nine pages

three-way interaction

the third of five taste stimuli

b. the numbers *zero* and *one* when the words would be easier to comprehend than the figures or when the words do not appear in context with numbers 10 and above.

zero-base budgeting

one-line sentence

However, one response was valid. [*but* However, 1 of 15 responses was valid.]

c. any number that begins a sentence, title, or text heading. (Whenever possible, reword the sentence to avoid beginning with a number.)

Ten participants answered the questionnaire

Forty-eight percent of the sample showed an increase; 2% showed no change.

Four patients improved, and 4 patients did not improve.

d. common fractions

one fifth of the class

two-thirds majority

reduced by three fourths

e. universally accepted usage

the Twelve Apostles

the Fourth of July

the Ten Commandments

3.44 *Combining Figures and Words to Express Numbers*
Use a combination of figures and words to express

a. rounded large numbers (starting with millions).

almost 3 million people

a budget of $2.5 billion

b. back-to-back modifiers.

2 two-way interactions

ten 7-point scales

twenty 6-year-olds

the first 10 items

A combination of figures and words in these situations increases the clarity and readability of the construction. In some situations, however, readability may suffer instead of benefit. In such a case, spelling out both numbers is preferred.

Poor:

1st two items

first 2 items

Better:

first two items

3.45 *Ordinal Numbers*

Treat ordinal numbers as you would cardinal numbers (see sections 3.42–3.44).

Ordinal	**Cardinal base**
second-order factor	two orders (3.43a)
the fourth graders	four grades (3.43a)
the fifth list for the 12th-grade students	five lists, 12 grades (3.42b)
the first item of the 75th trial	one item, 75 trials (3.42b)
the 2nd and 11th rows	2 rows, 11 rows (3.42b)
the first and third groups	one group, three groups (3.43a)
the third column	three columns (3.43a)
of 3rd-year students	3 years (3.42e)
4th and 5th years	4 years, 5 years (3.42e)

3.46 *Decimal Fractions*

Use a zero before the decimal point when numbers are less than 1.

0.23 cm, 0.48 s

Do not use a zero before a decimal fraction when the number cannot be greater than 1 (e.g., correlations, proportions, and levels of statistical significance).

$r(24) = -.43, p < .05$

The number of decimal places to use in reporting the results of experiments and data analytic manipulations of the data should be governed by three general principles: (a) a fundamental attitude to round as much as possible while keeping (b) prospective use and (c) statistical precision in mind. As a general rule, fewer decimal digits are easier to comprehend than more digits; therefore, in general, it is better to round to two decimal places or to rescale the measurement (in which case effect sizes should be presented in the same metric). For instance, a difference in distances that must be carried to four decimals to be seen when scaled in meters can be more effectively illustrated by conversion to millimeters, which would require only a few decimal digits to illustrate the same difference. As a rule, when properly scaled, most data can be effectively presented with two decimal digits of accuracy. Report correlations, proportions, and inferential statistics such as t, F, and chi-square to two decimals. In general, significance probabilities will be reported to two decimal places (i.e., the lowest reported significance probability being $p < .01$). There are, however, circumstances under which more decimals may be reported (e.g., Bonferroni tests, exact randomization probabilities).

3.47 *Roman Numerals*

If roman numerals are part of an established terminology, do not change to arabic numerals; for example, use Type II error. Use arabic, not roman, numerals for routine seriation (e.g., Step 1).

3.48 *Commas in Numbers*

Use commas between groups of three digits in most figures of 1,000 or more.

Exceptions:

page numbers	page 1029
binary digits	00110010
serial numbers	290466960
degrees of temperature	3071 °F
acoustic frequency designations	2000 Hz

| degrees of freedom | $F(24, 1000)$ |
| numbers to the right of a decimal point | 4,900.0744 |

3.49 *Plurals of Numbers*

To form the plurals of numbers, whether expressed as figures or as words, add *s* or *es* alone, without an apostrophe.

fours and sixes   1950s   10s and 20s

Metrication

3.50 *Policy on Metrication*

APA uses the metric system in its journals. All references to physical measurements, where feasible, should be expressed in metric units. The metric system outlined in this section is based, with some exceptions, on the International System of Units (SI), which is an extension and refinement of the traditional metric system and is supported by the national standardizing bodies in many countries, including the United States.

In preparing manuscripts, authors should use metric units if possible. Experimenters who use instruments that record measurements in nonmetric units may report the nonmetric units but also must report the established SI equivalents in parentheses immediately after the nonmetric units.

The rods were spaced 19 mm apart. [Measurement was made in metric units.]

The rod was 3 ft (0.91 m) long. [Measurement was made in nonmetric units and converted to the rounded SI equivalent.]

Journal editors reserve the right to return manuscripts if measurements are not expressed properly. Tables 3.4–3.8 provide guidelines on the use of metric expressions.

3.51 *Style for Metric Units*

Abbreviation. Use the metric symbol (see Tables 3.4–3.8) to express a metric unit when it appears with a numeric value (e.g., 4 m). When a metric unit does not appear with a numeric value, spell out the unit in text (e.g., measured in meters), and use the metric symbol in column and stub headings of tables to conserve space (e.g., lag in ms).

Capitalization. Use lowercase letters when writing out full names of units (e.g., meter, nanometer), unless the name appears in capitalized material or at the beginning of a sentence.

For the most part, use lowercase letters for symbols (e.g., cd), even in capitalized material. Symbols derived from the name of a person usually include uppercase letters (e.g., Gy), as do symbols for some prefixes that represent powers of 10: exa (E), peta (P), tera (T), giga (G), and mega (M). (See the list in section 3.25 for more examples.)

Use the symbol L for liter when it stands alone (e.g., 5 L, 0.3 mg/L) because a lowercase *l* may be misread as the numeral one (use lowercase *l* for fractions of a liter: 5 ml, 9 ng/dl).

Plurals. Make full names of units plural when appropriate. Example: meters

Do not make symbols of units plural. Example: 3 cm, *not* 3 cms

Periods. Do not use a period after a symbol, except at the end of a sentence.

Spacing. Never use a space between a prefix and a base unit. Examples: kg, kilogram

Use a space between a symbol and the number to which it refers, except for measures of angles (e.g., degrees, minutes, and seconds). Examples: 4.5 m, 12 °C, but 45° angle

Compound units. Use a centered dot between the symbols of a compound term formed by the multiplication of units. Example: Pa·s

Use a space between full names of units of a compound unit formed by the multiplication of units; do not use a centered dot. Example: pascal second

Table 3.4. International System (SI) Base and Supplementary Units

Quantity	Name	Symbol
Base units		
amount of substance	mole	mol
electrical current	ampere	A
length	meter	m
luminous intensity	candela	cd
mass	kilogram	kg
thermodynamic temperature[a]	kelvin	K
time	second	s
Supplementary units		
plane angle	radian	rad
solid angle	steradian	sr

[a]Celsius temperature is generally expressed in degrees Celsius (symbol: °C).

Table 3.5. International System (SI) Prefixes

Factor	Prefix	Symbol	Factor	Prefix	Symbol
10^{18}	exa	E	10^{-1}	deci	d
10^{15}	peta	P	10^{-2}	centi	c
10^{12}	tera	T	10^{-3}	milli	m
10^{9}	giga	G	10^{-6}	micro	μ
10^{6}	mega	M	10^{-9}	nano	n
10^{3}	kilo	k	10^{-12}	pico	p
10^{2}	hecto	h	10^{-15}	femto	f
10^{1}	deka	da	10^{-18}	atto	a

Table 3.6. *International System (SI) Derived Units With Special Names*

Quantity	Name	Symbol	Expression in terms of other units
absorbed dose, specific energy imparted, kerma, absorbed dose index	gray	Gy	J/kg
activity (of a radionuclide)	becquerel	Bq	s^{-1}
capacitance	farad	F	C/V
conductance	siemens	S	A/V
dose equivalent, dose equivalent index	sievert	Sv	J/kg
electric charge, quantity of electricity	coulomb	C	A·s
electric potential, potential difference, electromotive force, voltage	volt	V	W/A
electric resistance	ohm	Ω	V/A
energy work, quantity of heat	joule	J	N·m
force	newton	N	$(kg \cdot m)/s^2$
frequency	hertz	Hz	s^{-1}
illuminance	lux	lx	lm/m^2
inductance	henry	H	Wb/A
luminous flux	lumen	lm	cd·sr
magnetic flux	weber	Wb	V·s
magnetic flux density	tesla	T	Wb/m^2
pressure, stress	pascal	Pa	N/m^2
radiant flux, power	watt	W	J/s
volume (capacity)	liter	L	dm^3

Table 3.7. Other International System (SI) Derived Units

Quantity	Name	Symbol
absorbed dose rate	gray per second	Gy/s
acceleration	meter per second squared	m/s^2
angular acceleration	radian per second squared	rad/s^2
angular velocity	radian per second	rad/s
area	square meter	m^2
concentration (amount of substance)	mole per cubic meter	mol/m^3
current density	ampere per square meter	A/m^2
density, mass density	kilogram per cubic meter	kg/m^3
electric charge density	coulomb per cubic meter	kg/m^3
electric field strength	volt per meter	V/m
electric flux density	coulomb per square meter	C/m^2
energy density	joule per cubic meter	J/m^3
exposure (X and γ rays)	coulomb per kilogram	C/kg
heat capacity, entropy	joule per kelvin	J/K
luminance	candela per square meter	cd/m^2
magnetic field strength	ampere per meter	A/m
molar energy	joule per mole	J/mol
molar entropy, molar heat capacity	joule per mole kelvin	$J/(mol \cdot K)$
moment of force	newton meter	$N \cdot m$
permeability	henry per meter	H/m
permittivity	farad per meter	F/m
power density, heat flux density, irradiance	watt per square meter	W/m^2
radiance	watt per square meter steradian	$W/(m^2 \cdot sr)$
radiant intensity	watt per steradian	W/sr
specific energy	joule per kilogram	J/kg
specific heat capacity, specific entropy	joule per kilogram kelvin	$J/(kg \cdot K)$
specific volume	cubic meter per kilogram	m^3/kg
surface tension	newton per meter	N/m
thermal conductivity	watt per meter kelvin	$W/(m \cdot k)$
velocity, speed	meter per second	m/s
viscosity (dynamic)	pascal second	$Pa \cdot s$
viscosity (kinematic)	square meter per second	m^2/s
volume	cubic meter	m^3
wave number	one per meter	m^{-1}

Table 3.8. Examples of Conversions to International System (SI) Equivalents

Physical quantity	Traditional U.S. unit	SI equivalent
Area	acre	4,046.873 m^2
	square foot[a]	0.09290304 m^2
	square inch[a]	645.16 mm^2
	square mile (statute)	2.589998 km^2
	square yard	0.8361274 m^2
Energy	British thermal unit (IT)	1,055.056 J
	calorie (IT), thermochemical[a]	4.186800 J
	erg	10^{-7} J
	kilowatt hour[a]	3.6 × 10^6 J
Force	dyne	10^{-5} N
	kilogram force[a]	9.80665 N
	poundal	0.138255 N
Length	angstrom (Å)[a]	0.1 nm
	foot (international)[a]	0.3048 m
	inch[a]	2.54 cm
	micrometer[a]	1.0 μm
	mile (U.S. statute)	1.609347 km
	nautical mile (international; nmi)[a]	1,852.0 m
	yard[a]	0.9144 m
Light	footcandle	10.76391 lx
	footlambert	3.426359 cd/m^2
Mass	grain[a]	64.79891 mg
	ounce	28.34952 g
	pound (U.S.)[a]	0.45359237 kg
Power	horsepower (electric)[a]	0.746 kW
Pressure	atmosphere (normal)[a]	101,325.0 Pa
	pound per square inch (psi)	6.894757 kPa
	torr[a]	(101,325/760) Pa
	sound pressure level (SPL; 0.0002 dynes/cm^2)[b]	20 μN/m^2

(table continues)

Table 3.8. (*continued*)

Physical quantity	Traditional U.S. unit	SI equivalent
Volume	cubic foot	0.02831685 m^3
	cubic inch	16.38706 cm^3
	fluid ounce	29.57353 ml
	quart (liquid)	0.9463529 L

Note. IT = International Table.

[a]Conversion factors for these units are exact. (For conversion factors that are not exact, the precision with which the quantity was measured determines the number of decimal places.)

[b]A decibel value is a measure of the power of sound relative to a specific reference level. The most common reference level on which decibel values are based is at 20 μN/m^2. If decibel values are based on another reference level, specify the level. Also, always indicate how frequencies were weighted: If frequencies were equally weighted, write SPL (i.e., sound pressure level) in parentheses after the decibel value; if frequencies were unequally weighted, specify the standard weighting used (e.g., A, B, or C) in parentheses after the decibel value.

3.52 *Metric Tables*

Tables 3.4–3.8 are intended to assist authors in the conversion to the metric system. They are based on tables that appeared in the National Bureau of Standards' (1979) "Guidelines for Use of the Modernized Metric System." For more detailed information, consult the sources on metrication referenced in section 9.03.

Statistical and Mathematical Copy

APA style for presenting statistical and mathematical copy reflects both standards of content and form agreed on in the field and the requirements of the printing process.

3.53 *Selecting the Method of Analysis and Retaining Data*

Authors are responsible for the statistical method selected and for all supporting data. Access to computer analyses of data does not relieve the author of responsibility for selecting the appropriate data analytic techniques. To permit interested readers to verify the statistical analysis, an author should retain the raw data after publication of the research. Authors of manuscripts accepted for publication in APA journals are required to have available their raw data throughout the editorial review process and for at least 5 years after the date of publication (section 8.05 includes a discussion about sharing data in the subsection on data verification).

3.54 *Selecting Effective Presentation*

Statistical and mathematical copy can be presented in text, in tables, and in figures. Read sections 3.57, 3.62, and 3.75 to compare methods of presentation and to decide how best to present your data. A general rule that might prove useful is

- if you have 3 or fewer numbers, use a sentence;
- if you have from 4 to 20 numbers, use a table; and
- if you have more than 20 numbers, consider using a graph or figure instead of a table.

When you are in doubt about the clearest and most effective method of presentation, prepare tables or figures with the understanding that if the manuscript is accepted, they are to be published at the editor's discretion. In any case, be prepared to submit tables and figures of complex statistical and mathematical material if an editor requests them.

3.55 *References for Statistics*

Do not give a reference for statistics in common use; this convention applies to most statistics used in journal articles. Do give a reference for (a) less common statistics, especially those that have appeared in journals but that are not yet incorporated in textbooks, or (b) a statistic used in a controversial way (e.g., to justify a test of significance when the data do not meet the assumptions of the test). When the statistic itself is the focus of the article, give supporting references.

3.56 Formulas

Do not give a formula for a statistic in common use; do give a formula when the statistic or mathematical expression is new, rare, or essential to the paper. Presentation of equations is described in sections 3.60–3.61.

3.57 Statistics in Text

When reporting inferential statistics (e.g., t tests, F tests, chi-square tests), include sufficient information to allow the reader to fully understand the analyses conducted and possible alternative explanations for the results of these analyses. What constitutes sufficient information depends on the analytic approach selected. Examples of presentations follow (see section 5.14 on typing statistical and mathematical copy):

> For immediate recognition, the omnibus test of the main effect of sentence format was statistically significant, $F(2, 177) = 4.37$, $p = .03$. Regarding the 2 one-degree-of-freedom contrasts of interest (C1 and C2 above), both reached the specified .05 significance level, $F(1, 117) = 4.03$, $p = .05$, and $F(1, 117) = 4.71$, $p = .03$, respectively. In terms of effect sizes . . .

> For the autokinetic movement illusion, as predicted, people highly hypnotizable ($M = 8.19$, $SD = 7.12$) reported perceiving the stationary light as moving significantly more often than did the other participants ($M = 5.26$, $SD = 4.25$), $t(60) = 1.99$, $p = .03$ (one-tailed), $d = .50$. The high-hypnotizability group ($M = 21.41$, $SD = 10.35$) reported statistically greater occurrences of extreme, focused attention than did the low group ($M = 16.24$, $SD = 11.09$), $t(75) = 2.11$, $p = .02$ (one-tailed), $d = .48$.

If you present descriptive statistics in a table or figure, you do not need to repeat them in text, although highlighting particular data in the narrative may be helpful.

With chi-square, report degrees of freedom and sample size (i.e., the number of independent entries in the chi-square table) in parentheses:

$$\chi^2(4, N = 90) = 10.51, p = .03$$

When enumerating a series of similar statistics, be certain that the relation between the statistics and their referents is clear. Words such as *respectively* and *in order* can clarify this relationship.

> Means (with standard deviations in parentheses) for Trials 1 through 4 were 2.43 (0.50), 2.59 (1.21), 2.68 (0.39), and 2.86 (0.12), respectively.

> In order, means for Trials 1 through 4 were 2.43, 2.59, 2.68, and 2.86 (*SD*s = 0.50, 1.21, 0.39, and 0.12, respectively). The *n*s for each trial were 17.

3.58 *Statistical Symbols*

When using a statistical term in the narrative, use the term, not the symbol. For example, use The means were, *not* The *M*s were.

Symbols for population versus sample statistics. Population (i.e., theoretical) statistics, properly called *parameters,* are usually represented by lowercase Greek letters. A few sample (i.e., observed) statistics are also expressed by Greek letters (e.g., χ^2), but most sample statistics are expressed by italicized Latin letters (e.g., *SD*).

Symbols for number of subjects. Use an uppercase, italicized *N* to designate the number of members in a total sample (e.g., $N = 135$) and a lowercase, italicized *n* to designate the number of members in a limited portion of the total sample (e.g., $n = 30$).

Symbol for percent (%). Use the symbol for percent only when it is preceded by a numeral. Use the word *percentage* when a number is not given.

found that 18% of the rats

determined the percentage of rats

Exception: In table headings and figure legends, use the symbol % to conserve space.

Standard, boldface, and italic type. Statistical symbols and mathematical copy are typeset in three different typefaces: standard, **boldface,** and *italic.* The same typeface is used for a symbol whether the symbol appears in text, tables, or figures.

Greek letters, subscripts, and superscripts that function as identifiers (i.e., that are not variables) and abbreviations that are not variables (e.g., sin, log) are typeset in a standard typeface. On the manuscript, do not italicize them.

μ_{girls}, α, ε, β

Symbols for vectors are bold. Use the word processor boldface function (or a handwritten wavy underline).

v

All other statistical symbols are typeset in italic type.

N, M_X, df, p, SS_b, SE, MSE, t, F, a, b

A list of common statistical abbreviations is provided in Table 3.9.

Table 3.9. *Statistical Abbreviations and Symbols*

Abbreviation/ Symbol	Definition
ANCOVA	Analysis of covariance
ANOVA	Analysis of variance (univariate)
d	Cohen's measure of effect size
d'	(d prime) measure of sensitivity
D	Used in Kolmogorov–Smirnov test
df	degree of freedom
f	Frequency
f_e	Expected frequency
F	Fisher's F ratio
F_{max}	Hartley's test of variance homogeneity
g	Hedge's measure of effect size
H	Used in Kruskal–Wallis test; also used to mean *hypothesis*
H_0	Null hypothesis under test
H_1	Alternative hypothesis
HSD	Tukey's honestly significant difference (also referred to as the Tukey *a* procedure)
k	Coefficient of alienation
k^2	Coefficient of nondetermination
K-R 20	Kuder–Richardson formula
LR	Likelihood ratio (used with some chi-squares)
LSD	Fisher's least significant difference
M	Mean (arithmetic average)
MANOVA	Multivariate analysis of variance

(table continues)

Table 3.9. (*continued*)

Abbreviation/ Symbol	Definition
Mdn	Median
mle	Maximum likelihood estimate (used with programs such as LISREL)
MS	Mean square
MSE	Mean square error
n	Number in a subsample
N	Total number in a sample
ns	Nonsignificant
p	Probability; also the success probability of a binomial variable
P	Percentage, percentile
pr	Partial correlation
q	$1 - p$ for a binomial variable
Q	Quartile (also used in Cochran's test)
r	Pearson product–moment correlation
r^2	Pearson product–moment correlation squared; coefficient of determination
r_b	Biserial correlation
r_k	Reliability of mean *k* judges' ratings
r_1	Estimate reliability of the typical judge
r_{pb}	Point-biserial correlation
r_s	Spearman rank correlation coefficient (formerly rho [ρ])
R	Multiple correlation; also composite rank, a significance test
R^2	Multiple correlation squared; measure of strength of relationship

Table 3.9. (*continued*)

Abbreviation/ Symbol	Definition
SD	Standard deviation
SE	Standard error (of measurement)
SEM	Standard error of measurement
SEM	Structural equation modeling
sr	Semipartial correlation
SS	Sum of squares
t	Computed value of *t* test
T	Computed value of Wilcoxon's or McCall's test
T^2	Computed value of Hotelling's test
Tukey *a*	Tukey's HSD procedure
U	Computed value of Mann–Whitney test
V	Cramér's statistic for contingency tables; Pillai–Bartlett multivariate criterion
W	Kendall's coefficient of concordance
x	Abscissa (horizontal axis in graph)
y	Ordinate (vertical axis in graph)
z	A standard score; difference between one value in a distribution and the mean of the distribution divided by the *SD*
|*a*|	Absolute value of *a*
α	Alpha; probability of a Type I error; Cronbach's index of internal consistency
β	Beta; probability of a Type II error; $(1 - \beta$ is statistical power); standardized multiple regression coefficient

(*table continues*)

Table 3.9. (*continued*)

Abbreviation/ Symbol	Definition
γ	Gamma; Goodman–Kruskal's index of relationship
Δ	Delta (cap); increment of change
κ	Cohen's estimate of effect size
η^2	Eta squared; measure of strength of relationship
Θ	Theta (cap); Roy's multivariate criterion
λ	Lambda; Goodman–Kruskal's measure of predictability
Λ	Lambda (cap); Wilks's multivariate criterion
ν	Nu; degrees of freedom
ρ_I	Rho (with subscript); intraclass correlation coefficient
Σ	Sigma (cap); sum or summation
τ	Tau; Kendall's rank correlation coefficient; also Hotelling's multivariate trace criterion
ϕ	Phi; measure of association for a contingency table; also a parameter used in determining sample size or statistical power
ϕ^2	Phi squared; proportion of variance accounted for in a 2×2 contingency table
χ^2	Computed value of a chi-square tset
ψ	Psi; a statistical contrast
ω^2	Omega squared; measure of strength of relationship
$\char94$	(caret) when above a Greek letter (or parameter), indicates an estimate (or statistic)

Note. Greek symbols are lowercase unless noted otherwise.

Identifying letters and symbols. Some letters, numerals, and other characters may be ambiguous to the typesetter and should be clarified with notations made by hand (see Equation 1 in section 3.61). The following characters, for example, may be misread in typewritten and handwritten copy: 1 (the numeral one or the letter *l*), 0 (the numeral zero or the letter *o*), × (multiplication sign or the letter *x*), Greek letters (the letter *B* or beta), and letters that have the same shape in capital and lowercase forms, which can be especially confusing in subscripts and superscripts (e.g., *c*, *s*, and *x*). Identify ambiguous characters with a notation in the margin on their first appearance in the manuscript (e.g., "lowercase *l* throughout").

In general, remember that production staff usually do not have mathematical backgrounds and will reproduce what they see, not what a mathematician knows. If errors appear in the typeset proofs because of ambiguity in a manuscript, the author may be charged for correcting them. Avoid misunderstandings and corrections by preparing mathematical copy carefully and by reviewing the copyedited manuscript thoroughly before returning it to the production office for typesetting.

3.59 *Spacing, Alignment, and Punctuation*

Space mathematical copy as you would space words: $a+b=c$ is as difficult to read as wordswithoutspacing; $a + b = c$ is much better. Align mathematical copy carefully. Subscripts usually precede superscripts (x_a^2), but a prime is placed next to a letter or symbol (x'_a). Superscripts will be typeset directly above subscripts in APA journals unless the author gives specific instructions to the contrary when transmitting the accepted manuscript for production (see section 5.24).

Punctuate all equations, whether they are in the line of text or displayed (i.e., typed on a new line), to conform to their place in the syntax of the sentence (see the period following Equation 1 in section 3.61). If an equation exceeds the column width of a typeset page (approximately

55 characters, including spaces, will fit on one line in most APA journals), the typesetter will break it. For long equations, indicate on the final version of the accepted manuscript where breaks would be acceptable.

3.60 *Equations in Text*

Place short and simple equations, such as $\alpha = [(1 + b)/x]^{1/2}$, in the line of text. Equations in the line of text should not project above or below the line; for example, the equation above would be difficult to set in the line of text if it were in this form:

$$\alpha = \sqrt{\frac{1 + b}{x}}.$$

To present fractions in the line of text, use a slanted line (/) and appropriate parentheses and brackets: Use ( ) first, then [( )], and finally {[( )]}. Use parentheses and brackets to avoid ambiguity: Does $a/b + c$ mean $(a/b) + c$ or $a/(b + c)$?

3.61 *Displayed Equations*

To display equations, start them on a new line, and double-space twice above and twice below the equation. Simple equations should be displayed if they must be numbered for later reference. Display all complex equations.

Number displayed equations consecutively, with the number in parentheses near the right margin of the page:

$$\underset{\text{chi}}{X} = -2 \underset{\text{lc ex}}{\overset{\text{summation}}{\sum}} a_x^2 + \underset{\text{one}}{\overset{\text{zero}}{a_0}} + \frac{\cos x - 5ab}{1/n + a_x}. \tag{1}$$

When referring to numbered equations, spell out the reference; for example, write Equation 1 (do not abbreviate as Eq. 1), or write the first equation.

Tables

3.62 *Tabular Versus Textual Presentation*

Tables are efficient, enabling the researcher to present a large amount of data in a small amount of space. Tables usually show exact numerical values, and the data are arranged in an orderly display of columns and rows, which aids comparison. For several reasons, it is worthwhile to be selective in choosing how many tables to include in your paper. First, a reader may have difficulty sorting through a large number of tables and may lose track of your message (Scientific Illustration Committee, 1988). Second, a disproportionately large number of tables compared with a small amount of text can cause problems with the layout of typeset pages; text that is constantly broken up with tables will be hard for the reader to follow. Third, tables are complicated to set in type and are therefore more expensive to publish than text. For these reasons, reserve tables for crucial data that are directly related to the content of your article and for simplifying text that otherwise would be dense with numbers.

Dense:

The mean final errors (with standard deviations in parentheses) for the Age × Level of Difficulty interaction were .05 (.08), .05 (.07), and .11 (.10) for the younger participants and .14 (.15), .17 (.15), and .26 (.21) for the older participants at low, moderate, and high levels of difficulty, respectively.

The reader can more easily comprehend and compare these data when they are presented in tabular form, as in Table Example 1. However, the data in unusually short and simple tables (e.g., a table with two or fewer columns and rows) are more efficiently presented in text.

Determine the amount of data the reader needs to understand the discussion, and then decide whether those data are best presented in text or as a table or figure. Peripherally related or extremely detailed data should be omitted or, depending on their nature, presented in an appendix (see sections 3.90–3.93).

Tables usually present quantitative data. Occasionally, however, a table that consists of words is used to present qualitative comparisons. For additional information on word tables, see section 3.69.

Tables that communicate quantitative data are effective only when the data are arranged so that their meaning is obvious at a glance (Ehrenberg, 1977; Wainer, 1997). A table should be organized so that entries that are to be compared are next to one another. Following this principle, it is generally the case that different indices (e.g., means, standard deviations, sample sizes) should be segregated into different parts of tables. Table Example 1 illustrates these principles. An author's thoughtful preparation can result in tables that very effectively communicate the essential results of an empirical inquiry.

Table Example 2 shows the basic elements of a table and illustrates the advantage of including derivative values in a table—in this case, the differences between the *With* and *Without Pretraining* subsamples that are the focus of the discussion. Detailed information on the preparation of tables is presented in sections 3.63–3.74. Table Examples 3 and 4 are examples of different kinds of tables as they would appear in a manuscript, that is, as prepared with a personal computer or a typewriter. These tables show the proper form and arrangement of titles, headings, data in the body of the table, footnotes, and rules.

Many data tables have certain canonical forms. The advantage of using the canonical form is that the reader generally knows where to look in the table for certain kinds of information. Table Example 5 presents the canonical form for reporting correlations in two groups. There are situations, however, where presentation in noncanonical form can enhance the reader's understanding of the point being made. Consider, for example, the same data recast into Table Example 6. In this case a number of changes have been made in the form of the table; most noticeably, the order of the variables in the rows and columns is not the same. The column order has been rearranged to bring the high positive correlations together, thereby making the structure of the relationships clearer. In addition, the nonmeaningful correlations of the variable with itself have been eliminated, and the number of decimals has been reduced so that the essential features of the data are stressed (but at the cost of some detail and precision). The judicious use of noncanonical forms can be effective but must always be motivated by the special circumstances of the data array.

Additional information on ways to present data in specific kinds of tables is presented in section 3.69.

Table Example 1.

Table X

Error Rates of Older and Younger Groups

Level of difficulty	Mean error rate		Standard deviation		Sample size	
	Younger	Older	Younger	Older	Younger	Older
Low	.05	.14	.08	.15	12	18
Moderate	.05	.17	.07	.15	15	12
High	.11	.26	.10	.21	16	14

Table Example 2.

Table X

Mean Numbers of Correct Responses by Children With and Without Pretraining

Grade	Girls			Boys		
	With	Without	Difference	With	Without	Difference
Verbal tests						
3	280	240	40	281	232	49
4	297	251	46	290	264	26
5	301	260	41	306	221	85
n^a	18	19		19	20	
Mathematical tests						
3	201	189	12	210	199	11
4	214	194	20	236	210	26
5	221	216[b]	5	239	213	26
n^a	20	17		19	18	

Note. Maximum score = 320.

[a]Numbers of children out of 20 in each group who completed all tests. [b]One girl in this group gave only two correct responses.

(Annotations: stubhead, column spanner, decked head, column head, table spanner, stub, cell, table body, notes to table)

Tables

Table Example 3.

Table X

Mean Causality and Responsibility Attribution Scores

Personal similarity	Situational similarity	
	Low	High
Causality		
High	16	15
Low	32	20
Responsibility		
High	16	9
Low	38	19

Note. The higher the score, the greater the attribution. Actual scores have been multiplied by 10.

Tables

Table Example 4.

Table X

Recognition Memory for Words and Nonwords as a Function of Age and Viewing Condition

Viewing condition	Adults[a]	Children[b]	Difference
		Words	
Dim	91	73	18
Moderate	88	63	25
Bright	61	45	16
		Nonwords	
Dim	78	58	20
Moderate	65	62	3
Bright	80	51	29

Note. The values represent mean percentages of correctly recognized words or nonwords.

[a]Adults were 18–21 years old. [b]Children were 12–14 years old.

Table Example 5. **Sample correlation table**

Table X

Intercorrelations Between Subscales for Students and Older Adults

Subscale	1	2	3	4
		Students (*n* = 200)		
1. Tranquillity	—	.93	−.09	.73
2. Goodwill		—	−.34	.62
3. Happiness			—	.14
4. Elation				—
		Older adults (*n* = 189)		
1. Tranquillity	—	.42	−.07	.52
2. Goodwill		—	−.43	.62
3. Happiness			—	.47
4. Elation				—

Tables

Table Example 6.

Table X

Intercorrelations Between Subscales for Students and Older Adults

Subscale	Goodwill	Elation	Happiness
Students (*n* = 200)			
Tranquillity	.9	.7	−.1
Goodwill		.6	−.3
Elation			.1
Older adults (*n* = 189)			
Tranquillity	.4	.5	−.1
Goodwill		.6	−.4
Elation			.5

3.63 *Relation of Tables and Text*

Discussing tables in text. An informative table supplements—instead of duplicates—the text. In the text, refer to every table and tell the reader what to look for. Discuss only the table's highlights; if you discuss every item of the table in text, the table is unnecessary.

Ensuring that each table can be understood on its own. Each table should be an integral part of the text but also should be intelligible without reference to the text. Explain all abbreviations (except such standard statistical abbreviations as *M*, *SD*, and *df*) and special use of underlining, dashes, and parentheses. Always identify units of measurement.

Tables

Citing tables. In the text, refer to tables by their numbers:

as shown in Table 8, the responses were . . .

children with pretraining (see Table 5) . . .

Do not write "the table above" (or below) or "the table on page 32," because the position and page number of a table cannot be determined until the typesetter sets the pages. (Students preparing theses or dissertations in which tables and figures are integrated into the text may disregard this requirement; see chapter 6.)

3.64 *Relation Between Tables*

Consider combining tables that repeat data. Ordinarily, identical columns or rows of data should not appear in two or more tables. Be consistent in the presentations of all tables within a paper to facilitate comparisons. Use similar formats, titles, and headings, and use the same terminology throughout (e.g., *response time* or *reaction time*, not both).

3.65 *Table Numbers*

Number all tables with arabic numerals in the order in which the tables are first mentioned in text, regardless of whether a more detailed discussion of the tables occurs later in the paper (the typesetter lays out tables and figures closest to where they are first mentioned). Do not use suffix letters to number tables; that is, label tables as Tables 5, 6, and 7 instead of 5, 5a, and 5b, or combine the related tables into one table. If the manuscript includes an appendix with tables, identify the tables of the appendix with capital letters and arabic numerals (e.g., Table A1 is the first table of Appendix A or of a sole appendix, which is not labeled with a letter; Table C2 is the second table of Appendix C).

3.66 *Table Titles*

Give every table a brief but clear and explanatory title.

Too telegraphic:

Relation Between College Majors and Performance [It is unclear what data are presented in the table.]

Too detailed:

Mean Performance Scores on Test A, Test B, and Test C of Students With Psychology, Physics, English, and Engineering Majors [This duplicates information in the headings of the table.]

Good title:

Mean Performance Scores of Students With Different College Majors

Abbreviations that appear in the headings or the body of a table sometimes can be parenthetically explained in the table title. For example,

Hit and False-Alarm (FA) Proportions in Experiment 2

Abbreviations that require longer explanations or that do not relate to the table title are explained in a general note to the table (see section 3.70). Do not use a specific footnote to clarify an element of the title.

3.67 Headings

A table classifies related items and enables the reader to compare them. Data form the body of the table. Headings establish the logic of your organization of the data and identify the columns of data beneath them. Like a table title, a heading should be telegraphic and should not be many more characters in length than the widest entry of the column it spans. For example,

Poor:		*Better:*	
Grade level		Grade	
3		3	
4		4	
5		5	

You may use standard abbreviations and symbols for nontechnical terms (e.g., *no.* for *number*, % for *percent*) and for statistics (e.g., *M, SD,* χ^2) in table headings without explanation. Abbreviations of technical terms, group names, and the like must be explained in a note to the table (see section 3.70).

Each column of a table must have a heading, including the *stub column,* or leftmost column of the table (its heading is called the *stub head*). The stub column usually lists the major independent variables. In Table Example 2, for example, the stub lists the grades. Number elements only when they appear in a correlation matrix (see Table Example 5) or if the text refers to them by number.

Subordination within the stub is easier to comprehend by indenting stub items instead of by creating an additional column. This also simplifies the typesetting by keeping the number of columns to a minimum.

Poor:

Sex	Pretraining
Girls	With
	Without
Boys	With
	Without

Better:

Group
Girls
With
Without
Boys
With
Without

All headings identify items below them, not across from them. The headings just above the body of the table (called *column heads* and *column spanners*) identify the entries in the vertical columns in the body of the table. A column head covers just one column; a column spanner covers two or more columns, each with its own column head. Headings stacked in this way are called *decked heads*. Often decked heads can be used to avoid repetition of words in column headings (see Table Example 2). If possible, do not use more than two levels of decked heads.

Incorrect:

Temporal lobe:	Left	Right

Wordy:

Left temporal lobe	Right temporal lobe

Correct:

Temporal lobe	
Left	Right

A few tables may require *table spanners* in the body of the table. These table spanners cover the entire width of the body of the table, allowing for further divisions within the table (see Table Example 2). Also, table spanners can be used to combine two tables into one, provided they have similar column heads.

Any item within a column should be syntactically as well as conceptually comparable with the other items in that column, and all items should be described by the heading:

Nonparallel:

Condition
Functional psychotic
Drinks to excess
Character disorder

Parallel:

Condition
Functional psychosis
Alcoholism
Character disorder

Stubheads, column heads, and column spanners should be singular unless they refer to groups (e.g., *Children*), but table spanners may be plural. Use sentence style for capitalization: Capitalize only the first letter of the first word of all headings (column headings, column spanners, stub heads, and table spanners) and word entries. (All proper nouns should be in caps and lowercase.)

3.68 *Body of a Table*

Decimal values. The body of a table contains the data. Express numerical values in the number of decimal places that the precision of measurement justifies (see section 3.46), and, if possible, carry all comparable values to the same number of decimal places. Do not change the unit of measurement or the number of decimal places within a column.

Empty cells. If the point of intersection between a row and a column (called a *cell*) cannot be filled because data are not applicable, leave the cell blank. If a cell cannot be filled because data were not obtained or are not reported, insert a dash in that cell and explain the use of the dash in the general note to the table. By convention, a dash in a correlation matrix (see Table Example 5) usually indicates that the correlation of an item with itself was not computed. No explanation of this use of the dash in a correlation matrix is needed. If you need to explain that data in a correlation matrix are unavailable, unreported, or inapplicable, use a specific note (see section 3.70) rather than a dash.

Conciseness. Be selective in your presentation. Do not include columns of data that can be calculated easily from other columns:

Not concise:

	No. responses			
Participant	First trial	Second trial	Total	M
1	5	7	12	6

The example could be improved by (a) giving either the number of responses per trial or the total number of responses, whichever is more important to the discussion, and (b) not including the column of averages because their calculation is simple.

3.69 *Presenting Data in Specific Types of Tables*

Analysis of variance (ANOVA) tables. To avoid statistics-laden text that is difficult to read, you may want to present ANOVA statistics in a table. To do so, list the source in the stub column; report degrees of freedom in the first column after the stub column and the *F* ratios next. Stub entries should first show between-subjects variables and the error and then within-subject variables and any error. Enclose mean square errors in parentheses, and explain what the values in parentheses mean in a general note to the table. Identify statistically significant *F* ratios with asterisks, and provide the probability values in a probability footnote (see section 3.70); avoid columns of probability values. (See Table Example 7.)

Regression tables. List both raw or unstandardized (*B*) and standardized beta (β) coefficients unless the study is purely applied (in which case, list only *B*s) or purely theoretical (in which case, list only βs). Specify in the table what type of analysis (hierarchical or simultaneous) you used. For hierarchical regressions, be sure to provide the increments of change (see Table Example 8).

Path and LISREL (linear structural relations) tables. Present the means, standard deviations, and intercorrelations of the entire set of variables you use as input to path and LISREL analyses. These data are essential for the reader to replicate or confirm your analyses and are necessary for archival purposes, for example, if your study is included in meta-analyses. To help the reader interpret your table, give short descriptions instead of just a list of symbols of the *x* and *y* variables used in the models (see Table Example 9). If you need to use acronyms, be sure to define each one.

Occasionally, multiple models are compared in LISREL analyses. In cases like these, it may be useful to summarize the fit of these models and tests of model comparisons (see Table Example 10). (Results of analyses of structural models are often presented in a figure; see section 3.77.)

Word tables. Unlike most tables, which present quantitative data, some tables consist mainly of words. Word tables present qualitative comparisons or descriptive information. For example, a word table can enable the reader to compare characteristics of studies in an article that reviews many studies, or it can present questions and responses from a survey or show an outline of the elements of a theory. Word tables illustrate the discussion in the text; they should not repeat the discussion. (See Table Example 11.)

Word tables include the same elements of format as do other types of tables—table number and title, headings, rules, and possibly notes. Keep column entries brief and simple. Indent any runover lines in entries. *Double-space all parts of a word table.*

Table Example 7. **Sample ANOVA table**

Table X

Analysis of Variance for Classical Conditioning

Source	*df*	*F*	η	*p*
Between subjects				
Anxiety (A)	2	0.76	.22	.48
Shock (S)	1	0.01	.02	.92
A × S	2	0.18	.11	.84
S within-group				
error	30	(16.48)		
Within subjects				
Blocks (B)	4	3.27**	.31	.01
B × A	8	0.93	.24	.49
B × S	4	2.64*	.28	.04
B × A × S	8	0.58	.19	.79
B × S within-				
group error	120	(1.31)		

Note. Values enclosed in parentheses represent mean square errors. *S* = subjects. Adapted from "The Relation of Drive to Finger-Withdrawal Conditioning," by M. F. Elias, 1965, *Journal of Experimental Psychology, 70*, p. 114.

*p < .05. **p < .01.

Table Example 8. **Sample regression table**

Table X

Summary of Hierarchical Regression Analysis for Variables Predicting Adult Daughters' Belief in Paternalism (N = 46)

Variable	B	SE B	β
Step 1			
Daughter's education	−5.89	1.93	−.41*
Mother's age	0.67	0.31	.21*
Step 2			
Daughter's education	−3.19	1.81	−.22
Mother's age	0.31	0.28	.14
Attitude toward elders	1.06	0.28	.54*
Affective feelings	1.53	0.60	.31*
Dogmatism	−0.03	0.10	−.04

Note. R^2 = .26 for Step 1; ΔR^2 = .25 for Step 2 (ps < .05). From "Relationship of Personal–Social Variables to Belief in Paternalism in Parent Caregiving Situations," by V. G. Cicirelli, 1990, *Psychology and Aging, 5,* 436. Copyright 1990 by the American Psychological Association. Adapted with permission of the author.
*p < .05.

Table Example 9. **Sample LISREL table**

Table X

Factor Loadings and Uniqueness for Confirmatory Factor Model of Type A Behavior Pattern Variables

Measure and variable	Unstandardized factor loading	SE	Uniqueness
SI—Speech Characteristics			
Loud and explosive	.60	—	.32
Rapid and accelerating	.63	.04	.29
Response latency	.71	.04	.16
Verbal competitiveness	.82	.05	.25
SI—Answer Content			
Competitiveness	.60	—	.34
Speed	.59	.04	.27
Impatience	.67	.05	.28
SI—Hostility			
Stylistic rating	.60	—	.22
Content rating	.60	.05	.17

Table Example 9 (continued). **Sample LISREL table**

Measure and variable	Unstandardized factor loading	SE	Uniqueness
Thurstone Activity Scale			
Variable 1	.60	—	.73
Variable 2	.88	.08	.39
Variable 3	.71	.07	.54
Variable 4	.69	.07	.74
Variable 5	.74	.07	.31

Note. Dashes indicate the standard error was not estimated. SI = Structured Interview. From "The Nomological Validity of the Type A Personality Among Employed Adults," by D. C. Ganster, J. Schaubroeck, W. E. Sime, and B. T. Mayes, 1991, *Journal of Applied Psychology, 76,* p. 154. Copyright 1991 by the American Psychological Association. Reprinted with permission of the author.

Table Example 10. **Sample model comparison table**

Table X

Fit Indices for Nested Sequence of Cross-Sectional Models

Model	χ^2	NFI	PFI	χ^2_{diff}	ΔNFI
1. Mobley's (1977) measurement model	443.18*	.92	.67		
2. Quit & search intentions	529.80*	.89	.69		
Difference between Model 2 & Model 1				86.61*	.03
3. Search intentions & thoughts of quitting	519.75*	.90	.69		
Difference between Model 3 & Model 1				76.57*	.02
4. Intentions to quit & thoughts of quitting	546.97*	.89	.69		
Difference between Model 4 & Model 1				103.78*	.03
5. One withdrawal cognition	616.97*	.87	.70		
Difference between Model 5 & Model 1				173.79*	.05

Table Example 10 (continued). **Sample model comparison table**

Model	χ^2	NFI	PFI	χ^2_{diff}	ΔNFI
6. Hom et al.'s (1984)					
structural model	754.37*	.84	.71		
Difference between					
Model 6 & Model 5				137.39*	.03
7. Structural null model	2,741.49*	.23	.27		
Difference between					
Model 7 & Model 6				1,987.13*	.61
8. Null model	3,849.07*				

Note. NFI = normed fit index; PFI = parsimonious fit index. From "Structural Equations Modeling Test of a Turnover Theory: Cross-Sectional and Longitudinal Analyses," by P. W. Hom and R. W. Griffeth, 1991, *Journal of Applied Psychology, 76,* p. 356. Copyright 1991 by the American Psychological Association. Reprinted with permission of the author.

*$p < .05$.

Table Example 11. **Sample word table**

Table X

Some Memorial and Processing Advantages of the
Fuzzy-Processing Preference

Advantage	Description
Trace availability	Gist has a memorial stability advantage over verbatim detail; therefore, reasoning is engineered to operate on the types of information that tend to be available in memory.
Trace accessibility	Gist has a retrieval advantage over verbatim traces because it can be accessed by a broader range of retrieval cues.
Trace malleability	The schematic, patternlike nature of gist makes it easier to manipulate than verbatim traces during the course of reasoning.

Table Example 11 (continued). **Sample word table**

Advantage	Description
Processing simplicity	Less elaborate representations call for less complicated processing operations, and gist is less elaborate than verbatim traces.
Processing accuracy	Processing verbatim details typically produces no accuracy gains, especially with respect to the functional goals that reasoning serves, and the reverse is often true.
Processing effort	The fuzzy-processing preference comports with the law of least effort in that reasoning gravitates toward processing activities that are easier to execute.

Note. From "Memory Independence and Memory Interference in Cognitive Development," by C. J. Brainerd and V. F. Reyna, 1993, *Psychological Review, 100*, p. 48. Copyright 1993 by the American Psychological Association. Adapted with permission of the author.

Tables

3.70 *Notes to a Table*

Tables have three kinds of notes, which are placed below the table: general notes, specific notes, and probability notes.

A general note qualifies, explains, or provides information relating to the table as a whole and ends with an explanation of abbreviations, symbols, and the like.

General notes are designated by the word *Note* (italicized) followed by a period. (See section 3.73 and Table Examples 7–11 for examples of general notes indicating that a table is from another source.)

> *Note.* All nonsignificant three-way interactions were omitted. M = match process; N = nonmatch process.

A specific note refers to a particular column, row, or individual entry. Specific notes are indicated by superscript lowercase letters (e.g., [a, b, c]). Within the headings and table body, order the superscripts from left to right and from top to bottom, starting at the top left. Specific notes to a table do not apply to any other table, and each table's first footnote begins with a superscript lowercase *a*. (See Table Examples 2 and 4 for examples of this kind of note.)

> [a]$n = 25$. [b]This participant did not complete the trials.

A probability note indicates the results of tests of significance. Asterisks indicate those values for which the null hypothesis is rejected, with the probability (*p* value) specified in the probability note. Include a probability note only when relevant to specific data within the table. Assign a given alpha level the same number of asterisks from table to table within your paper, such as $*p < .05$ and $**p < .01$; the largest probability receives the fewest asterisks.

$F(1, 52)$
6.95*
12.38**

*$p < .05$. **$p < .01$.

Ordinarily, you will use asterisks to identify probability values; occasionally, however, you may need to distinguish between one-tailed and two-tailed tests in the same table. To do so, use asterisks for the two-tailed p values and an alternate symbol (e.g., daggers) for the one-tailed p values.

*$p < .05$, two-tailed. **$p < .01$, two-tailed. †$p < .05$, one-tailed. ††$p < .01$, one-tailed.

Asterisks attached to the obtained value of a statistical test in a table indicate probability. To indicate significant differences between two or more table entries—for example, means that are compared with procedures such as a Tukey test—use lowercase *sub*scripts (see Table Example 12). Explain the use of the subscripts in the table note (see the following sample table notes).

Note. Means having the same subscript are not significantly different at $p < .01$ in the Tukey honestly significant difference comparison.

or

Note. Means with different subscripts differ significantly at $p < .01$ by the Fisher least significant difference test.

Table Example 12. **Sample of data comparison**

Table X

Judgments of Agency of Life Events by Condition

	Anger		Sadness	
Target judgment	Hot	Cold	Hot	Cold
Future problems	4.10_a	4.35_a	5.46_b	3.81_a
Future successes	4.31_a	4.55_a	4.55_a	3.85_a
Life circumstances	3.80_a	4.50_b	5.40_c	3.46_a

Note. Judgments were made on 9-point scales (1 = *completely due to people's actions*, 9 = *completely due to impersonal forces*). Means in the same row that do not share subscripts differ at $p < .05$ in the Tukey honestly significant difference comparison. From "Beyond Simple Pessimism: Effects of Sadness and Anger on Social Perception," by D. Keltner, P. C. Ellsworth, and K. Edwards, 1993, *Journal of Personality and Social Psychology, 64,* p. 751. Copyright 1993 by the American Psychological Association. Adapted with permission of the author.

Order the notes to a table in the following sequence: *general* note, *specific* note, *probability* note.

Note. The participants . . . responses.

$^a n = 25.$ $^b n = 42.$

$^* p < .05.$ $^{**} p < .01.$

Each type of note begins flush left (i.e., no paragraph indentation) on a new line below the table and is double-spaced. The first *specific* note begins flush left on a new line under the *general* note; subsequent specific notes follow one after the other on the same line (lengthy specific notes may be set on separate lines when typeset). The first *probability* note begins flush left on a new line; subsequent probability notes are run in.

Notes are useful for eliminating repetition from the body of a table. Certain types of information may be appropriate either in the table or in a note. To determine the placement of such material, remember that clearly and efficiently organized data enable the reader to focus on the significance of the data. Thus, if probability values or subsample sizes are numerous, use a column rather than many notes. Conversely, if a row or column contains few entries (or the same entry), eliminate the column by adding a note to the table:

Poor:

Group	n
Anxious	15
Depressed	15
Control	15

Better:

Group[a]
Anxious
Depressed
Control

[a]n = 15 for each group.

3.71 *Ruling of Tables*

Typesetting requirements restrict the use of rules (i.e., lines) in a table. Limit the rules to those that are necessary for clarity, and use horizontal rather than vertical rules. (Vertical rules are rarely used in APA journals.) Appropriately positioned white space can be an effective substitute for rules; for example, long, uninterrupted columns of numbers or words are more readable if a horizontal line of space is inserted after every fourth or fifth entry.

In the manuscript, use generous spacing between columns and rows and strict alignment to clarify relationships within a table.

3.72 *Size of Tables*

Turning a journal sideways to read a table is an inconvenience to readers. You can design a table to fit the width of a journal page or column if you count characters (i.e., letters, numbers, and spaces). Count characters in the widest entry in each column (whether in the table body or in a heading), and allow 3 characters for spaces between columns. If the count exceeds 60, the table will not fit across the width of most APA journal columns. If the count exceeds 125, the table will not fit across the width of most APA journal pages. To determine the exact fit, count the characters that fit across a column or page in the journal for which you are writing, and adjust your table if necessary. When typing tables, it is acceptable to turn them sideways (landscape orientation for setting up a laser printer) on the page or run them over several pages, but do not single-space or reduce the type size.

3.73 *Tables From Another Source*

Authors must obtain permission to reproduce or adapt all or part of a table (or figure) from a copyrighted source. It is not necessary to obtain permission from APA to reproduce one table (or figure) from an APA article provided you obtain the author's permission and give full credit to APA as copyright holder and to the author through a complete and accurate citation. When you wish to reproduce material from sources not copyrighted by APA, contact the copyright holders to determine their requirements for both print and electronic reuse. If you have any doubt about the policy of the copyright holder, you should request permission. Always enclose the letter of permission when transmitting the final version of the accepted manuscript for production (see section 7.01).

Any reproduced table (or figure) must be accompanied by a note at the bottom of the reprinted table (or in the figure caption) giving credit to the original author and to the copyright holder. If the table (or figure) contains test items, see the cautionary note in section 3.93. Use the following form for tables or figures. (For copyright permission footnotes in text [see section 3.41 for permission to quote], use the following form, but substitute the indented superscript footnote number for the word *Note.*)

Material reprinted from a journal article:

Note. From [*or* The data in column 1 are from] "Title of Article," by A. N. Author and C. O. Author, 2000, *Title of Journal, 50,* p. 22. Copyright 2000 by the Name of Copyright Holder. Reprinted [*or* Adapted] with permission.

Material reprinted from a book:

Note. From [*or* The data in column 1 are from] *Title of Book* (p. 103), by A. N. Author and C. O. Author, 1999, Place of Publication: Publisher. Copyright 1999 by the Name of Copyright Holder. Reprinted [*or* Adapted] with permission.

3.74 *Table Checklist*

- Is the table necessary?
- Is the entire table—including the title, headings, and notes—double-spaced?
- Are all comparable tables in the manuscript consistent in presentation?
- Is the title brief but explanatory?
- Does every column have a column heading?
- Are all abbreviations; special use of italics, parentheses, and dashes; and special symbols explained?
- Are all probability level values correctly identified, and are asterisks attached to the appropriate table entries? Is a probability level assigned the same number of asterisks in all tables in the same article?
- Are the notes in the following order: general note, specific note, probability note?

- Are all vertical rules eliminated?
- Will the table fit across the width of a journal column or page?
- If all or part of a copyrighted table is reproduced, do the table notes give full credit to the copyright owner? Have you received written permission for reuse (in print and electronic form) from the copyright holder and sent a copy with the final version of your paper?
- Is the table referred to in text?

Figures

3.75 *Deciding to Use Figures*

In APA journals, any type of illustration other than a table is called a *figure*. (Because tables are typeset, rather than photographed from artwork supplied by the author, they are not considered figures.) A figure may be a chart, graph, photograph, drawing, or other depiction.

Consider carefully whether to use a figure. Tables are often preferred for the presentation of quantitative data in archival journals because they provide exact information; figures typically require the reader to estimate values. On the other hand, figures convey at a quick glance an overall pattern of results. They are especially useful in describing an interaction —or lack thereof—and nonlinear relations. A well-prepared figure can also convey structural or pictorial concepts more efficiently than can text.

During the process of drafting a manuscript, and in deciding whether to use a figure, ask yourself these questions:

- What idea do you need to convey?
- Is the figure necessary? If it duplicates text, it is not necessary. If it complements text or eliminates lengthy discussion, it may be the most efficient way to present the information.
- What type of figure (e.g., graph, chart, diagram, drawing, map, or photograph) is most suited to your purpose? Will a simple, relatively inexpensive figure (e.g., line art) convey the point as well as an elaborate, expensive figure (e.g., photographs combined with line art, figures that are in color instead of in black and white)?

3.76 *Standards for Figures*

The standards for good figures are simplicity, clarity, and continuity. A good figure

- augments rather than duplicates the text;
- conveys only essential facts;
- omits visually distracting detail;
- is easy to read—its elements (type, lines, labels, symbols, etc.) are large enough to be read with ease in the printed form;
- is easy to understand—its purpose is readily apparent;
- is consistent with and is prepared in the same style as similar figures in the same article; that is, the lettering is of the same size and typeface, lines are of the same weight, and so forth; and
- is carefully planned and prepared.

Types of figures and guidelines for preparing them are described in sections 3.77–3.82 so that you can select the figure most appropriate to the information being presented and ensure the preparation of a figure of professional quality. If you engage a professional artist, supply the artist with the guidelines in this section. (See the references in section 9.03 for more on the preparation of figures.)

3.77 *Types of Figures*

Several types of figures can be used to present data to the reader. Sometimes the choice of which type to use will be obvious, but at other times it will not. Figure Examples 1 and 2 and Figure Examples 3 and 4 illustrate this point by showing that there are different methods for depicting the same data in a figure. Well-designed figures can convey a memorable image of the overall pattern of results. They also can be the best way to reveal what the reader is not expecting. (See the references in section 9.03 for additional source materials on graphing and visualizing data.)

Graphs show relations—comparisons and distributions—in a set of data and may show, for example, absolute values, percentages, or index

Figures

numbers. Keep the lines clean and simple, and eliminate extraneous detail. The presentation of information on the horizontal (or x) and vertical (or y) axes should be orderly (e.g., small to large) and consistent (e.g., in comparable units of measurement).

- **Scatter plots** consist of single dots plotted to represent the values of single events on the two variables scaled on the abscissa and ordinates (see Figure Example 5). Meaningful clusters of dots imply correlations. For example, a cluster of dots along a diagonal implies a linear relationship, and if all the dots fall on a diagonal line, the coefficient of correlation is 1.00.

- **Line graphs** are used to show the relation between two quantitative variables. The independent variable is plotted on the horizontal axis, and the dependent variable is plotted on the vertical axis (see Figure Examples 1, 2, and 4). Grid marks on the axes demarcate units of measurement; scales on the axes can be linear (with equal numerical and visual increments, e.g., 25, 30, 35), logarithmic, or log-linear.

- **Bar graphs** are used when the independent variable is categorical (e.g., as with different experimental conditions; see Figure Example 3). Solid horizontal or vertical bars each represent one kind of datum. In a subdivided bar graph, each bar shows two or more divisions of data (note that comparison across bars is difficult for all but the first layer because they do not have a common baseline). Other bar graphs include multiple bar graphs (in which whole bars represent different single variables in one set of data) and sliding bar graphs (in which bars are split by a horizontal line that serves as the reference for each bar, such as to show less-than-zero and greater-than-zero relations).

- **Pictorial graphs** are used to represent simple quantitative differences between groups. All symbols representing equal values should be the same size. Keep in mind that if you double the height of a symbol, you quadruple its area.

3.77 APA EDITORIAL STYLE

- **Circle (or pie) graphs,** or 100% graphs, are used to show percentages and proportions. The number of items compared should be kept to five or fewer. Order the segments from large to small, beginning the largest segment at 12 o'clock. A good way to highlight differences is to shade the segments from light to dark, making the smallest segment the darkest. Use patterns of lines and dots to shade the segments.

Charts can describe the relations between parts of a group or object or the sequence of operations in a process; charts are usually boxes connected with lines. For example, organizational charts show the hierarchy in a group, flowcharts show the sequence of steps in a process, and schematics show components in a system. Figure Example 6 shows the elements of a theoretical model in a path analysis.

Dot maps can show population density, and **shaded maps** can show averages or percentages. In these cases, plotted data are superimposed on a map. Maps should always be prepared by a professional artist, who should clearly indicate the compass orientation (e.g., north–south) of the map, fully identify the map's location, and provide the scale to which the map is drawn. Use arrows to help readers focus on reference points.

Drawings are selective and give the author the flexibility to emphasize any aspect of an image or idea (see Figure Example 7). They can be done from any of several views, for instance, a two-dimensional view of one side of an object or a view of an object rotated and tipped forward to show several sides at once. Drawings should be prepared by a professional artist and should use the least amount of detail necessary to convey the point.

Photographs have excellent eye appeal. They should be of professional quality and should be prepared with a background that produces the greatest amount of contrast. A photographer can highlight a particular aspect of the photograph by manipulating the camera angle or by choosing a particular type of lighting or film. (For more on photographs, see section 3.82.)

Figure Example 1. Sample line graph.[1]

- Lines are smooth and sharp.
- Typeface is simple (sans serif) and legible.
- Unit of measure is indicated in axis label.
- Axis labels are shared by both panels to decrease clutter.
- Legends are contained within the borders of the graph.
- Symbols are easy to differentiate.
- Caption explains error bars.

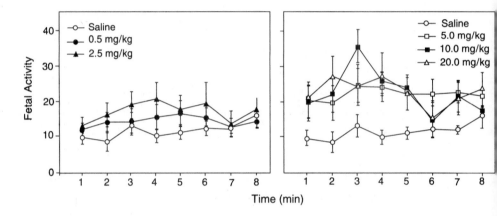

Figure X. Overall motor activity during the first 8 min of the observation session of E21 (Embryonic Day 21) rat fetuses treated with isotonic saline or varying dosages of cocaine. Cocaine groups in the left panel did not differ significantly from the saline-treated control group; cocaine groups in the right panel exhibited significantly elevated activity compared with the control group. Points represent the mean number of movements per minute; vertical lines depict standard errors of the means.

[List captions together on a separate page.]

---

[1] From "Cocaine Alters Behavior in the Rat Fetus," by D. K. Simonik, S. R. Robinson, and W. P. Smotherman, 1993, *Behavioral Neuroscience, 107,* p. 870. Copyright 1993 by the American Psychological Association. Adapted with permission of the author.

Figures

Figure Example 2. Alternative line graph to left panel of previous figure.

- Expanding the scale makes differences within the data more visible.
- A single error bar shows the only significant difference.

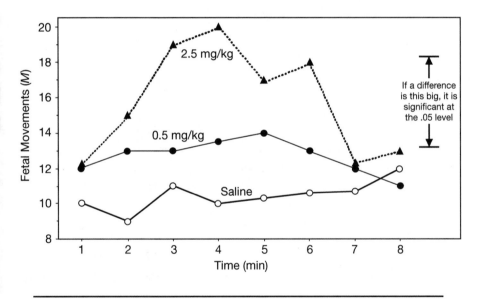

Figure Example 3. Sample bar graph.[2]

- Bars are easy to differentiate by fill pattern.
- Zero point is indicated on ordinate axis.
- Axes are labeled with legible type; ordinate axis indicates unit of measure.
- Legend appears within dimensions of the graph.
- Axes are just long enough to accommodate bar length.
- Caption explains error bars and sample sizes.

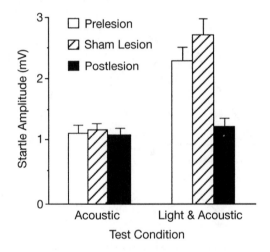

Figure X. Mean amplitude startle response (+*SE*) for prelesion (*n* = 4), sham lesion (*n* = 2), and postlesion (*n* = 2) groups in acoustic and light-and-acoustic test conditions.

[List captions together on a separate page.]

Figure Example 4. A line graph as an alternative to a bar graph.

- Figure is simpler.
- More than one comparison at a time can be perceived.

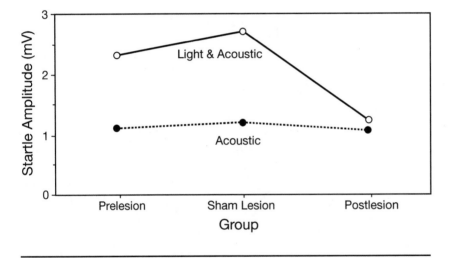

Figure Example 5. Sample scatter plot.[3]

- Solid circles represent data points.
- Zero point indicated on axes.
- Axis labels are in a legible typeface.

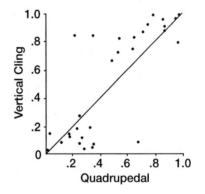

Figure X. Proportion of left-hand reaches by squirrel monkeys from horizontal quadrupedal and vertical cling postures in Experiment 1. [List captions together on a separate page.]

---

[3] From "Postural Effects on Manual Reaching Laterality in Squirrel Monkeys (*Saimiri sciureus*) and Cotton-Top Tamarins (*Saguinus oedipus*)," by L. S. Roney and J. E. King, 1993, *Journal of Comparative Psychology, 107*, p. 382. Copyright 1993 by the American Psychological Association. Adapted with permission of the author.

Figures

Figure Example 6. Sample chart (path model).[4]

- Names of variables are indicated with the variable symbols.
- Size of numbers is proportional to lettering, enabling complex figure to be placed in a small space on page.

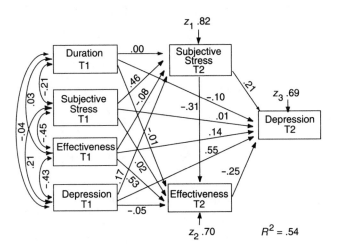

Figure X. Initial path-analytic model: Influence of caregiving dura-tion, subjective caregiving stress, and subjective caregiving effec-tiveness on changes in depression.

[List captions together on a separate page.]

Figure Example 7. Sample line drawing.[5]

- Lines are simple; no extraneous detail.
- Type is legible.
- Arrangement of components of figure is compact.

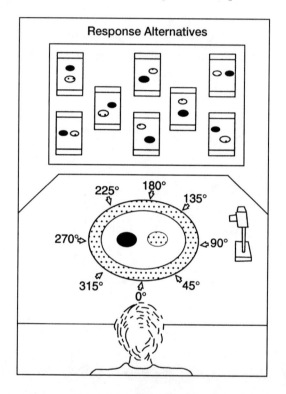

Figure X. The perspective-taking task. In the item depicted, the disks are in the horizontal orientation, the camera is at 90°, and the correct response is shown in the upper left corner of the response alternatives.

[List captions together on a separate page.]

---

[5] From "Understanding Person–Space–Map Relations: Cartographic and Developmental Perspectives," by L. S. Liben and R. M. Downs, 1993, *Developmental Psychology, 29,* p. 744. Copyright 1993 by the American Psychological Association. Reprinted with permission of the author.

3.78 *Line Art Versus Halftone*

Although there are many types of figures, usually only two printing processes are involved in reproducing them: line art processing and halftone processing. Line art is any material that will reproduce only in black and white, for example, type, lines, boxes, and dots; such material includes line graphs, charts, and bar graphs. Halftones are figures that have shades of gray—photographs and photomicrographs, for example (see Figure Example 8). Halftones require a special printing process, which makes them more expensive than line drawings to reproduce.

Figure Example 8. Sample photograph (halftone).[6]

- Cropped to omit extraneous detail and to fit in one column.
- Good contrast for reproduction.
- Panel label has good contrast to background.
- Scale bar included and labeled in 14-pt sans serif font.

Figures

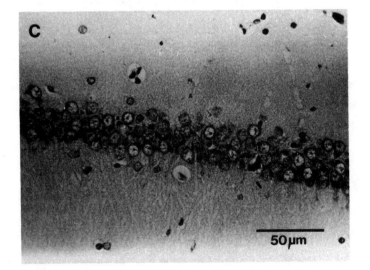

Figure X. Photomicrograph of part of the CA1 cell field from the control rat.

[List captions together on a separate page.]

---

[6] Panel from "Impaired Object Recognition Memory in Rats Following Ischemia-Induced Damage to the Hippocampus," by E. R. Wood, D. G. Mumby, J. P. J. Pinel, and A. G. Phillips, 1993, *Behavioral Neuroscience, 107,* p. 55. Copyright 1993 by the American Psychological Association. Reprinted with permission of the author.

3.79 *Overall Size and Proportion*

When planning a figure, consider that

■ All published figures must fit the dimensions of the journal in which your article will be published. Size your figures to fit within a single journal column unless multiple panels or fine detail require them to be the width of the journal page (see Table 3.10).

■ Parallel figures or figures of equal importance should be of equal size; that is, they should be prepared according to the same scale.

■ Combining like figures (e.g., two line graphs with identical axes) facilitates comparisons between them. For example, if each of two figures can be reduced to fit in a single column, place one above the other and treat them as one figure. Two line graphs with identical axes might be combined horizontally and treated as one figure (see Figure Example 1).

■ All elements of a figure, including plot points and subscripts, must be large enough to be legible (as a general rule, type should be no smaller than 8 point and no larger than 14 point).

■ A figure legend, which is a key to symbols used in the figure, should be positioned within the borders of the figure (see Figure Examples 1 and 3). Place labels for parts of a figure as close as possible to the components being indentified.

3.80 *Preparation of Figures*

Figures may be mechanically produced or computer generated. Mechanical figure preparation usually should be done by graphic arts professionals because they have the technical skill to produce a figure that meets printing requirements. A graphic arts professional also may produce a figure with sophisticated computer software and hardware that typically are unavailable to authors. A glossy or high-quality laser print of any professional-quality figure is acceptable, however, whether created by a graphics specialist or generated by computer. If you generate figures by computer, resist the temptation to use special effects (e.g., three-dimensional effects in bar graphs and line graphs); although special ef-

Table 3.10. *Sizing and Type Specifications for Figures for APA Journals*

A. *Standard Figure Sizes*

| APA journal dimension | Standard figure width | | | |
| | 1 column | | 2 columns | |
	Minimum	Maximum	Minimum	Maximum
Inches				
$8\frac{1}{4} \times 11$	2	$3\frac{1}{4}$	$4\frac{1}{4}$	$6\frac{7}{8}$
$6\frac{3}{4} \times 10$	2	$2\frac{5}{8}$	$3\frac{5}{8}$	$5\frac{1}{2}$
Centimeters				
21×28	5.0	8.45	10.60	17.50
17×25.4	5.0	6.70	9.30	14.00
Picas				
49.5×66	13	20	25	41.5
40.5×60	12	16	22	33

Note. Figures are sized to fit within the ranges shown. Simple line graphs and bar graphs will be reduced to fit into one column.

B. *Minimum and Maximum Type Sizes*

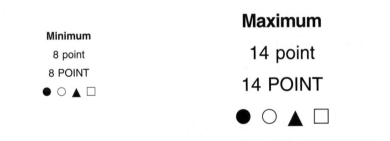

Note. For legibility, a sans serif typeface, such as Helvetica used above, is recommended. Other common sans serif typefaces are Futura, Univers, Geneva, and Optima. A combination of circles and triangles is recommended to distinguish curves on line graphs; the shapes remain distinctive after reduction, whereas circles and squares can look similar when reduced.

Figures

fects may have eye-catching appeal and are popular in newsletters and magazines, they can distort data and distract the reader.

Whether prepared by graphic artist or author, drawn by hand or generated by a graphics software or statistical package, all figures must adhere to the following mechanical specifications to be acceptable for reproduction (camera ready).

Size and proportion of elements. Each element must be large enough and sharp enough to be legible (see Figure Example 9 for examples of good and poor proportions). The size of lettering should be no smaller than 8-point type and no larger than 14-point type (see Table 3.10 for examples of each). As a general guideline, plot symbols should be about the size of a lowercase letter of an average label within the figure. Also consider the weight (i.e., size, density) of each element in a figure in relation to that of every other element, making the most important elements the most prominent. For example, curves on line graphs and outlines of bars on bar graphs should be bolder than axis labels, which should be bolder than the axes and tick marks (Scientific Illustration Committee, 1988).

Materials. For mechanical figure preparation, use black india ink and a good grade of bright white drawing paper. The higher the contrast, the sharper the detail. If you draw a graph on tracing paper over a dark grid, use high-quality tracing paper. Professional artists also use pencil, scratchboard (white lines on a black field), carbon dust (to show shades of gray), and ink wash. If you are creating your own figures and need to show shaded areas, you may use patterns of lines or dots on pressure-sensitive adhesive paper (e.g., Zipatone, Letraset, Formatt), which are available from art supply stores. Keep in mind that pen-and-ink figures, which can almost always be reproduced as line art, often will be less expensive to prepare and reproduce than, for example, halftone pencil drawings.

For computer-generated figures, use high-quality, bright white paper or other paper stock that is designed to produce high-quality output from your equipment. The output must have a minimum resolution of

300 dots per inch (600 to 1200 dots per inch is preferable). In addition, the software and hardware used must produce smooth curves and crisp lines showing no jagged areas. See Figure Example 10 for examples of acceptable and unacceptable computer-generated art.

Shading. Drawings and graphs should be shaded in such a way that they can be reproduced as line art rather than as more expensive halftones. If different shadings are used to distinguish bars or segments of a graph, choose shadings that are distinct (e.g., the best option to distinguish two sets of bars is no shading [open] and black [solid]). Limit the number of different shadings used in one bar graph to two or three. If more are required, a table may be a better presentation of the data. Instead of using fine dot screens to create shades of gray in a bar graph, use a pattern of diagonal lines (hatching) or heavier dots (stippling). Diagonal lines produce the best effect; fine stippling and shading can "drop out," or disappear, when reproduced. If you use fine dot screens, be sure that different bars contrast with each other by at least 30% of gray tone (Scientific Illustration Committee, 1988). Computer-generated art will typically be produced as line art, as long as the image has been created through a digital process that places dots on the page.

Lettering. For either mechanical or computer-generated type, use a simple, sans serif typeface (such as Arial, Futura, or Helvetica) with enough space between letters to avoid crowding. Letters should be clear, sharp, and uniformly dark and should be as consistent a size as possible throughout the figure. Point size should vary by no more than 4 points; for example, if axis labels are 12 points, legend labels should be no smaller than 8 points, the minimum acceptable size of lettering.

Style of type also affects legibility: For example, type in boldface tends to thicken and become less legible when reproduced. Initial capitals and lowercase letters generally are easier to read than all capital letters, but if the figure requires several distinctions (i.e., levels) of lettering, occasional use of capitals is acceptable. If the figure consists of several panels, label each panel with a capital letter in the top left corner (the letter should be 14 point: **A**).

Figure Example 9. Proportion examples.

Examples of poor (top) and good (bottom) proportions on originals (left) and their reductions at 80% (right). In the poor original, the type size varies from 4 to 16 points and is in an illegible "jagged," condensed style, which worsens with reduction; the shading, symbols, and lines improve slightly but are still too difficult to distinguish. The professional sans serif type in the good original holds up on reduction, as do the symbols and lines.[7]

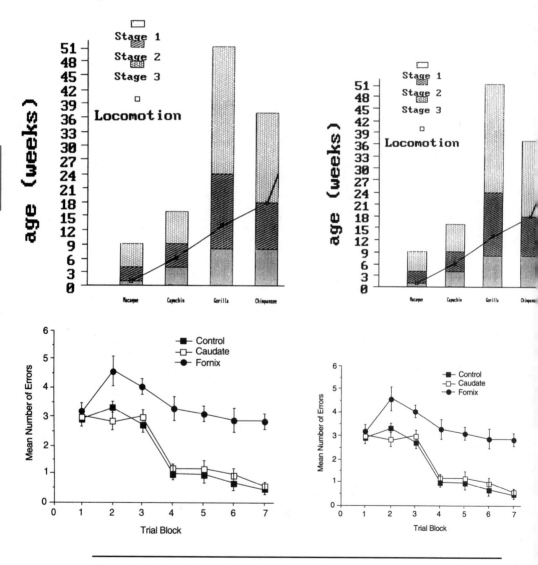

[7] Top panel used with permission from P. Poti and G. Spinozzi, whose revised art appeared in "Early Sensorimotor Development in Chimpanzees (*Pan troglodytes*)," 1994, *Journal of Comparative Psychology, 108,* p. 100. Bottom panel from "Double Dissociation of Fornix and Caudate Nucleus Lesions on Acquisition of Two Water Maze Tasks: Further Evidence for Multiple Memory Systems," by M. G. Packard and J. L. McGaugh, 1992, *Behavioral Neuroscience, 106,* p. 442. Copyright 1992 by the American Psychological Association. Adapted with permission of the author.

Figure Example 10. Examples of unacceptable computer-generated art (left) and the revision (right).

Unacceptable
- Type is jagged and illegible.
- Curves are jagged.
- Axes labels are in all caps, and ordinate label reads vertically.
- Units of measure are not specified.

Acceptable
- Lettering is professional.
- Curves are smooth.
- Lettering is in caps and lowercase and runs parallel to axes.
- Units of measure are specified.
- Top border and right axis were removed.

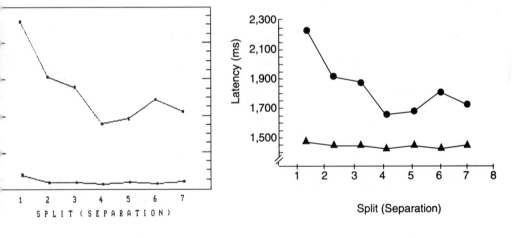

Typewritten or nonprofessional freehand lettering is not acceptable for publication. Computer-generated lettering that has a resolution of less than 300 dots per inch (such as dot-matrix printer output) or that has jagged edges, regardless of the resolution, is unacceptable.

Three methods of mechanical lettering are acceptable: professional lettering, stencil, and dry-transfer sheets. Professional lettering includes typeset or hand lettering. A stencil (e.g., Chartpak, Leroy, Wrico, or Ames lettering devices) provides a guide to the size and proportion of all lettering on the figure. Align letters from dry-transfer or pressure-sensitive sheets carefully, and press the letters securely onto the original figure so that they do not rub off. You can apply a light coat of spray fixative to protect the lettering until you photograph the figure to make a glossy print or photostat.

Preparing the final print. The final print that you supply for publication must have high contrast and be reasonably sturdy. For mechanically prepared figures, and for the best results with computer-generated figures, have a photographic proof or photostat of the figure made on gloss-coated photographic paper. Check that the glossy print is in sharp focus and that the background is bright white, not grainy or gray. For computer-generated figures, the output from your computer equipment is often acceptable for reproduction. Use bright white, high-quality paper or other high-quality materials (such as transparencies) that are designed to get the best possible quality of output from your equipment. Check that the final print is sharp and free from smudges. If your computer-generated art includes shading, check the printout to make sure that all shading has an even tone so that "bald spots" do not occur in reproduction. (For additional information on submitting final prints, see section 3.85.)

Submitting an electronic version of a figure. APA is open to receiving digital art files, if you are interested in providing them. Printers are not at this time fully successful in using author-supplied digital art, so you will still need to provide a high-quality print as well (see previous section).

The graphic files with which we are the most successful are TIFF files generated from a professional-level graphics program (such as Adobe Photoshop or Illustrator) in accordance with the following guidelines:

- *Line art*—black-and-white (or bitmap), with a resolution of 1200 dots per inch.
- *Halftones*—grayscale, with a resolution of 300 dots per inch.
- *Combination halftones* (halftones with superimposed labels or lettering)—grayscale, with a resolution of 600 dots per inch.

Files created in standard office software (e.g., for word processing, spreadsheet functions, or presentations) cannot be used for printing, primarily because the resolution of the files is too low. Files created in presentation software are unacceptable because the maximum resolution is only 72 dots per inch.

3.81 *Creating Graphs*

Follow these guidelines in creating a graph mechanically or with a computer. Computer software that generates graphs will often handle most of these steps automatically. Nevertheless, you should examine the resulting graph to ensure that it follows these guidelines and make any needed adjustments.

- Use bright white paper.
- Use medium lines for the vertical and horizontal axes. The best aspect ratio of the graph may depend on the data.
- Choose the appropriate grid scale. Consider the range and scale separation to be used on both axes and the overall dimensions of the figure so that plotted curves span the entire illustration.
- In line graphs, a change in the proportionate sizes of the x units to

the *y* units changes the slant of the line. Thus, for example, disproportionately large units on the vertical axis will exaggerate differences. Be sure the curve or slant of the line accurately reflects the data.

- Indicate units of measurement by placing tick marks on each axis at the appropriate intervals. Use equal increments of space between tick marks on linear scales.
- If the units of measurement on the axes do not begin at zero, break the axes with a double slash.
- Clearly label each axis with both the quantity measured and the units in which the quantity is measured. Carry numerical labels for axis intervals to the same number of decimal places.
- Position the axis label parallel to its axis. Do not stack letters so that the label reads vertically; do not place a label perpendicular to the vertical (*y*) axis unless it is very short (i.e., two words or a maximum of 10 characters). The numbering and lettering of grid points should be horizontal on both axes.

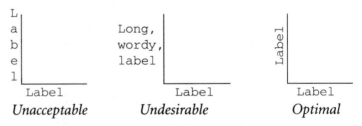

- Use legibility as a guide in determining the number of curves to place on a figure—usually no more than four curves per graph. Allow adequate space between and within curves, remembering that the figure may need to be reduced.
- Use distinct, simple geometric forms for plot points; good choices are open and solid circles and triangles. Combinations of squares and circles or squares and diamonds are not recommended because they can be difficult to differentiate if the art is reduced, as can open symbols with dots inside (e.g., ⊙).

3.82 *Using Photographs*

Because reproduction softens contrast and detail in photographs, starting with rich contrast and sharp prints is important. The camera view and the lighting should highlight the subject and provide high contrast; a light or dark background can provide even more contrast.

Photographs must be of professional quality and on black-and-white film. Do not submit color prints because the transition from color to black and white for reproduction is unpredictable and usually inaccurate in tone. Have a color negative, slide, or print developed as a black-and-white print before submitting it for publication. (If you intend to have a photograph printed in color, be sure to consult your publisher or the publication's instructions to authors.)

Photographs usually benefit from cropping (i.e., eliminating what is not to be reproduced). Cropping recomposes the photograph, eliminates extraneous detail, and recenters the image. Cropping can also remove blemishes.

To prepare for cropping a photograph, first determine the ideal area to be reproduced, that is, the part of the photograph that will appear on the printed page. The area to be reproduced need not be the same shape as the larger photograph, but the edges should be straight lines at right angles to each other.

Next, mark the area to be reproduced. One way to indicate the area is to outline it on a piece of acetate or tissue paper covering the photograph. Write lightly with a felt-tipped pen on tissue overlays. Never write directly on the face of the photograph.

Finally, have a print made of the outlined area of the photograph, and submit the new print with the manuscript.

If you group photographs for purposes of comparison or to save space, butt the photographs right next to each other. The printer can insert a thin white or black line between the photographs to separate them. Some printers prefer unmounted photographs for compatibility with reproduction equipment; be sure to consult the publication's instructions to authors for this information.

Photomicrographs are produced with specialized equipment. Photomicrographs should be submitted so that they can be reproduced at their exact size for optimal print quality. Therefore, be sure to find out which dimensions are acceptable for the journal to which you are submitting your manuscript (for APA journals, see Table 3.10). If you mark on a tissue or acetate overlay the most important areas of the photomicrograph, the printer can pay particular attention to them when making the halftone. Indicate the degree of magnification by including a scale line on the photograph. Also, indicate in the figure caption the type of staining materials and any unusual lighting used.

If you photograph a person, get a signed release from that person to use the photograph. If you use a photograph from another source, try to obtain the original photograph because photographs of photographs do not print clearly. Obtain written permission for reuse (in both print and electronic form) from the copyright holder, and acknowledge the author and the copyright holder in the figure caption (see section 3.73).

3.83 *Identifying and Citing Figures*

Number all figures consecutively with arabic numerals throughout an article in the order in which they are first mentioned in text (i.e., Figure 1, Figure 2). Write this number lightly with a pencil or pen (but do not use a ballpoint pen) as close to the top right edge of the figure print as possible, taking care to write *outside* of the image area. If the image area takes up the entire print, write the number on the back of the figure instead. Also on the back of the print, write the article's short title and the word *TOP* to designate the top of the figure.

In the text, refer to figures by their numbers:

as shown in Figure 2, the relationships are

data are related (see Figure 5)

Never write "the figure above" (or below) or "the figure on page 12," because the position and page number of a figure cannot be determined until the typesetter lays out the pages.

3.84 *Figure Legends and Captions*

In APA journals, a legend explains the symbols used in the figure; it is placed within and photographed as part of the figure. A caption is a concise explanation of the figure; it is typeset and placed below the figure.

On the final print, make certain that the symbols, abbreviations, and terminology in the caption and legend agree with the symbols, abbreviations, and terminology in the figure, in other figures in the article, and in the text. When preparing the final version for production and again when proofing the typeset article, compare the caption with the figure; proofread all lettering, and make sure no labels are missing.

Legends. The legend is an integral part of the figure; therefore, it should have the same kind and proportion of lettering that appear in the rest of the figure. Because it is scanned as part of the figure, the legend must appear on the final print, preferably within the axis area (if any). Capitalize major words in the legend.

Captions. The caption serves both as an explanation of the figure and as a figure title; therefore, the artwork should not include a title. The caption should be a brief but descriptive phrase. Compare the following captions.

Too brief:

Figure 3. Fixation duration.

Sufficiently descriptive:

Figure 3. Fixation duration as a function of the delay between the beginning of eye fixation and the onset of the stimulus in Experiment 1.

After the descriptive phrase, add any information needed to clarify the figure: A reader should not have to refer to the text to decipher the figure's message. Always explain units of measurement, symbols, and abbreviations that are not included in the legend. If your graph includes error bars, explain whether they represent standard deviations, standard errors, confidence limits, or ranges; it is also helpful to define the sample sizes used (see Figure Example 1). If statistically significant values are marked in the figure, explain the probability in the caption (follow the same system used for table notes; see section 3.70).

Because the caption is typeset and placed outside the figure, type all figure captions, with their numbers, double-spaced starting on a separate sheet (see section 5.22 for typing instructions).

If you reproduced or adapted your figure from a copyrighted source, you must obtain written permission for print and electronic reuse from the copyright holder and give credit in the figure caption to the original author and copyright holder. Use the wording shown in section 3.73, and place this notice at the end of the caption.

3.85 *Submitting Figures*

With the original submitted manuscript, paper copies of figures are acceptable. Glossy or final prints must be prepared before the manuscript is accepted for publication. Final figures must be photographed and submitted as 8 × 10 in. (20 × 25 cm) glossy prints or submitted as final prints on bright white paper. Computer-generated figures should be on 8½ × 11 in. (22 × 28 cm) high-quality, bright white paper or other material that produces a sharp image and high contrast. If it is necessary to submit smaller prints, remount them on 8½ × 11 in. (22 × 28 cm) paper.

To reproduce the figure, the printer scans the glossy or final print to create a digital image file. Flaws in the glossy or final print will appear in the published figure. Therefore, do not attach anything to the print with staples or paper clips, and avoid pressing down on the print when you write the identification information on the back. Protect the figure by putting a piece of tissue paper over it. Place the prints between pieces of cardboard to protect them.

3.86 *Figure Checklist*

- Is the figure necessary?
- Is the figure simple, clean, and free of extraneous detail?
- Are the data plotted accurately?
- Is the grid scale correctly proportioned?
- Is the lettering large and dark enough to read? Is the lettering compatible in size with the rest of the figure? (Freehand, typewritten, or jagged computer-generated lettering is not acceptable.)
- Are parallel figures or equally important figures prepared according to the same scale?
- Are terms spelled correctly?
- Are all abbreviations and symbols explained in a figure legend or figure caption? Are the symbols, abbreviations, and terminology in the figure consistent with those in the figure caption? In other figures? In the text?
- Are digital files in TIFF format at the appropriate resolution and accompanied by a high-quality laser printout?
- Are all figure captions typed together on a separate page?
- Are the figures numbered consecutively with arabic numerals?
- Are all figures mentioned in the text?
- Is each figure an 8 × 10 in. (20 × 25 cm) glossy print or photostat or an 8½ × 11 in. (22 × 28 cm) final print?
- Are all figures identified lightly in pencil or felt-tip pen on the back by figure number (on the front or back) and short article title (on the back)?
- Is TOP written on the back of figures to show orientation?
- Is written permission for print and electronic reuse enclosed for figures that are being reproduced or adapted from another source? Is proper credit given in the figure caption?

Footnotes and Notes

Notes may be substantive or explanatory or may identify sources, according to where they are used and what information needs to be conveyed. Sections 3.87–3.89 define the kinds of notes in APA journals.

3.87 *Footnotes in Text*

Footnotes in text are of two kinds: content footnotes and copyright permission footnotes.

Content footnotes supplement or amplify substantive information in the text; they should not include complicated, irrelevant, or nonessential information. Because they are distracting to readers and expensive to include in printed material, such footnotes should be included only if they strengthen the discussion. A content footnote should convey just one idea; if you find yourself creating paragraphs or displaying equations as you are writing a footnote, then the main text or an appendix probably would be a more suitable place to present your information (see sections 1.14 and 3.90–3.93 for more information on appendixes; for typing instructions, see section 5.19). Another alternative to consider is to indicate in a short footnote that the material is available from the author. In most cases, an author integrates an article best by presenting important information in the text, not in a footnote.

Copyright permission footnotes acknowledge the source of quotations (see section 3.41 on permission to quote). Use the suggested wording for reprinted tables or figures (see section 3.73). All other kinds of reference citations, including legal citations and citations to material of limited availability, should appear in the reference list (see sections 4.01–4.15 and Appendix D).

Number content and copyright permission footnotes consecutively throughout an article with superscript arabic numerals. Type these footnotes on a separate page (see section 5.20 for typing instructions). Subsequent references to a footnote are by parenthetical note:

the same results (see Footnote 3)

3.88 *Notes to Tables*

Table notes, which are placed below the bottom rule of a table, explain the table data or provide additional information (see section 3.70 on notes to a table). They also acknowledge the source of a table if the table is reprinted (see section 3.73 for suggested wording).

3.89 *Author Note*

An author note appears with each printed article to identify each author's departmental affiliation, provide acknowledgments, state any disclaimers or perceived conflict of interest, and provide a point of contact for the interested reader. (Students should note that an author note is usually not a requirement for theses and dissertations; see chapter 6.) Notes should be arranged as follows.

First paragraph: Complete departmental affiliation. Identify departmental affiliations at the time of the study for all authors. Format as follows: name of the author as it appears in the byline, comma, department name, comma, university name, semicolon, next author name, and so on, and end with a period. Because the order of authorship is shown in the byline, the copy editor may edit the departmental affiliations paragraph to conserve space (e.g., if some authors are in identically named departments). If an author is not affiliated with an institution, provide the city and state (provide city and country for authors whose affiliations are outside of the United States, and include province for authors in Canada or Australia). No degrees should be given, and state names should be spelled out.

Second paragraph: Changes of affiliation (if any). Identify any changes in author affiliation subsequent to the time of the study. Use the following wording: [author's name] is now at [affiliation].

Third paragraph: Acknowledgments. Identify grants or other financial support (and the source, if appropriate) for your study; do not precede grant numbers by No. or #. Next, acknowledge colleagues who assisted you in conducting the study or critiquing your manuscript (see the subsection on publication credit in section 8.05 for a discussion of criteria for authorship). Do not acknowledge the persons routinely involved in the review and acceptance of manuscripts—peer reviewers or editors, associate editors, and consulting editors of the journal in which the article is to appear. (If you would like to acknowledge a specific idea raised by a reviewer, do so in the text where the idea is discussed.) In this paragraph you may also explain any special agreements concerning authorship, such as if you and your colleagues contributed equally to the study. You may end this paragraph with thanks for personal assistance, such as in manuscript preparation.

This paragraph is the appropriate place to disclose any special circumstances; explain them before providing the routine information described in the previous paragraph. For example, if your paper is based on an earlier study (e.g., a longitudinal study), a doctoral dissertation, or a paper presented at a meeting, state that information in this paragraph. Also, acknowledge the publication of related reports (e.g., reports on the same database). If any relationships may be perceived as a conflict of interest (e.g., if you own stock in a company that manufactures a drug used in your study), explain them here. If your employer or granting organization requires a disclaimer stating, for example, that the research reported does not reflect the views of that organization, such a statement is included in this paragraph.

Fourth paragraph: Point of contact (*mailing address, e-mail*). Provide a complete mailing address for correspondence (see the example that follows for appropriate wording); names of states should be written out, not abbreviated, for ease of international mailing. You may end this paragraph with an e-mail address.

John Doe, Department of Psychology, University of Illinois at Urbana–Champaign; Jane Smith, Department of Educational Psychology, University of Chicago.

Jane Smith is now at Department of Psychology and Family Studies, University of California, San Diego.

This research was supported in part by grants from the National Institute on Aging and from the John D. and Catherine T. MacArthur Foundation.

Correspondence concerning this article should be addressed to John Doe, Department of Psychology, University of Illinois, Champaign, Illinois 61820. E-mail: jdoe@uiuc.edu

Unlike content footnotes, the author note is not numbered; the note should be typed on a page separate from the main text and from any content footnotes. If the manuscript is to receive a masked review, type the author note on the title page (see section 5.20 for typing instructions).

Appendixes

An appendix serves two purposes: It allows the author to provide the reader with detailed information that would be distracting to read in the main body of the article, and it enables production staff to be more flexible with rules of style and layout. If you submit a list of words as a table, for example, the copy editor may (a) request column and stub headings to make the list fit APA style for tables or (b) suggest placing the list in an appendix.

Common kinds of appendixes include a mathematical proof, a large table, lists of words, a sample of a questionnaire or other survey instrument used in the research, and a computer program. A paper may include more than one appendix.

3.90 *Identifying and Citing Appendixes*

If your paper has only one appendix, label it Appendix; if your paper has more than one appendix, label each one with a capital letter (Appendix A, Appendix B, etc.) in the order in which it is mentioned in the main text. Each appendix must have a title. In the text, refer to appendixes by their labels:

produced the same results for both studies (see Appendixes A and B for complete proofs).

3.91 *Body and Headings*

Like the main text, an appendix may include headings and subheadings. (To determine levels of heading within an appendix, treat the appendix separate from the main text: For example, the main text may have four levels of heading, but if the appendix has only two levels of heading, treat the appendix as if it were a two-level paper; see section 3.32.) Like the main text, an appendix also may include tables, figures, and displayed equations. Number each appendix table and figure, and number displayed equations if necessary for later reference; precede the number with the letter of the appendix in which it is included (e.g., Table A1). In a sole appendix, which is not labeled with a letter, precede all tables, figures, and equation numbers with the letter *A* to distinguish them from those of the main text. The same rules for citation that apply to the main text apply to appendixes: All appendix tables and figures must be cited within the appendix and numbered in order of citation.

3.92 *Tables as Appendixes*

If one table constitutes an entire appendix, the centered appendix label and title serve in lieu of a table number and title. Generally, treat multiple tables as separate appendixes. If multiple tables (but no text) are combined into one appendix, number the tables.

3.93 *Tests and Questionnaires*

If you would like to publish a new test or questionnaire in an APA journal, APA will own the copyright. (Authors who wish to retain copyright to a measure they believe might have commercial value can do so by indicating "copyright [year] by [author name].")

If you want to reprint another author's test or questionnaire, you must determine whether permission is required from the copyright holder, obtain permission for print and electronic reuse when it is required, and give full credit in your article to the copyright holder. When permission is required, send the permission letter (see section 7.01) when transmitting your accepted manuscript for publication.

Cautionary Note: A number of commercial instruments—for example, intelligence tests and projective measures—are highly protected. Permission is required, and may be denied, to republish even one item from such instruments. You should seek permission from the copyright holder before submission of papers containing such items. Publishers will require written evidence that such permission has been obtained. If there is *any* question concerning the copyright protection of such items, permission should be requested early in the process of writing the paper.

Reference Citations in Text

Document your study throughout the text by citing by author and date the works you used in your research. This style of citation briefly identifies the source for readers and enables them to locate the source of information in the alphabetical reference list at the end of the article. (See sections 4.03 to 4.15 on the preparation of the reference list.)

3.94 *One Work by One Author*

APA journals use the author–date method of citation; that is, the surname of the author (do not include suffixes such as *Jr.*) and the year of publication are inserted in the text at the appropriate point:

Walker (2000) compared reaction times

In a recent study of reaction times (Walker, 2000)

If the name of the author appears as part of the narrative, as in the first example, cite only the year of publication in parentheses. Otherwise, place both the name and the year, separated by a comma, in parentheses (as in the second example). Even if the reference includes month and year, include only the year in the text citation. In the rare case in which both the year and the author are given as part of the textual discussion, do not add parenthetical information:

In 2000 Walker compared reaction times

Within a paragraph, you need not include the year in subsequent references to a study as long as the study cannot be confused with other studies cited in the article:

In a recent study of reaction times, Walker (2000) described the method. . . . Walker also found

3.95 *One Work by Multiple Authors*

When a work has two authors, always cite both names every time the reference occurs in text.

When a work has three, four, or five authors, cite all authors the first time the reference occurs; in subsequent citations, include only the surname of the first author followed by et al. (not italicized and with a period after "al") and the year if it is the first citation of the reference within a paragraph:

Wasserstein, Zappulla, Rosen, Gerstman, and Rock (1994) found [Use as first citation in text.]

Wasserstein et al. (1994) found [Use as subsequent first citation per paragraph thereafter.]

Wasserstein et al. found [Omit year from subsequent citations after first citation within a paragraph.]

Exception: If two references with the same year shorten to the same form (e.g., both Bradley, Ramirez, & Soo, 1994, and Bradley, Soo, Ramirez, & Brown, 1994, shorten to Bradley et al., 1994), cite the surnames of the first authors and of as many of the subsequent authors as necessary to distinguish the two references, followed by a comma and et al.

Bradley, Ramirez, and Soo (1994) and Bradley, Soo, et al. (1994)

When a work has six or more authors, cite only the surname of the first author followed by et al. (not italicized and with a period after "al") and the year for the first and subsequent citations. (In the reference list, however, provide the initials and surnames of the first six authors, and shorten any remaining authors to et al.)

If two references with six or more authors shorten to the same form, cite the surnames of the first authors and of as many of the subsequent authors as necessary to distinguish the two references, followed by a comma and et al. For example, suppose you have entries for the following references:

> Kosslyn, Koenig, Barrett, Cave, Tang, and Gabrieli (1996)
>
> Kosslyn, Koenig, Gabrieli, Tang, Marsolek, and Daly (1996)

In text you would cite them, respectively, as

> Kosslyn, Koenig, Barrett, et al. (1996) and Kosslyn, Koenig, Gabrieli, et al. (1996)

Join the names in a multiple-author citation in running text by the word *and.* In parenthetical material, in tables and captions, and in the reference list, join the names by an ampersand (&):

> as Nightlinger and Littlewood (1993) demonstrated
>
> as has been shown (Jöreskog & Sörbom, 1989)

3.96 *Groups as Authors*

The names of groups that serve as authors (e.g., corporations, associations, government agencies, and study groups) are usually spelled out each time they appear in a text citation. The names of some group authors (e.g., associations, government agencies) are spelled out in the first citation and abbreviated thereafter. In deciding whether to abbreviate the name of a group author, use the general rule that you need to give enough information in the text citation for the reader to locate the entry in the reference list without difficulty. If the name is long and cumbersome and if the abbreviation is familiar or readily understandable, you may abbreviate the name in the second and subsequent citations. If the name is short or if the abbreviation would not be readily understandable, write out the name each time it occurs.

For example, the following group author is readily identified by its abbreviation:

Entry in reference list:

National Institute of Mental Health. (1999).

First text citation:

(National Institute of Mental Health [NIMH], 1999)

Subsequent text citations:

(NIMH, 1999)

The name of the following group author should be written out in full:

Entry in reference list:

University of Pittsburgh. (1993).

All text citations:

(University of Pittsburgh, 1993)

3.97 *Works With No Author (Including Legal Materials) or With an Anonymous Author*

When a work has no author, cite in text the first few words of the reference list entry (usually the title) and the year. Use double quotation marks around the title of an article or chapter, and italicize the title of a periodical, book, brochure, or report:

on free care ("Study Finds," 1982)

the book *College Bound Seniors* (1979)

Treat references to legal materials like references to works with no author; that is, in text, cite materials such as court cases, statutes, and legislation by the first few words of the reference and the year (see Appendix D for the format of text citations and references for legal materials).

When a work's author is designated as "Anonymous," cite in text the word *Anonymous* followed by a comma and the date:

(Anonymous, 1998)

In the reference list, an anonymous work is alphabetized by the word *Anonymous* (see section 4.04).

3.98 *Authors With the Same Surname*

If a reference list includes publications by two or more primary authors with the same surname, include the first author's initials in all text citations, even if the year of publication differs. Initials help the reader to avoid confusion within the text and to locate the entry in the list of references (see section 4.04 for the order of appearance in the reference list):

R. D. Luce (1959) and P. A. Luce (1986) also found

J. M. Goldberg and Neff (1961) and M. E. Goldberg and Wurtz (1972) studied

3.99 *Two or More Works Within the Same Parentheses*

Order the citations of two or more works within the same parentheses in the same order in which they appear in the reference list (see section 4.04), according to the following guidelines.

Arrange two or more works by the same authors (in the same order) by year of publication. Place in-press citations last. Give the authors' surnames once; for each subsequent work, give only the date.

> Past research (Edeline & Weinberger, 1991, 1993)
>
> Past research (Gogel, 1984, 1990, in press)

Identify works by the same author (or by the same two or more authors in the same order) with the same publication date by the suffixes a, b, c, and so forth after the year; repeat the year. The suffixes are assigned in the reference list, where these kinds of references are ordered alphabetically by title (of the article, chapter, or complete work).

> Several studies (Johnson, 1991a, 1991b, 1991c; Singh, 1983, in press-a, in press-b)

List two or more works by different authors who are cited within the same parentheses in alphabetical order by the first author's surname. Separate the citations with semicolons:

> Several studies (Balda, 1980; Kamil, 1988; Pepperberg & Funk, 1990)

Exception: You may separate a major citation from other citations within parentheses by inserting a phrase, such as see also, before the first of the remaining citations, which should be in alphabetical order:

> (Minor, 2001; see also Adams, 1999; Storandt, 1997)

3.100 *Classical Works*

When a work has no date of publication (see section 4.09), cite in text the author's name, followed by a comma and n.d. for "no date." When a date of publication is inapplicable, such as for some very old works, cite the year of the translation you used, preceded by trans., or the year of the version you used, followed by version. When you know the original date of publication, include this in the citation.

(Aristotle, trans. 1931)

James (1890/1983)

Reference entries are not required for major classical works, such as ancient Greek and Roman works and the Bible; simply identify in the first citation in the text the version you used. Parts of classical works (e.g., books, chapters, verses, lines, cantos) are numbered systematically across all editions, so use these numbers instead of page numbers when referring to specific parts of your source:

1 Cor. 13:1 (Revised Standard Version)

3.101 *Specific Parts of a Source*

To cite a specific part of a source, indicate the page, chapter, figure, table, or equation at the appropriate point in text. Always give page numbers for quotations (see section 3.34). Note that the words *page* and *chapter* are abbreviated in such text citations:

(Cheek & Buss, 1981, p. 332)

(Shimamura, 1989, chap. 3)

For electronic sources that do not provide page numbers, use the paragraph number, if available, preceded by the ¶ symbol or the abbreviation para. If neither paragraph nor page numbers are visible, cite the heading and the number of the paragraph following it to direct the reader to the location of the material (see section 3.39).

(Myers, 2000, ¶ 5)

(Beutler, 2000, Conclusion section, para. 1)

To cite parts of classical works (see section 3.100), use the specific line, book, and section numbers as appropriate, and *do not* provide page numbers, even for direct quotations.

3.102 *Personal Communications*

Personal communications may be letters, memos, some electronic communications (e.g., e-mail or messages from nonarchived discussion groups or electronic bulletin boards), personal interviews, telephone conversations, and the like. Because they do not provide recoverable data, personal communications are not included in the reference list. Cite personal communications in text only. Give the initials as well as the surname of the communicator, and provide as exact a date as possible:

T. K. Lutes (personal communication, April 18, 2001)

(V.-G. Nguyen, personal communication, September 28, 1998)

For information on electronic media that may be listed in the References, see section I of chapter 4. Use your judgment in citing other electronic forms as personal communications; computer networks (including the Internet) currently provide a casual forum for communicating, and what you cite should have scholarly relevance.

3.103 *Citations in Parenthetical Material*

In a citation that appears in parenthetical text, use commas (not brackets) to set off the date:

(see Table 2 of Hashtroudi, Chrosniak, & Schwartz, 1991, for complete data)

CHAPTER FOUR

Reference List

The reference list at the end of a journal article documents the article and provides the information necessary to identify and retrieve each source. Authors should choose references judiciously and must include only the sources that were used in the research and preparation of the article. Note that a reference list cites works that specifically support a particular article. In contrast, a bibliography cites works for background or for further reading and may include descriptive notes, as in section 9.03 of this *Publication Manual*. APA journals require reference lists, not bibliographies.

References in APA publications are cited in text with an author–date citation system and are listed alphabetically in the References section in APA style or, for legal materials, in accordance with *The Bluebook: A Uniform System of Citation* (2000). Elements of APA-style references, such as author names, titles, and dates of publication, are described beginning in section 4.06; examples of how these elements and their variations go together to form an APA-style reference are given in this chapter. (Examples of references to legal materials, which are prepared in a different way, are included in Appendix D.)

4.01 *Agreement of Text and Reference List*

References cited in text must appear in the reference list; conversely, each entry in the reference list must be cited in text (see sections 3.94–3.103 and Appendix D, section D.02 for citation of references in text). The author must make certain that each source referenced appears in both places and that the text citation and reference list entry are identical in spelling and year. Failure to do so can result in expensive changes after a manuscript is set in type; the author bears the cost of these changes.

4.02 *Construction of an Accurate and Complete Reference List*

Because one purpose of listing references is to enable readers to retrieve and use the sources, reference data must be correct and complete. Each entry usually contains the following elements: author, year of publication, title, and publishing data—all the information necessary for unique identification and library search. The best way to ensure that information is accurate and complete is to check each reference carefully against the original publication. Give special attention to spelling of proper names and of words in foreign languages, including accents or other special marks, and to completeness of journal titles, years, volume numbers, and page numbers. Authors are responsible for all information in their reference lists. Accurately prepared references help establish your credibility as a careful researcher. An inaccurate or incomplete reference "will stand in print as an annoyance to future investigators and a monument to the writer's carelessness" (Bruner, 1942, p. 68).

4.03 *APA Style*

APA style for the preparation of references is detailed in this chapter. In APA journals, legal materials are also given in the reference list, not in text footnotes, and their preparation is discussed in Appendix D. Because a reference list includes only references that document the article and provide recoverable data, do not include personal communications, such as letters, memoranda, and informal electronic communication. Instead, cite personal communications only in text (see section 3.102 for format).

The reference list must be double-spaced, and entries should have a hanging indent. Incomplete or improperly prepared references will be returned to authors for correction.

Abbreviations. Acceptable abbreviations in the reference list for parts of books and other publications include

chap.	chapter
ed.	edition
Rev. ed.	revised edition
2nd ed.	second edition
Ed. (Eds.)	Editor (Editors)
Trans.	Translator(s)
n.d.	no date
p. (pp.)	page (pages)
Vol.	Volume (as in Vol. 4)
vols.	volumes (as in 4 vols.)
No.	Number
Pt.	Part
Tech. Rep.	Technical Report
Suppl.	Supplement

Publishers' locations. Give the location (city and state for U.S. publishers, city, state or province if applicable, and country for publishers outside of the United States) of the publishers of books, reports, brochures, and other separate, nonperiodical publications. If the publisher is a university and the name of the state (or province) is included in the name of the university, do not repeat the name in the publisher location. The names of U.S. states and territories are abbreviated in the reference list and in the Method section (suppliers' locations); use the official two-letter U.S. Postal Service abbreviations listed in Table 4.1. The following locations can be listed without a state abbreviation or country because they are major cities that are well known for publishing:

Baltimore	New York	Amsterdam	Paris
Boston	Philadelphia	Jerusalem	Rome
Chicago	San Francisco	London	Stockholm
Los Angeles		Milan	Tokyo
		Moscow	Vienna

Arabic numerals. Although some volume numbers of books and journals are given in roman numerals, APA journals use arabic numerals

Table 4.1. *Abbreviations for States and Territories*

Location	Abbreviation	Location	Abbreviation
Alabama	AL	Missouri	MO
Alaska	AK	Montana	MT
American Samoa	AS	Nebraska	NE
Arizona	AZ	Nevada	NV
Arkansas	AR	New Hampshire	NH
California	CA	New Jersey	NJ
Canal Zone	CZ	New Mexico	NM
Colorado	CO	New York	NY
Connecticut	CT	North Carolina	NC
Delaware	DE	North Dakota	ND
District of Columbia	DC	Ohio	OH
		Oklahoma	OK
Florida	FL	Oregon	OR
Georgia	GA	Pennsylvania	PA
Guam	GU	Puerto Rico	PR
Hawaii	HI	Rhode Island	RI
Idaho	ID	South Carolina	SC
Illinois	IL	South Dakota	SD
Indiana	IN	Tennessee	TN
Iowa	IA	Texas	TX
Kansas	KS	Utah	UT
Kentucky	KY	Vermont	VT
Louisiana	LA	Virginia	VA
Maine	ME	Virgin Islands	VI
Maryland	MD	Washington	WA
Massachusetts	MA	West Virginia	WV
Michigan	MI	Wisconsin	WI
Minnesota	MN	Wyoming	WY
Mississippi	MS		

(e.g., Vol. 3, not Vol. III) because they use less space and are easier to comprehend than roman numerals. A roman numeral that is part of a title should remain roman (e.g., *Attention and Performance XIII*).

4.04 *Order of References in the Reference List*
The principles for arranging entries in a reference list are described next. You will probably also find it helpful to look at the reference list in the sample manuscript in chapter 5 (Figure 5.1) and at reference lists in journals that are published in APA style.

Alphabetizing names. Arrange entries in alphabetical order by the surname of the first author, using the following rules for special cases:

- Alphabetize letter by letter. Remember, however, that "nothing precedes something": Brown, J. R., precedes Browning, A. R., even though *i* precedes *j* in the alphabet.
- Alphabetize the prefixes M', Mc, and Mac literally, not as if they were all spelled *Mac*. Disregard the apostrophe: MacArthur precedes McAllister, and MacNeil precedes M'Carthy.
- Alphabetize surnames that contain articles and prepositions (de, la, du, von, etc.) according to the rules of the language of origin. If you know that a prefix is commonly part of the surname (e.g., De Vries), treat the prefix as part of the last name and alphabetize by the prefix (e.g., DeBase precedes De Vries). If the prefix is not customarily used (e.g., Helmholtz rather than von Helmholtz), disregard it in the alphabetization and place the prefix following the initials (e.g., Helmholtz, H. L. F. von). The biographical section of *Merriam-Webster's Collegiate Dictionary* is a helpful guide on surnames with articles or prepositions.
- Alphabetize entries with numerals as if the numerals were spelled out.

Order of several works by the same first author. When ordering several works by the same first author, give the author's name in the first and all subsequent references, and use the following rules to arrange the entries:

- One-author entries by the same author are arranged by year of publication, the earliest first:

  Hewlett, L. S. (1996).

  Hewlett, L. S. (1999).

- One-author entries precede multiple-author entries beginning with the same surname:

  Alleyne, R. L. (2001).

  Alleyne, R. L., & Evans, A. J. (1999).

- References with the same first author and different second or third authors are arranged alphabetically by the surname of the second author or, if the second author is the same, the surname of the third author, and so on:

  Gosling, J. R., Jerald, K., & Belfar, S. F. (2000).

  Gosling, J. R., & Tevlin, D. F. (1996).

  Hayward, D., Firsching, A., & Brown, J. (1999).

  Hayward, D., Firsching, A., & Smigel, J. (1999).

- References with the same authors in the same order are arranged by year of publication, the earliest first:

  Cabading, J. R., & Wright, K. (2000).

  Cabading, J. R., & Wright, K. (2001).

■ References by the same author (or by the same two or more authors in the same order) with the same publication date are arranged alphabetically by the title (excluding *A* or *The*) that follows the date.

Exception: If the references with the same authors published in the same year are identified as articles in a series (e.g., Part 1 and Part 2), order the references in the series order, not alphabetically by title.

Lowercase letters—*a, b, c,* and so on—are placed immediately after the year, within the parentheses:

Baheti, J. R. (2001a). Control. . . .

Baheti, J. R. (2001b). Roles of. . . .

Order of several works by different first authors with the same surname. Works by different authors with the same surname are arranged alphabetically by the first initial:

Mathur, A. L., & Wallston, J. (1999).

Mathur, S. E., & Ahlers, R. J. (1998).

Note: Include initials with the surname of the first author in the text citations (see section 3.98).

Order of works with group authors or with no authors. Occasionally a work will have as its author an agency, association, or institution, or it will have no author at all.

Alphabetize group authors, such as associations or government agencies, by the first significant word of the name. Full official names should be used (e.g., American Psychological Association, not APA). A parent body precedes a subdivision (e.g., University of Michigan, Department of Psychology).

If, *and only if,* the work is signed "Anonymous," the entry begins with

Refs

the word *Anonymous* spelled out, and the entry is alphabetized as if Anonymous were a true name.

If there is no author, the title moves to the author position, and the entry is alphabetized by the first significant word of the title.

Treat legal references like references with no author; that is, alphabetize legal references by the first significant item in the entry (word or abbreviation). See Appendix D for the format of references for legal materials and the ways to cite them in the text.

4.05 *References Included in a Meta-Analysis*

To conserve journal pages, do not list the studies included in a meta-analysis in a separate appendix. Instead, integrate these studies alphabetically within the References section, and identify each by preceding it with an asterisk.

> Bandura, A. J. (1977). *Social learning theory*. Englewood Cliffs, NJ: Prentice Hall.
>
> *Bretschneider, J. G., & McCoy, N. L. (1968). Sexual interest and behavior in healthy 80- to 102-year-olds. *Archives of Sexual Behavior, 14*, 343–350.

Add the following statement before the first reference entry: References marked with an asterisk indicate studies included in the meta-analysis. The in-text citations to studies selected for meta-analysis are not preceded by asterisks.

4.06 *Introduction to APA Reference Style*

Sections 4.07–4.15 describe the main elements of the most common types of references in the order in which they would appear in an entry. Detailed notes on style and punctuation accompany the description of each element, and example numbers given in parentheses correspond to examples in section 4.16.

4.07 *General Forms*

Periodical:

> Author, A. A., Author, B. B., & Author, C. C. (1994). Title of article. *Title of Periodical, xx,* xxx–xxx.

Periodicals include items published on a regular basis: journals, magazines, scholarly newsletters, and so on.

Nonperiodical:

> Author, A. A. (1994). *Title of work.* Location: Publisher.

Part of a nonperiodical (e.g., book chapter):

> Author, A. A., & Author, B. B. (1994). Title of chapter. In A. Editor, B. Editor, & C. Editor (Eds.), *Title of book* (pp. xxx–xxx). Location: Publisher.

Nonperiodicals include items published separately: books, reports, brochures, certain monographs, manuals, and audiovisual media.

Online periodical:

> Author, A. A., Author, B. B., & Author, C. C. (2000). Title of article. *Title of Periodical, xx,* xxx–xxx. Retrieved month day, year, from source.

Online document:

> Author, A. A. (2000). *Title of work.* Retrieved month day, year, from source.

Electronic sources include aggregated databases, online journals, Web sites or Web pages, newsgroups, Web- or e-mail-based discussion groups, and Web- or e-mail-based newsletters.

4.08 *Authors*

Periodical:

> **Kernis, M. H., Cornell, D. P., Sun, C.-R., Berry, A., & Harlow, T.** (1993). There's more to self-esteem than whether it is high or low: The importance of stability of self-esteem. *Journal of Personality and Social Psychology, 65,* 1190–1204.

Nonperiodical:

> **Robinson, D. N. (Ed.).** (1992). *Social discourse and moral judgment.* San Diego, CA: Academic Press.

- Invert all authors' names; give surnames and initials for only up to and including six authors. When authors number seven or more, abbreviate the seventh and subsequent authors as et al. [not italicized and with a period after "al"]. In text, follow the citation guidelines in section 3.95.
- If an author's first name is hyphenated, retain the hyphen and include a period after each initial.
- Use commas to separate authors, to separate surnames and initials, and to separate initials and suffixes (e.g., Jr. and III); with two or more authors, use an ampersand (&) before the last author.
- Spell out the full name of a group author (e.g., Australian In Vitro Fertilization Collaborative Group; National Institute of Mental Health).
- If authors are listed with the word *with*, include them in the reference in parentheses, for example, Bulatao, E. (with Winford, C. A.). The text citation, however, refers to the primary author only.

- In a reference to an edited book, place the editors' names in the author position, and enclose the abbreviation Ed. or Eds. in parentheses after the last editor's name.
- In a reference to a work with no author, move the title to the author position, before the date of publication (see Example 26).
- Finish the element with a period. In a reference to a work with a group author (e.g., study group, government agency, association, corporation), the period follows the author element. In a reference to an edited book, the period follows the parenthetical abbreviation (Eds.). In a reference to a work with no author, the period follows the title, which is moved to the author position. (When an author's initial with a period ends the element, do not add an extra period.)

4.09 *Publication Date*

Fowers, B. J., & Olson, D. H. **(1993).** ENRICH Marital Satisfaction Scale: A brief research and clinical tool. *Journal of Family Psychology, 7,* 176–185. [journals, books, audiovisual media]

(1993, June). [meetings; monthly magazines, newsletters, and newspapers]

(1994, September 28). [dailies and weeklies]

(in press). [any work accepted for publication but not yet printed]

(n.d.). [work with no date available]

- Give in parentheses the year the work was copyrighted (for unpublished works, give the year the work was produced).
- For magazines, newsletters, and newspapers, give the year followed by the exact date on the publication (month or month and day; see Examples 6–11), in parentheses.
- Write in press in parentheses for articles that have been accepted for publication but that have not yet been published. Do not give a date until the article has actually been published. (To reference a

paper that is still in revision and under review, use Example 60. See Examples 58–61 for references to unpublished manuscripts.)

■ For papers and posters presented at meetings, give the year and month of the meeting, separated by a comma and enclosed in parentheses.

■ If no date is available, write n.d. in parentheses.

■ Finish the element with a period after the closing parenthesis.

4.10 *Title of Article or Chapter*

Periodical:

Deutsch, F. M., Lussier, J. B., & Servis, L. J. (1993). **Husbands at home: Predictors of paternal participation in childcare and housework.** *Journal of Personality and Social Psychology, 65,* 1154–1166.

Nonperiodical:

O'Neil, J. M., & Egan, J. (1992). **Men's and women's gender role journeys: Metaphor for healing, transition, and transformation.** In B. R. Wainrib (Ed.), *Gender issues across the life cycle* (pp. 107–123). New York: Springer.

■ Capitalize only the first word of the title and of the subtitle, if any, and any proper nouns; do not italicize the title or place quotation marks around it.

■ Enclose nonroutine information that is important for identification and retrieval in brackets immediately after the article title. Brackets indicate a description of form, not a title. Following are some of the more common notations that help identify works.

Notation	Example
[Letter to the editor]	11
[Special issue]	12
[Monograph]	15
[Abstract]	16

■ Finish the element with a period.

4.11 *Title of Work and Publication Information: Periodicals*

Journal:

Buss, D. M., & Schmitt, D. P. (1993). Sexual strategies theory: An evolutionary perspective on human mating. **Psychological Review, 100, 204–232.**

Magazine:

Henry, W. A., III. (1990, April 9). Beyond the melting pot. **Time, 135, 28–31.**

■ Give the periodical title in full, in uppercase and lowercase letters.
■ Give the volume number of journals, magazines, and newsletters. Do not use Vol. before the number. If, and only if, each issue of a journal begins on page 1, give the issue number in parentheses immediately after the volume number (see Example 2).
■ If a journal or newsletter does not use volume numbers, include the month, season, or other designation with the year, for example (1994, April).
■ Italicize the name of the periodical and the volume number, if any.
■ Give inclusive page numbers. Use pp. before the page numbers in references to newspapers. (Note that in electronic sources, page numbers are often not relevant—see Examples 72–74).

- Use commas after the title and volume number.
- Finish the element with a period.

4.12 *Title of Work: Nonperiodicals*

Saxe, G. B. (1991). **Cultural and cognitive development: Studies in mathematical understanding.** Hillsdale, NJ: Erlbaum.

- Capitalize only the first word of the title and of the subtitle, if any, and any proper nouns; italicize the title.
- Enclose additional information given on the publication for its identification and retrieval (e.g., edition, report number, volume number) in parentheses immediately after the title. Do not use a period between the title and the parenthetical information; do not italicize the parenthetical information.
- Enclose a description of the form of the work in brackets (after any parenthetical information) if the information is necessary for identification and retrieval; some examples follow.

Notation	Example
[Brochure]	33
[Motion picture]	65
[Videotape]	65
[CD]	69
[Computer software]	92
[Data file]	94, 95

- If a volume is part of a larger, separately titled series or collection, treat the series and volume titles as a two-part title (see Example 35).
- Finish the element with a period.

4.13 *Title of Work: Part of a Nonperiodical (Book Chapters)*

The title element for an edited book consists of (a) the name of the editor (if any) preceded by the word In and (b) the book title with parenthetical information.

Editor:

> Baker, F. M., & Lightfoot, O. B. (1993). Psychiatric care of ethnic elders. **In A. C. Gaw (Ed.),** *Culture, ethnicity, and mental illness* (pp. 517–552). Washington, DC: American Psychiatric Press.

- Because the editor's name is not in the author position, do not invert the name; use initials and surname. Give initials and surnames for *all* editors (for substantial reference works with a large editorial board, naming the lead editor followed by et al. is acceptable).
- With two names, use an ampersand (&) before the second surname, and do not use commas to separate the names. With three or more names, use an ampersand before the final surname, and use commas to separate the names.
- Identify the editor by the abbreviation Ed. in parentheses after the surname.
- For a book with no editor, simply include the word In before the book title.
- Finish this part of the element with a comma.

Book title with parenthetical information:

> Baker, F. M., & Lightfoot, O. B. (1993). Psychiatric care of ethnic elders. In A. C. Gaw (Ed.), **Culture, ethnicity, and mental illness (pp. 517–552).** Washington, DC: American Psychiatric Press.

- Give inclusive page numbers of the article or chapter in parentheses after the title. (Note that in electronic sources, page numbers may not be relevant—see Example 76).
- If additional information is necessary for retrieval (e.g., edition, report number, or volume number), this information precedes the page numbers within the parentheses and is followed by a comma (see Example 36).
- Finish the element with a period.

4.14 *Publication Information: Nonperiodicals*

Location, ST:	**Hillsdale, NJ:**
Publisher.	**Erlbaum.**
Location, Province, Country:	**Toronto, Ontario, Canada:**
Publisher.	**University of Toronto Press.**
Location, Country:	**Oxford, England:**
Publisher.	**Basil Blackwell.**
Major City:	**Amsterdam:**
Publisher.	**Elsevier.**

- Give the city and, if the city is not well known for publishing (see section 4.03) or could be confused with another location, the state or province (and/or country) where the publisher is located as noted on the title page of the book. Use U.S. Postal Service abbreviations for states (see Table 4.1). Use a colon after the location.
- If the publisher is a university and the name of the state or province is included in the name of the university, do not repeat the state or province in the publisher location.
- Give the name of the publisher in as brief a form as is intelligible. Write out the names of associations, corporations, and university presses, but omit superfluous terms, such as *Publishers, Co.,* or *Inc.,* which are not required to identify the publisher. Retain the words *Books* and *Press.*

- If two or more publisher locations are given, give the location listed first in the book or, if specified, the location of the publisher's home office.
- Finish the element with a period.

4.15 *Retrieval Information: Electronic Sources*

The retrieval statement provides the date the information was retrieved, along with the name and/or address of the source.

> *Electronic reference formats recommended by the American Psychological Association.* (2000, October 12). **Retrieved October 23, 2000, from http://www.apa.org/journals/webref.html**

> Eid, M., & Langeheine, R. (1999). The measurement of consistency and occasion specificity with latent class models: A new model and its application to the measurement of affect. *Psychological Methods, 4,* 100–116. **Retrieved November 19, 2000, from the PsycARTICLES database.**

- If information is obtained from a document on the Internet, provide the Internet address for the document at the end of the retrieval statement.
- If information is retrieved from an aggregated database, providing the name of the database is sufficient; no address is needed.
- Use available from to indicate that the URL leads to information on how to obtain the cited material, rather than to the material itself (see Example 95).
- Finish the retrieval element with a period, *unless* it ends with an Internet address.

4.16 *Elements and Examples of References in APA Style*

This section contains examples of references in APA style. The examples are grouped into the following categories: periodicals; books, brochures, and book chapters; technical and research reports; proceedings of meetings and symposia; doctoral dissertations and master's theses; unpublished works and publications of limited circulation; reviews; audiovisual media; and electronic media.

For periodicals, books, articles or chapters in edited books, technical research reports, and reviews (the most common kinds of references), this section provides a model reference and identifies the elements of the reference, such as the author and the date of publication.

Examples are also provided for less common categories of references. Notes on style, if needed, follow each example.

An index of reference examples precedes the examples in this section. By category, the index lists types of works (e.g., periodical, technical report) referenced and then variations in specific elements (e.g., author name, title of article). The numbers after each index entry refer to the numbered examples in this section.

How to proceed if a reference example you need is not in this section. The most common kinds of references are illustrated herein. Occasionally, however, you may need to use a reference for a source for which this section does not provide a specific example. In such a case, look over the general forms in section 4.07 and the examples throughout chapter 4; choose the example that is most like your source, and follow that format. When in doubt, provide more information rather than less. Because one purpose of listing references is to enable readers to retrieve and use the sources, each entry usually contains the following elements: author, year of publication, title, and publishing data—all the information necessary for unique identification and library search.

Type of work referenced: Print (sections A–G), audiovisual (section H), electronic media (section I)

A. Periodicals

abstract, 16, 17
annually published, 19

Refs

Elements of a reference

Author variations

Refs

Throughout this chapter, the primary examples showing *elements of a reference* are double-spaced. The *examples of references*, however, are single-spaced to save space in this *Publication Manual*. In a manuscript for publication, all references are to be double-spaced; when typeset, they will be converted to a single-spaced printed page.

A. *Periodicals*

Elements of a reference to a periodical

Herman, L. M., Kuczaj, S. A., III, & Holder, M. D. (1993). Responses to anomalous gestural sequences by a language-trained dolphin: Evidence for processing of semantic relations and syntactic information. *Journal of Experimental Psychology: General, 122,* 184–194.

Note: For treatment of electronic periodicals, see section I.

Article authors: Herman, L. M., Kuczaj, S. A., III, & Holder, M. D.

Date of publication: (1993).

Article title: Responses to anomalous gestural sequences by a language-trained dolphin: Evidence for processing of semantic relations and syntactic information.

- Capitalize only the first word of the title and of the subtitle, if any, and any proper nouns; do not italicize the title or place quotation marks around it.
- Enclose nonroutine information that is important for identification and retrieval in brackets immediately after the article title (e.g., [Letter to the editor], see Example 11). Brackets indicate a description of form, not a title.
- Finish the element with a period.

Periodical title and publication information: *Journal of Experimental Psychology: General, 122*, 184–194.

Examples of references to periodicals

1. Journal article, one author

Mellers, B. A. (2000). Choice and the relative pleasure of consequences. *Psychological Bulletin, 126*, 910–924.

2. Journal article, two authors, journal paginated by issue

Klimoski, R., & Palmer, S. (1993). The ADA and the hiring process in organizations. *Consulting Psychology Journal: Practice and Research, 45*(2), 10–36.

3. Journal article, three to six authors

Saywitz, K. J., Mannarino, A. P., Berliner, L., & Cohen, J. A. (2000). Treatment for sexually abused children and adolescents. *American Psychologist, 55*, 1040–1049.

4. Journal article, more than six authors

Wolchik, S. A., West, S. G., Sandler, I. N., Tein, J., Coatsworth, D., Lengua, L., et al. (2000). An experimental evaluation of theory-based mother and mother–child programs for children of divorce. *Journal of Consulting and Clinical Psychology, 68,* 843–856.

■ After the sixth author's name and initial, use et al. to indicate the remaining authors of the article.

■ In text, use the following parenthetical citation each time (including the first) the work is cited: (Wolchik et al., 2000).

5. Journal article in press

Zuckerman, M., & Kieffer, S. C. (in press). Race differences in face-ism: Does facial prominence imply dominance? *Journal of Personality and Social Psychology.*

■ A paper that has been submitted to a journal and accepted for publication is considered in press. (If the paper is still undergoing revision and review, use Example 60 for the appropriate reference format.)

■ Do not give a year, a volume, or page numbers until the article is published. In text, use the following parenthetical citation: (Zuckerman & Kieffer, in press).

■ If another reference by the same author (or same order of authors for multiple authors) is included in the list of references, place the in-press entry after the published entry. If there is more than one in-press reference, list the entries alphabetically by the first word after the date element, and assign lowercase letter suffixes to the date element (e.g., in press-a).

6. Magazine article

Kandel, E. R., & Squire, L. R. (2000, November 10). Neuroscience: Breaking down scientific barriers to the study of brain and mind. *Science, 290,* 1113–1120.

- Give the date shown on the publication—month for monthlies or month and day for weeklies.
- Give the volume number.

7. Newsletter article

Brown, L. S. (1993, Spring). Antidomination training as a central component of diversity in clinical psychology education. *The Clinical Psychologist, 46,* 83–87.

- Give the date as it appears on the issue.
- Give the volume number.

8. Newsletter article, no author

The new health-care lexicon. (1993, August/September). *Copy Editor, 4,* 1–2.

- Alphabetize works with no author by the first significant word in the title (in this case, new).
- In text, use a short title (or the full title if it is short) for the parenthetical citation: ("The New Health-Care Lexicon," 1993).
- Give the volume number.

9. Daily newspaper article, no author

New drug appears to sharply cut risk of death from heart failure. (1993, July 15). *The Washington Post,* p. A12.

- Alphabetize works with no author by the first significant word in the title.
- In text, use a short title for the parenthetical citation: ("New Drug," 1993).

■ Precede page numbers for newspaper articles with p. or pp.

10. Daily newspaper article, discontinuous pages

Schwartz, J. (1993, September 30). Obesity affects economic, social status. *The Washington Post*, pp. A1, A4.

■ If an article appears on discontinuous pages, give all page numbers, and separate the numbers with a comma (e.g., pp. B1, B3,
B5–B7).

11. Weekly newspaper article, letter to the editor

Berkowitz, A. D. (2000, November 24). How to tackle the problem
of student drinking [Letter to the editor]. *The Chronicle of
Higher Education*, p. B20.

12. Entire issue or special section of a journal

Barlow, D. H. (Ed.). (1991). Diagnoses, dimensions, and *DSM-IV*:
The science of classification [Special issue]. *Journal of Abnormal Psychology, 100*(3).

■ To cite an entire issue or special section of a journal (in this
example, a special issue), give the editors of the issue and the
title of the issue.
■ If the issue has no editors, move the issue title to the author
position, before the year of publication, and end the title with
a period. Alphabetize the reference entry by the first significant
word in the title. In text, use a short title for the parenthetical
citation, for example: ("Diagnoses," 1991).
■ For retrievability, provide the issue number for special issues but
the page range for special sections.

- To reference an article within a special issue, simply follow the format shown in Examples 1–4.

13. Monograph with issue number and serial (or whole) number

Harris, P. L., & Kavanaugh, R. D. (1993). Young children's understanding of pretense. *Monographs of the Society for Research in Child Development, 58*(1, Serial No. 231).

- Give the volume number and, immediately after in parentheses, the issue and serial (or whole) numbers. Use Whole instead of Serial if the monograph is identified by a whole number.
- For a monograph that is treated as a separate nonperiodical, see Example 47.

14. Monograph bound separately as a supplement to a journal

Battig, W. F., & Montague, W. E. (1969). Category norms for verbal items in 56 categories: A replication and extension of the Connecticut category norms. *Journal of Experimental Psychology Monographs, 80*(3, Pt. 2).

- Give the issue number and supplement or part number in parentheses immediately after the volume number.

15. Monograph bound into journal with continuous pagination

Ganster, D. C., Schaubroeck, J., Sime, W. E., & Mayes, B. T. (1991). The nomological validity of the Type A personality among employed adults [Monograph]. *Journal of Applied Psychology, 76,* 143–168.

- Include Monograph in brackets as a description of form.

Refs

16. Abstract as original source

Woolf, N. J., Young, S. L., Fanselow, M. S., & Butcher, L. L. (1991). MAP-2 expression in cholinoceptive pyramidal cells of rodent cortex and hippocampus is altered by Pavlovian conditioning [Abstract]. *Society for Neuroscience Abstracts, 17*, 480.

■ Place the description Abstract in brackets between the abstract title and the period.

17. Abstract from a secondary source (print periodical)

Nakazato, K., Shimonaka, Y., & Homma, A. (1992). Cognitive functions of centenarians: The Tokyo Metropolitan Centenarian Study. *Japanese Journal of Developmental Psychology, 3*, 9–16. Abstract obtained from *PsycSCAN: Neuropsychology*, 1993, 2, Abstract No. 604.

■ The term *secondary source* refers to such things as abstracts, article summaries, book reviews, and so forth. These are derived from *primary sources* (journal articles, books), often by someone other than the original author(s). In scholarly research, it is preferable to read and cite primary sources whenever possible.

■ Cite the secondary source in a retrieval statement at the end of the reference, beginning with the words Abstract obtained from, followed by the title of the secondary source, the year of publication, the volume number, and the abstract identifier (if applicable).

■ If the date of the secondary source is different from the date of the original publication, cite in text both dates, separated by a slash, with the original date first: Nakazato, Shimonaka, and Homma (1992/1993).

Refs

18. Journal supplement

Regier, A. A., Narrow, W. E., & Rae, D. S. (1990). The epidemiology of anxiety disorders: The epidemiologic catchment area (ECA) experience. *Journal of Psychiatric Research, 24*(Suppl. 2), 3–14.

■ Give the supplement number in parentheses immediately after the volume number.

19. Periodical published annually

Fiske, S. T. (1993). Social cognition and social perception. *Annual Review of Psychology, 44,* 155–194.

■ Treat series that have regular publication dates and titles as periodicals, not books. If the subtitle changes in series published regularly, such as topics of published symposia (e.g., the Nebraska Symposium on Motivation and the *Annals of the New York Academy of Sciences*), treat the series as a book or chapter in an edited book (see Examples 49 and 50).

20. Non-English journal article, title translated into English

Ising, M. (2000). Intensitätsabhängigkeit evozierter Potenzial im EEG: Sind impulsive Personen Augmenter oder Reducer? [Intensity dependence in event-related EEG potentials: Are impulsive individuals augmenters or reducers?]. *Zeitschrift für Differentielle und Diagnostische Psychologie, 21,* 208–217.

■ If the original version of a non-English article is used as the source, cite the original version. Give the original title and, in brackets, the English translation.

- Use diacritical marks and capital letters for non-English words as done in the original language (umlauts and capitals for the nouns in this example).

21. English translation of a journal article, journal paginated by issue

Stutte, H. (1972). Transcultural child psychiatry. *Acta Paedopsychiatrica, 38*(9), 229–231.

- If the English translation of a non-English article is used as the source, cite the English translation. Give the English title without brackets (for use of brackets with non-English works, see Examples 20, 31, and 37).

22. Citation of a work discussed in a secondary source

- Give the secondary source in the reference list; in text, name the original work, and give a citation for the secondary source. For example, if Seidenberg and McClelland's work is cited in Coltheart et al. and you did not read the work cited, list the Coltheart et al. reference in the References. In the text, use the following citation:

Text citation:

Seidenberg and McClelland's study (as cited in Coltheart, Curtis, Atkins, & Haller, 1993)

Reference list entry:

Coltheart, M., Curtis, B., Atkins, P., & Haller, M. (1993). Models of reading aloud: Dual-route and parallel-distributed-processing approaches. *Psychological Review, 100*, 589–608.

B. *Books, Brochures, and Book Chapters*

Elements of a reference to an entire book

Beck, C. A. J., & Sales, B. D. (2001). *Family mediation: Facts, myths, and future prospects.* Washington, DC: American Psychological Association.

Book authors or editors: Beck, C. A. J., & Sales, B. D.
Date of publication: (2001).
Book title: *Family mediation: Facts, myths, and future prospects.*
Publication information: Washington, DC: American Psychological Association.

■   If a book has more than six authors, follow the rule for journals (see Example 4) and abbreviate remaining authors as et al. [not italicized and with a period after "al"] in the first and subsequent text citations.

Examples of references to entire books

23. Book, third edition, Jr. in name

Mitchell, T. R., & Larson, J. R., Jr. (1987). *People in organizations: An introduction to organizational behavior* (3rd ed.). New York: McGraw-Hill.

24. Book, group author (government agency) as publisher

Australian Bureau of Statistics. (1991). *Estimated resident population by age and sex in statistical local areas, New South*

Wales, June 1990 (No. 3209.1). Canberra, Australian Capital Territory: Author.

- Alphabetize group authors by the first significant word of the name.
- When the author and publisher are identical, use the word Author as the name of the publisher.

25. Edited book

Gibbs, J. T., & Huang, L. N. (Eds.). (1991). *Children of color: Psychological interventions with minority youth.* San Francisco: Jossey-Bass.

- *Note.* For a book with just one author and an editor as well, list the editor in parentheses after the title, as a translator is treated (see Example 32).

26. Book, no author or editor

Merriam-Webster's collegiate dictionary (10th ed.). (1993). Springfield, MA: Merriam-Webster.

- Place the title in the author position.
- Alphabetize books with no author or editor by the first significant word in the title (Merriam in this case).
- In text, use a few words of the title, or the whole title if it is short, in place of an author name in the citation: (Merriam-Webster's Collegiate Dictionary, 1993).

27. Book, revised edition

Rosenthal, R. (1987). *Meta-analytic procedures for social research* (Rev. ed.). Newbury Park, CA: Sage.

28. Several volumes in a multivolume edited work, publication over period of more than 1 year

> Koch, S. (Ed.). (1959–1963). *Psychology: A study of science* (Vols. 1–6). New York: McGraw-Hill.

- ■ In text, use the following parenthetical citation: (Koch, 1959–1963).

29. *Diagnostic and Statistical Manual of Mental Disorders*

> American Psychiatric Association. (1994). *Diagnostic and statistical manual of mental disorders* (4th ed.). Washington, DC: Author.

- ■ The association is both author and publisher.
- ■ Cite the edition you used, with arabic numerals, in parentheses.
- ■ In text, cite the name of the association and the name of the manual in full at the first mention in the text; thereafter, you may refer to the traditional *DSM* form (italicized) as follows:

DSM–III	(1980)	third edition
DSM–III–R	(1987)	third edition, revised
DSM–IV	(1994)	fourth edition
DSM–IV–TR	(2000)	text revision

30. Encyclopedia or dictionary

> Sadie, S. (Ed.). (1980). *The new Grove dictionary of music and musicians* (6th ed., Vols. 1–20). London: Macmillan.

- ■ For major reference works with a large editorial board, you may list the name of the lead editor, followed by et al.

4.16   REFERENCE LIST EXAMPLES

31. Non-English book

Piaget, J., & Inhelder, B. (1951). *La genèse de l'idée de hasard chez l'enfant* [The origin of the idea of chance in the child]. Paris: Presses Universitaires de France.

■ If the original version of a non-English book is used as the source, cite the original version: Give the original title and, in brackets, the English translation.

32. English translation of a book

Laplace, P.-S. (1951). *A philosophical essay on probabilities* (F. W. Truscott & F. L. Emory, Trans.). New York: Dover. (Original work published 1814)

■ If the English translation of a non-English work is used as the source, cite the English translation: Give the English title without brackets (for use of brackets with non-English works, see Examples 20, 31, and 37).
■ In text, cite the original publication date and the date of the translation: (Laplace, 1814/1951).

33. Brochure, corporate author

Research and Training Center on Independent Living. (1993). *Guidelines for reporting and writing about people with disabilities* (4th ed.) [Brochure]. Lawrence, KS: Author.

■ Format references to brochures in the same way as those to entire books.
■ In brackets, identify the publication as a brochure.

Elements of a reference to an article or chapter in an edited book

Massaro, D. (1992). Broadening the domain of the fuzzy logical model of perception. In H. L. Pick Jr., P. van den Broek, & D. C. Knill (Eds.), *Cognition: Conceptual and methodological issues* (pp. 51–84). Washington, DC: American Psychological Association.

Article or chapter author: Massaro, D.

Date of publication: (1992).

Article or chapter title: Broadening the domain of the fuzzy logical model of perception.

Book editors: In H. L. Pick Jr., P. van den Broek, & D. C. Knill (Eds.),

Book title and article or chapter page numbers: *Cognition: Conceptual and methodological issues* (pp. 51–84).

Publication information: Washington, DC: American Psychological Association.

Examples of references to articles or chapters in edited books

34. Article or chapter in an edited book, two editors

Bjork, R. A. (1989). Retrieval inhibition as an adaptive mechanism in human memory. In H. L. Roediger III & F. I. M. Craik (Eds.), *Varieties of memory & consciousness* (pp. 309–330). Hillsdale, NJ: Erlbaum.

- For a chapter in a book that is not edited, include the word In before the book title.

35. Article or chapter in an edited book in press, separately titled volume in a multivolume work (two-part title)

Auerbach, J. S. (in press). The origins of narcissism and narcissistic personality disorder: A theoretical and empirical reformulation. In J. M. Masling & R. F. Bornstein (Eds.), *Empirical studies of psychoanalytic theories: Vol. 4. Psychoanalytic perspectives on psychopathology.* Washington, DC: American Psychological Association.

- Do not give the year unless the book is published. In text, use the following parenthetical citation: (Auerbach, in press).
- Page numbers are not available until a work is published; therefore, you cannot give inclusive page numbers for articles or chapters in books that are in press.

36. Chapter in a volume in a series

Maccoby, E. E., & Martin, J. (1983). Socialization in the context of the family: Parent–child interaction. In P. H. Mussen (Series Ed.) & E. M. Hetherington (Vol. Ed.), *Handbook of child psychology: Vol. 4. Socialization, personality, and social development* (4th ed., pp. 1–101). New York: Wiley.

- List the series editor first and the volume editor second so that they will be parallel with the titles of the works.

37. Non-English article or chapter in an edited book, title translated into English

Davydov, V. V. (1972). De introductie van het begrip grootheid in de eerste klas van de basisschool: Een experimenteel on-

derzoek [The introduction of the concept of quantity in the
first grade of the primary school: An experimental study].
In C. F. Van Parreren & J. A. M. Carpay (Eds.), *Sovjetpsy-
chologen aan het woord* (pp. 227–289). Groningen, The
Netherlands: Wolters-Noordhoff.

- If the original version of a non-English article or chapter is used
  as the source, cite the original version: Give the original title
  and, in brackets, the English translation.

38. Entry in an encyclopedia

Bergmann, P. G. (1993). Relativity. In *The new encyclopaedia
Britannica* (Vol. 26, pp. 501–508). Chicago: Encyclopaedia
Britannica.

- If an entry has no byline, place the title in the author position.

39. English translation of an article or chapter in an edited book, volume in a multivolume work, republished work

Freud, S. (1961). The ego and the id. In J. Strachey (Ed. & Trans.),
*The standard edition of the complete psychological works
of Sigmund Freud* (Vol. 19, pp. 3–66). London: Hogarth
Press. (Original work published 1923)

- If the English translation of a non-English work is used as the
  source, cite the English translation: Give the English title without
  brackets (for use of brackets with non-English works, see Examples 20, 31, and 37).
- To identify a translator, use Trans., and place the translator's
  name after the editor's name. When the editor is also the translator, identify both roles in parentheses after the editor's name.

- In text, use the following parenthetical citation: (Freud, 1923/ 1961).

40. English translation of an article or chapter in an edited book, reprint from another source

Piaget, J. (1988). Extracts from Piaget's theory (G. Gellerier & J. Langer, Trans.). In K. Richardson & S. Sheldon (Eds.), *Cognitive development to adolescence: A reader* (pp. 3–18). Hillsdale, NJ: Erlbaum. (Reprinted from *Manual of child psychology*, pp. 703–732, by P. H. Mussen, Ed., 1970, New York: Wiley)

- If the English translation of a non-English work is used as the source, cite the English translation: Give the English title without brackets (for use of brackets with non-English works, see Examples 20, 31, and 37).
- In text, use the following parenthetical citation: (Piaget, 1970/ 1988).

C. *Technical and Research Reports*

Mazzeo, J., Druesne, B., Raffeld, P. C., Checketts, K. T., & Muhlstein, A. (1991). *Comparability of computer and paper-and-pencil scores for two CLEP general examinations* (College Board Rep. No. 91–5). Princeton, NJ: Educational Testing Service.

Elements of a reference to a report

Report authors: Mazzeo, J., Druesne, B., Raffeld, P. C., Checketts, K. T., & Muhlstein, A.

Date of publication: (1991).

Report title: *Comparability of computer and paper-and-pencil scores for two CLEP general examinations* (College Board Rep. No. 91-5).

- If the issuing organization assigned a number (e.g., report number, contract number, monograph number) to the report, give that number in parentheses immediately after the title. Do not use a period between the report title and the parenthetical material; do not italicize the parenthetical material. If the report carries two numbers, give the number that best aids identification and retrieval.

Publication information: Princeton, NJ: Educational Testing Service.

- Give the name, exactly as it appears on the publication, of the specific department, office, agency, or institute that published or produced the report. Also, give the higher department, office, agency, or institute if the office that produced the report is not well known. For example, if the National Institute on Drug Abuse, an institute of the U.S. Department of Health and Human Services, produced the report, give only the institute as publisher. Because this institute is well known, it is not necessary to give the higher department as well. If you include the higher department, give the higher department first, then the specific department (see Examples 46 and 47).
- For reports from a document deposit service (e.g., NTIS or ERIC), enclose the document number in parentheses at the end of the entry (see Examples 42 and 43). Do not use a period after the document number.

Examples of references to reports

41. Report available from the Government Printing Office (GPO), government institute as group author

National Institute of Mental Health. (1990). *Clinical training in serious mental illness* (DHHS Publication No. ADM 90-1679). Washington, DC: U.S. Government Printing Office.

■ Government documents available from GPO should show GPO as the publisher.

42. Report available from the National Technical Information Service (NTIS)

Osgood, D. W., & Wilson, J. K. (1990). *Covariation of adolescent health problems.* Lincoln: University of Nebraska. (NTIS No. PB 91-154 377/AS)

■ Give the NTIS number in parentheses at the end of the entry.

43. Report available from the Educational Resources Information Center (ERIC)

Mead, J. V. (1992). *Looking at old photographs: Investigating the teacher tales that novice teachers bring with them* (Report No. NCRTL-RR-92-4). East Lansing, MI: National Center for Research on Teacher Learning. (ERIC Document Reproduction Service No. ED346082)

■ Give the ERIC number in parentheses at the end of the entry.

44. Government report not available from GPO or a document deposit service

U.S. Department of Health and Human Services. (1992). *Pressure ulcers in adults: Prediction and prevention* (AHCPR Publication No. 92-0047). Rockville, MD: Author.

45. Government report not available from GPO or a document deposit service, article or chapter in an edited collection

> Matthews, K. A. (1985). Assessment of Type A behavior, anger, and hostility in epidemiologic studies of cardiovascular disease. In A. M. Ostfield & E. D. Eaker (Eds.), *Measuring psychological variables in epidemiologic studies of cardiovascular disease* (NIH Publication No. 85-2270, pp. 153–183). Washington, DC: U.S. Department of Health and Human Services.

■ In parentheses immediately after the title of the collection, give the inclusive page numbers of the article or chapter as well as the number of the report.

46. Report from a university

> Broadhurst, R. G., & Maller, R. A. (1991). *Sex offending and recidivism* (Tech. Rep. No. 3). Nedlands, Western Australia: University of Western Australia, Crime Research Centre.

■ If the name of the state, province, or country is included in the name of the university, do not repeat the state, province, or country in the publisher location.
■ Give the name of the university first, then the name of the specific department or organization that produced the report.

47. Report from a university, edited report, monograph

> Shuker, R., Openshaw, R., & Soler, J. (Eds.). (1990). *Youth, media, and moral panic in New Zealand: From hooligans to video nasties* (Delta Research Monograph No. 11). Palmerston North, New Zealand: Massey University, Department of Education.

48. Report from a private organization

> Employee Benefit Research Institute. (1992, February). *Sources of health insurance and characteristics of the uninsured* (Issue Brief No. 123). Washington, DC: Author.

- ■ Use this form for issue briefs, working papers, and other corporate documents, with the appropriate document number for retrieval in parentheses.

D. *Proceedings of Meetings and Symposia*

49. Published proceedings, published contribution to a symposium, article or chapter in an edited book

> Deci, E. L., & Ryan, R. M. (1991). A motivational approach to self: Integration in personality. In R. Dienstbier (Ed.), *Nebraska Symposium on Motivation: Vol. 38. Perspectives on motivation* (pp. 237–288). Lincoln: University of Nebraska Press.

- ■ Capitalize the name of the symposium, which is a proper noun.
- ■ If the name of the state, province, or country is included in the name of the university, do not repeat the state, province, or country in the publisher location.

50. Proceedings published regularly

> Cynx, J., Williams, H., & Nottebohm, F. (1992). Hemispheric differences in avian song discrimination. *Proceedings of the National Academy of Sciences, USA, 89,* 1372–1375.

- ■ Treat regularly published proceedings as periodicals.
- ■ *Note.* If only an abstract of the article appears in the proceedings, insert [Abstract] after the article title and before the period.

Use brackets to show that the material is a description of form, not a title.

51. Unpublished contribution to a symposium

Lichstein, K. L., Johnson, R. S., Womack, T. D., Dean, J. E., & Childers, C. K. (1990, June). Relaxation therapy for polypharmacy use in elderly insomniacs and noninsomniacs. In T. L. Rosenthal (Chair), *Reducing medication in geriatric populations*. Symposium conducted at the meeting of the First International Congress of Behavioral Medicine, Uppsala, Sweden.

■ Give the month of the symposium.

52. Unpublished paper presented at a meeting

Lanktree, C., & Briere, J. (1991, January). *Early data on the Trauma Symptom Checklist for Children (TSC-C)*. Paper presented at the meeting of the American Professional Society on the Abuse of Children, San Diego, CA.

53. Poster session

Ruby, J., & Fulton, C. (1993, June). *Beyond redlining: Editing software that works*. Poster session presented at the annual meeting of the Society for Scholarly Publishing, Washington, DC.

■ Give the month of the meeting.

E. *Doctoral Dissertations and Master's Theses*

54. Doctoral dissertation abstracted in *Dissertation Abstracts International (DAI)* and obtained from UMI

Bower, D. L. (1993). Employee assistant programs supervisory referrals: Characteristics of referring and nonreferring supervisors. *Dissertation Abstracts International, 54* (01), 534B. (UMI No. 9315947)

- If the dissertation is obtained from UMI, give the UMI number as well as the volume and page numbers of *DAI* (see Example 56 for an unpublished doctoral dissertation).
- Prior to Volume 30, the title of *DAI* was *Dissertation Abstracts.*
- Beginning with Volume 27, *Dissertation Abstracts* (and then *DAI*) paginates in two series: *A. The Humanities and Social Sciences* and *B. The Physical Sciences and Engineering.*
- In 1976, a third and independent series (beginning with Volume 1) was added to *DAI: C. European Abstracts.* Beginning with Volume 14, the title of the series was changed to *C. Worldwide.*
- For a master's thesis abstracted in *Masters Abstracts International* and obtained from UMI, use the format shown here, and give as publication information the title, volume number, and page number as well as the UMI number (see Example 57 for an unpublished master's thesis).
- Prior to Volume 24, the title of *Masters Abstracts International* was *Masters Abstracts.*

55. Doctoral dissertation abstracted in *DAI* and obtained from the university

Ross, D. F. (1990). Unconscious transference and mistaken identity: When a witness misidentifies a familiar but innocent person from a lineup (Doctoral dissertation, Cornell University, 1990). *Dissertation Abstracts International, 51,* 417.

- If a manuscript copy of the dissertation from the university was used as the source, give the university and year of the dissertation as well as the volume and page numbers of *DAI.*

- For a master's thesis abstracted in *Masters Abstracts International* and obtained from the university, use the format shown here and give as publication information the title, volume number, and page number of *Masters Abstracts International* as well as the university and year of the thesis (see Example 57 for an unpublished master's thesis).

56. Unpublished doctoral dissertation

Wilfley, D. E. (1989). *Interpersonal analyses of bulimia: Normal-weight and obese.* Unpublished doctoral dissertation, University of Missouri, Columbia.

- If a dissertation does not appear in *DAI*, use the format shown here. (For dissertations that appear in *DAI*, see Examples 54 and 55.)

57. Unpublished master's thesis, university outside the United States

Almeida, D. M. (1990). *Fathers' participation in family work: Consequences for fathers' stress and father–child relations.* Unpublished master's thesis, University of Victoria, Victoria, British Columbia, Canada.

- Give the name of the city and, except for the cities listed in section 4.03, the name of the state. (Do not give the name of the state if it is included in the name of the university.)
- Give the city and, except for the cities listed in section 4.03, state or province (if applicable) and country of a university outside the United States.

F. *Unpublished Work and Publications of Limited Circulation*

58. Unpublished manuscript not submitted for publication

Stinson, C., Milbrath, C., Reidbord, S., & Bucci, W. (1992). *Thematic segmentation of psychotherapy transcripts for convergent analyses.* Unpublished manuscript.

■ For an unpublished manuscript with a university cited, see Example 59.

59. Unpublished manuscript with a university cited

Dépret, E. F., & Fiske, S. T. (1993). *Perceiving the powerful: Intriguing individuals versus threatening groups.* Unpublished manuscript, University of Massachusetts at Amherst.

■ Give the name of the city and, if the city is not listed in section 4.03, the name of the state or province. If the university is located outside the United States, identify the country as well. *Exception:* Do not give the name of the state, province, or country if it is included in the name of the university. In this example, both the city and state are included in the name of the university, so neither is repeated.

60. Manuscript in progress or submitted for publication but not yet accepted

McIntosh, D. N. (1993). *Religion as schema, with implications for the relation between religion and coping.* Manuscript submitted for publication.

■ Do not give the name of the journal or publisher to which the manuscript has been submitted.

- Treat a manuscript *accepted* for publication but not yet published as an in-press reference (see Examples 5 and 35).
- Use the same format for a draft or work in progress, but substitute the words Manuscript in preparation for the final sentence. Use the year of the draft you read (not "in preparation") in the text citation.
- Give the university if applicable.

61. Unpublished raw data from study, untitled work

Bordi, F., & LeDoux, J. E. (1993). [Auditory response latencies in rat auditory cortex]. Unpublished raw data.

- Do not italicize the topic; use brackets to indicate that the material is a description of content, not a title.

62. Publication of limited circulation

Klombers, N. (Ed.). (1993, Spring). *ADAA Reporter*. (Available from the Anxiety Disorders Association of America, 6000 Executive Boulevard, Suite 513, Rockville, MD 20852)

- For a publication of limited circulation, give in parentheses immediately after the title a name and address from which the publication can be obtained.
- If a publication can be obtained via the Web, a Web address may be given in place of or in addition to a mailing address (see section I for examples of Web addresses).

G. *Reviews*

Elements of a reference to a review

Mroczek, D. K. (2000). The emerging study of midlife [Review of

the book *Life in the middle: Psychological and social de-*

velopment in middle age]. *Contemporary Psychology: APA Review of Books, 45,* 482–485.

Review author: Mroczek, D. K.

Date of publication: (2000).

Review title: The emerging study of midlife

Medium being reviewed: Review of the book

Work being reviewed: *Life in the middle: Psychological and social development in middle age.*

Periodical title and publication information: *Contemporary Psychology: APA Review of Books, 45,* 482–485.

Examples of references to reviews

63. Review of a book

Schatz, B. R. (2000). Learning by text or context? [Review of the book *The social life of information*]. *Science, 290,* 1304.

- If the review is untitled, use the material in brackets as the title; retain the brackets to indicate that the material is a description of form and content, not a title.
- Identify the type of medium being reviewed in brackets (book, motion picture, television program, etc.).

64. Review of a motion picture

Kraus, S. J. (1992). Visions of psychology: A videotext of classic studies [Review of the motion picture *Discovering Psychology*]. *Contemporary Psychology, 37,* 1146–1147.

H. *Audiovisual Media*

65. Motion picture

Scorsese, M. (Producer), & Lonergan, K. (Writer/Director). (2000). *You can count on me* [Motion picture]. United States: Paramount Pictures.

Harrison, J. (Producer), & Schmiechen, R. (Director). (1992). *Changing our minds: The story of Evelyn Hooker* [Motion picture]. (Available from Changing Our Minds, Inc., 170 West End Avenue, Suite 25R, New York, NY 10023)

American Psychological Association (Producer). (2000). *Responding therapeutically to patient expressions of sexual attraction: A stimulus training tape* [Motion picture]. (Available from the American Psychological Association, 750 First Street, NE, Washington, DC 20002–4242)

- Give the name and, in parentheses, the function of the originator or primary contributors (the director or the producer, or both).
- Identify the work as a motion picture in brackets immediately after the title.
- Give the motion picture's country of origin (where it was primarily made and released) as well as the name of the movie studio. Note that depending on the film, a movie studio can be represented by different countries. In the example, the primary production and release of *You Can Count on Me* took place in the United States, but Miramax Films's *Il Postino (The Postman)* was primarily made in Italy and released there first, so the country of origin listed for that film would be Italy.
- When a motion picture is of limited circulation, provide the distributor's name and complete address in parentheses at the end of the reference.

66. Television broadcast

Crystal, L. (Executive Producer). (1993, October 11). *The MacNeil/ Lehrer news hour* [Television broadcast]. New York and Washington, DC: Public Broadcasting Service.

67. Television series

Miller, R. (Producer). (1989). *The mind* [Television series]. New York: WNET.

68. Single episode from a television series

Hall, B. (Writer), & Bender, J. (Director). (1991). The rules of the game [Television series episode]. In J. Sander (Producer), *I'll fly away*. New York: New York Broadcasting Company.

■ In the author position, list script writers first, followed by the director (identify his or her function in parentheses after the name).
■ Place the producer of the series in the editor position.

69. Music recording

General form:

Writer, A. (Date of copyright). Title of song [Recorded by artist if different from writer]. On *Title of album* [Medium of recording: CD, record, cassette, etc.]. Location: Label. (Recording date if different from copyright date)

Recording:

> Shocked, M. (1992). Over the waterfall. On *Arkansas traveler* [CD]. New York: PolyGram Music.

Rerecording by artist other than writer:

> Goodenough, J. B. (1982). Tails and trotters [Recorded by G. Bok, A. Mayo, & E. Trickett]. On *And so will we yet* [CD]. Sharon, CT: Folk-Legacy Records. (1990)

- In text citations, include side and band or track numbers: "Tails and Trotters" (Goodenough, 1982, track 5).

70. Audio recording

> Costa, P. T., Jr. (Speaker). (1988). *Personality, continuity, and changes of adult life* (Cassette Recording No. 207-433-88A-B). Washington, DC: American Psychological Association.

- Give the name and function of the originators or primary contributors (in this example, Costa, who is the speaker).
- Specify the medium in brackets immediately after the title (in this example, cassette recording). Give a number in parentheses for the recording if it is necessary for identification and retrieval. Brackets are used to identify medium. If medium is indicated as part of retrieval ID, brackets are not needed.
- Give the location and name of the distributor (in this example, American Psychological Association).

I. *Electronic Media*

Sources on the Internet. The Internet is a worldwide network of interconnected computers. Although there are a number of methods for navigating and sharing information across the Internet, by far the most popular and familiar is the graphical interface of the World Wide Web. The vast majority of Internet sources cited in APA journals are those that are accessed via the Web.

The variety of material available on the Web, and the variety of ways in which it is structured and presented, can present challenges for creating usable and useful references. Regardless of format, however, authors using and citing Internet sources should observe the following two guidelines:

1. Direct readers as closely as possible to the information being cited —whenever possible, reference specific documents rather than home or menu pages.
2. Provide addresses that work.

Documents available via the Internet include articles from periodicals (e.g., newspaper, newsletter, or journal); they may stand on their own (e.g., research paper, government report, online book or brochure); or they may have a quintessentially Web-based format (e.g., Web page, newsgroup).

At a minimum, a reference of an Internet source should provide a document title or description, a date (either the date of publication or update or the date of retrieval), and an address (in Internet terms, a uniform resource locator, or URL). Whenever possible, identify the authors of a document as well.

The URL is the most critical element—if it doesn't work, readers won't be able to find the cited material, and the credibility of your paper or argument will suffer. The most common reason URLs fail is that they are transcribed or typed incorrectly; the second most common reason is that the document they point to has been moved or deleted.

The components of a URL are as follows:

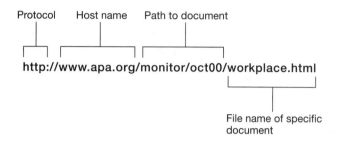

The protocol indicates what method a Web browser (or other type of Internet software) should use to exchange data with the file server on which the desired document resides. The protocols recognized by most browsers are hypertext transfer protocol (http), hypertext transfer protocol secure (https), and file transfer protocol (ftp); other Internet protocols include telnet and gopher. In a URL, all of the protocols listed in this paragraph should be followed by a colon and two forward slashes (e.g., http://).

The host name identifies the server on which the files reside. On the Web, it is often the address for an organization's home page (e.g., http://www.apa.org is the address for APA's home page). Although most host names start with "www," not all do (for example, http://journals.apa.org is the home page for APA's electronic journals, and http://members .apa.org is the entry page to the members-only portion of the APA site). The host name is not case sensitive; for consistency and ease of reading, always type it in lowercase letters.

The rest of the address indicates the directory path leading to the desired document. This part of the URL is case sensitive; faithfully reproduce uppercase and lowercase letters and all punctuation. It is important to provide the directory path, and not just the host name, because home pages and menu pages typically consist mainly of links, only one of which may be to the document or information you want the readers to find. If there are hundreds of links (or even just 10 to 20), readers may give up in frustration before they have located the material you are citing.

If you are using a word-processing program, the easiest way to transcribe a URL correctly is to copy it directly from the address window in your browser and paste it into your paper (make sure the automatic hyphenation feature of your word processor is turned off). Do not insert a hyphen if you need to break a URL across lines; instead, break the URL after a slash or before a period.

Test the URLs in your references regularly—when you first draft a paper, when you submit it for peer review, when you're preparing the final version for publication, and when you're reviewing the proofs. If the document you are citing has moved, update the URL so that it points to the correct location. If the document is no longer available, you may want to substitute another source (e.g., if you originally cited a draft and a formally published version now exists) or drop it from the paper altogether.

Periodicals

71. **Internet articles based on a print source**

At present, the majority of the articles retrieved from online publications in psychology and the behavioral sciences are exact duplicates of those in their print versions and are unlikely to have additional analyses and data attached. This is likely to change in the future. In the meantime, the same basic primary journal reference (see Examples 1–5) can be used, but if you have viewed the article only in its electronic form, you should add in brackets after the article title [Electronic version] as in the following fictitious example:

> VandenBos, G., Knapp, S., & Doe, J. (2001). Role of reference elements in the selection of resources by psychology undergraduates [Electronic version]. *Journal of Bibliographic Research, 5,* 117–123.

If you are referencing an online article that you have reason to believe has been changed (e.g., the format differs from the print version or page numbers are not indicated) or that includes additional data or commentaries, you will need to add the date you retrieved the document and the URL.

> VandenBos, G., Knapp, S., & Doe, J. (2001). Role of reference elements in the selection of resources by psychology undergraduates. *Journal of Bibliographic Research, 5,* 117–123. Retrieved October 13, 2001, from http://jbr.org/articles.html

72. Article in an Internet-only journal

> Fredrickson, B. L. (2000, March 7). Cultivating positive emotions to optimize health and well-being. *Prevention & Treatment, 3,* Article 0001a. Retrieved November 20, 2000, from http://journals.apa.org/prevention/volume3/pre0030001a.html

73. Article in an Internet-only journal, retrieved via file transfer protocol (ftp)

> Crow, T. J. (2000). Did *Homo sapiens* speciate on the y chromosome? *Psycoloquy, 11.* Retrieved March 25, 2001, from ftp://ftp.princeton.edu/harnad/Psycoloquy/2000.volume.11/psyc.00.11.001.language-sex-chromosomes.1.crow

74. Article in an Internet-only newsletter

> Glueckauf, R. L., Whitton, J., Baxter, J., Kain, J., Vogelgesang, S., Hudson, M., et al. (1998, July). Videocounseling for families of rural teens with epilepsy—Project update. *Telehealth News, 2*(2). Retrieved June 6, 2000, from http://www.telehealth.net/subscribe/newslettr_4a.html#1

- Use the complete publication date given on the article.
- Note that there are no page numbers.

- In an Internet periodical, volume and issue numbers often are not relevant. If they are not used, the name of the periodical is all that can be provided in the reference.
- Whenever possible, the URL should link directly to the article.
- Break a URL that goes to another line after a slash or before a period. Do not insert (or allow your word-processing program to insert) a hyphen at the break.

Nonperiodical documents on the Internet

75. Multipage document created by private organization, no date

> Greater New Milford (Ct) Area Healthy Community 2000, Task Force on Teen and Adolescent Issues. (n.d.). *Who has time for a family meal? You do!* Retrieved October 5, 2000, from http://www.familymealtime.org

- When an Internet document comprises multiple pages (i.e., different sections have different URLs), provide a URL that links to the home (or entry) page for the document.
- Use n.d. (no date) when a publication date is not available.

76. Chapter or section in an Internet document

> Benton Foundation. (1998, July 7). Barriers to closing the gap. In *Losing ground bit by bit: Low-income communities in the information age* (chap. 2). Retrieved August 18, 2001, from http://www.benton.org/Library/Low-Income/two.html

- Use a chapter or section identifier (if available) in place of page numbers.
- Provide a URL that links directly to the chapter or section.

77. Stand-alone document, no author identified, no date

> *GVU's 8th WWW user survey.* (n.d.). Retrieved August 8, 2000,
> from http://www.cc.gatech.edu/gvu/user_surveys/survey-
> 1997-10/

■ If the author of a document is not identified, begin the reference
with the title of the document.

78. Document available on university program or department Web site

> Chou, L., McClintock, R., Moretti, F., & Nix, D. H. (1993). *Technol-*
> *ogy and education: New wine in new bottles: Choosing*
> *pasts and imagining educational futures.* Retrieved August
> 24, 2000, from Columbia University, Institute for Learn-
> ing Technologies Web site: http://www.ilt.columbia.edu/
> publications/papers/newwine1.html

■ If a document is contained within a large and complex Web site
(such as that for a university or a government agency), identify
the host organization and the relevant program or department
before giving the URL for the document itself. Precede the URL
with a colon.

Technical and research reports

79. Report from a university, available on private organization Web site

> University of California, San Francisco, Institute for Health and
> Aging. (1996, November). *Chronic care in America: A 21st*
> *century challenge.* Retrieved September 9, 2000, from the

Robert Wood Johnson Foundation Web site: http://www.rwjf
.org/library/chrcare/

- When the author of a document is markedly different from the provider (e.g., the host organization), explicitly identify the latter in the retrieval statement.
- *Note.* This document is no longer available on this site. In most papers, such a reference should be updated or deleted.

80. U.S. government report available on government agency Web site, no publication date indicated

United States Sentencing Commission. (n.d.). *1997 sourcebook of federal sentencing statistics.* Retrieved December 8, 1999, from http://www.ussc.gov/annrpt/1997/sbtoc97.htm

81. Report from a private organization, available on organization Web site

Canarie, Inc. (1997, September 27). *Towards a Canadian health IWAY: Vision, opportunities and future steps.* Retrieved November 8, 2000, from http://www.canarie.ca/press/publications/pdf/health/healthvision.doc

82. Abstract of a technical report retrieved from university Web site

Kruschke, J. K., & Bradley, A. L. (1995). *Extensions to the delta rule of associative learning* (Indiana University Cognitive Science Research Report No. 14). Abstract retrieved October 21, 2000, from http://www.indiana.edu/~kruschke/deltarule_abstract.html

- If the document retrieved is an abstract rather than a full paper, begin the retrieval statement with Abstract retrieved.

Proceedings of meetings and symposia

83. Paper presented at a symposium, abstract retrieved from university Web site

> Cutler, L. D., Frölich, B., & Hanrahan, P. (1997, January 16). *Two-handed direct manipulation on the responsive workbench.* Paper presented at the 1997 Symposium on Interactive 3D Graphics. Abstract retrieved June 12, 2000, from http://www.graphics.stanford.edu/papers/twohanded/

84. Paper presented at a virtual conference

> Tan, G., & Lewandowsky, S. (1996). *A comparison of operator trust in humans versus machines.* Paper presented at the CybErg 96 virtual conference. Retrieved May 16, 2000, from http://www.curtin.edu.au/conference/cyberg/centre/outline .cgi/frame?dir=tan

■ Note that there is no geographic location for a virtual conference (i.e., a conference that takes place entirely online).

E-mail. E-mail sent from one individual to another should be cited as a personal communication (see section 3.102).

Newsgroups, online forums and discussion groups, and electronic mailing lists. The Internet offers several options for people around the world to sponsor and join discussions devoted to particular subjects. These options include newsgroups, online forums and discussion groups, and electronic mailing lists. (The last are often referred to as "listservs." However, LISTSERV is a trademarked name for a particular software program; "electronic mailing list" is the appropriate generic term.)

Refs

Newsgroups can be accessed via Usenet (usually through an e-mail program or news reader); archives of many Usenet newsgroups are also maintained on the Web at http://groups.google.com. Online forums or discussion groups are primarily Web based. Many, but not all, also operate as electronic mailing lists in that messages posted to the forum or discussion are e-mailed to participants.

Care should be taken when citing electronic discussion sources—as a rule, these are not referenced in formal publications because they are generally not peer reviewed, are not regarded as having scholarly content, and are not archived for a significant length of time. Any message or communication you cite should have scholarly value and should be retrievable. Although some newsgroups, online forums and discussion groups, and electronic mailing lists do maintain archives for a limited time, not all do. If no archives are maintained, then the message will not be retrievable and should not be included in the reference list. At best, it can be cited as a personal communication (see section 3.102).

85. Message posted to a newsgroup

Chalmers, D. (2000, November 17). Seeing with sound [Msg 1]. Message posted to news://sci.psychology.consciousness

- If the author's full name is available, list the last name first followed by initials. If only a screen name is available, use the screen name.
- Provide the exact date of the posting.
- Follow the date with the subject line of the message (also referred to as the "thread"); do not italicize it. Provide any identifier for the message in brackets after the title.
- Finish the reference with Message posted to followed by the address of the newsgroup. Note that the protocol is news.

86. Message posted to online forum or discussion group

Simons, D. J. (2000, July 14). New resources for visual cognition [Msg 31]. Message posted to http://groups.yahoo.com/group/visualcognition/message/31

87. Message posted to an electronic mailing list

Hammond, T. (2000, November 20). YAHC: Handle Parameters, DOI Genres, etc. Message posted to Ref-Links electronic mailing list, archived at http://www.doi.org/mail-archive/ref-link/msg00088.html

- ■ Provide the name of the mailing list and the address for the archived version of the message.

Other Electronic Sources

Aggregated databases. Researchers and students are increasingly making use of aggregated, searchable databases to find and retrieve abstracts, articles, and other types of information. The format specified in the previous edition of this manual required information about the source and format of the database in addition to information about the material retrieved. These days, however, most databases are available from a variety of sources or suppliers and in a variety of formats (e.g., on CD-ROM, mounted on a university server, available through a supplier Web site). Moreover, the distinctions between these various sources and formats are usually not apparent to the end user.

Therefore, when referencing material obtained by searching an aggregated database, follow the format appropriate to the work retrieved and add a retrieval statement that gives the date of retrieval and the proper name of the database. An item or accession number also may be provided but is not required. If you wish to include this number, put it in parentheses at the end of the retrieval statement.

88. Electronic copy of a journal article, three to five authors, retrieved from database

Borman, W. C., Hanson, M. A., Oppler, S. H., Pulakos, E. D., & White, L. A. (1993). Role of early supervisory experience in supervisor performance. *Journal of Applied Psychology, 78,* 443–449. Retrieved October 23, 2000, from PsycARTICLES database.

89. Daily newspaper article, electronic version available by search

Hilts, P. J. (1999, February 16). In forecasting their emotions, most people flunk out. *New York Times.* Retrieved November 21, 2000, from http://www.nytimes.com

90. Electronic copy of an abstract obtained from a secondary database

Fournier, M., de Ridder, D., & Bensing, J. (1999). Optimism and adaptation to multiple sclerosis: What does optimism mean? *Journal of Behavioral Medicine, 22,* 303–326. Abstract retrieved October 23, 2000, from PsycINFO database.

91. Electronic version of U.S. government report available by search from GPO Access database (on the Web)

U.S. General Accounting Office. (1997, February). *Telemedicine: Federal strategy is needed to guide investments* (Publication No. GAO/NSAID/HEHS-97–67). Retrieved September 15, 2000, from General Accounting Office Reports Online via GPO Access: http://www.access.gpo.gov/su_docs/aces/aces160.shtml?/gao/index.html

- The retrieval statement should provide a URL that links directly to the search screen for the database.

Computer programs, software, and programming languages. Reference entries are not necessary for standard off-the-shelf software and programming languages, such as Microsoft Word, Excel, Java, Adobe Photoshop, and even SAS and SPSS. In text, give the proper name of the software, along with the version number.

Do provide reference entries for specialized software or computer programs with limited distribution.

92. Computer software

Miller, M. E. (1993). The Interactive Tester (Version 4.0) [Computer software]. Westminster, CA: Psytek Services.

93. Computer software and manual available on university Web site

Schwarzer, R. (1989). Statistics software for meta-analysis [Computer software and manual]. Retrieved from http://www.yorku.ca/faculty/academic/schwarze/meta_e.htm

- Do not italicize names of software, programs, or languages.
- If an individual has proprietary rights to the software, name him or her as the author; otherwise, treat such references as unauthored works.
- In brackets immediately after the title, identify the source as a computer program, language, or software. Do not use a period between the title and the bracketed material.
- Give the location and the name of the organization that produced the work, if applicable, in the publisher position.
- To reference a manual, give the same information. However, in the brackets after the title, identify the source as a computer program or software manual.

Raw data

94. Data file, available from government agency

*National Health Interview Survey—Current health topics: 1991
—Longitudinal study of aging* (Version 4) [Data file]. Hyattsville, MD: National Center for Health Statistics.

■ In brackets at the end of the title (before the period), give a description of the material (e.g., Data file).

95. Data file, available from NTIS Web site

Department of Health and Human Services, National Center for Health Statistics. (1991). *National Health Provider Inventory: Home health agencies and hospices, 1991* [Data file]. Available from National Technical Information Service Web site, http://www.ntis.gov

■ Use available from to indicate that the URL leads to information on how to obtain the cited material, rather than to the material itself.

CHAPTER FIVE

Manuscript Preparation and Sample Papers to Be Submitted for Publication

The physical appearance of a manuscript can enhance the manuscript's effect or detract from it. A well-prepared manuscript looks professional to editors and reviewers and influences their decisions in a positive manner. On the other hand, mechanical flaws can sometimes lead reviewers to misinterpret content. Once accepted for publication, a properly prepared manuscript facilitates the work of the copy editor and the typesetter, minimizes the possibility of errors, and is more economical to publish.

This chapter describes the mechanical details of producing a typical paper manuscript. The instructions given here apply to manuscript preparation on both a standard typewriter and a personal computer with word-processing software. The focus throughout this chapter is on production of a manuscript that meets requirements for peer review and publication in an APA journal. If you are preparing a thesis or dissertation, some of these instructions may not apply; see chapter 6, and consult with your advisor.

When possible, APA and many other publishers prefer to produce the typeset version of your article directly from your word-processing disk or file, should your paper be accepted for publication. Effective and economical use of your word-processing file depends on its being consistently prepared. Therefore, from the outset of your first draft, you or your typist needs to follow certain conventions. The instructions given

Ms Prep

in this chapter on preparing the paper manuscript lay the groundwork for producing a usable electronic file. (See section 7.02 for further instructions on preparing an electronic file for publication.)

The Author's Responsibilities

Whether you type the manuscript yourself or have a typist prepare it, as author you are ultimately responsible for the quality of presentation of all aspects of the paper: correct spelling and punctuation, accurate quotations with page numbers, complete and accurate references, relevant content, coherent organization, proper format, legible appearance, and so forth. If the manuscript is to receive masked review, you are responsible for preparing the manuscript to conceal your and your colleagues' identities. You will need to

- proofread the manuscript after it is typed, making all corrections and changes before submitting the manuscript for consideration (see sections 5.07 and 5.27);
- examine the manuscript, using the checklist in Appendix A to ensure that the manuscript has been prepared according to APA style; and
- prepare a cover letter to accompany the submitted manuscript (see section 5.26 and Appendix E).

General Instructions for Preparing the Paper Manuscript

5.01 *Paper*

Type the manuscript or print it from your computer on one side of standard-sized ($8\frac{1}{2} \times 11$ in. [22×28 cm]), heavy white bond paper. All pages of the manuscript must be the same size. Do not use half sheets or strips of paper glued, taped, or stapled to the pages; these often get torn or lost in shipment and handling. Do not use onionskin or erasable paper, because these papers do not withstand handling.

5.02 *Typeface*

Use a typeface that is similar to one of the following examples:

Preferred typefaces:

12-pt Times Roman

That the probability of aggressive acts is high (all things being equal)

`12-pt Courier`

`That the probability of aggressive acts is high`
`(all things being equal)`

A **serif** typeface is preferred for text because it improves readability and reduces eye fatigue. (A **sans serif** type is used in figures, however, to provide a clean and simple line that enhances the visual presentation —see section 3.80.) The size of the type should be one of the standard typewriter sizes (pica or elite) or, if produced from a word-processing program, 12 points. Do not use a compressed typeface or any settings in your word-processing software that would decrease the spacing between letters or words. The default settings are normally acceptable. The type on paper must be dark, clear, and readable. It must also photocopy well.

Ohs, els, and special characters. Unless you are using a typewriter that does not have separate keys for the numeral one and the letter *l* and for the numeral 0 and the letter *o*, do not mistakenly type one of these characters when you mean the other. Although upper- and lowercase *o* and 0 may appear similar on your computer screen or printout, these characters appear very different when set into type (O, o, 0). The same is true of the numeral 1 and the lowercase letter *l* (see sections 3.58 and 5.14 on identifying symbols). Remember that if the manuscript is to be published from your word-processing file, your actual keystrokes are preserved and set into type. Errors you make in typing can become costly and difficult to correct during the publication process.

Special characters are accented letters and other diacriticals, Greek letters, math signs, and symbols. Type all special characters that you can, using a special typewriter element or the special character functions of your word-processing program. For a multiplication sign, use a lowercase x (x) or multiplication symbol preceded and followed by a space. For a minus sign, always use a hyphen with a space before and after. (See section 5.11 for more on hyphens and dashes; see section 5.14 for more on mathematical copy.)

Italics versus underlining. In a manuscript intended for publication, use the functions of your word-processing program to create italic, bold, or other special fonts or styles of type following the style guidelines specified in this *Publication Manual.* (See section 3.19 on the use of italics in APA journals.)

5.03 *Double-Spacing*

Double-spacing means leaving one full-size line blank between each line of type on the page. For most word-processing software, this means setting the line spacing to 2 or double. If your software specifies between-line spacing in terms of point size, you should specify line spacing, or *leading,* that is the point size of the type plus 2 points, multiplied by 2. That is, for 12-point type, you should set line spacing at 28 points. In any case, the result should be at least $^3/_{16}$ to $^1/_4$ in. (0.5 to 0.65 cm) of space between the typed lines on the paper manuscript.

Double-space between all lines of the manuscript. Double-space after every line in the title, headings, footnotes, quotations, references, figure captions, and all parts of tables. Although you may apply triple- or quadruple-spacing in special circumstances, such as immediately before and after a displayed equation, never use single-spacing or one-and-a-half spacing.

5.04 *Margins*

Leave uniform margins of at least 1 in. (2.54 cm) at the top, bottom, left, and right of every page. In most word-processing programs, 1 in. is the default setting for margins. This is the minimum margin for writing

instructions and queries. Uniform margins also help copy editors estimate the length of the printed article from the manuscript.

Line length and alignment. The length of each typed line is a maximum
of $6\frac{1}{2}$ in. (16.51 cm). Set a pica typewriter for 65 characters and an elite
machine for 78 characters. Do not justify lines; that is, do not use the
word-processing feature that adjusts spacing between words to make all
lines the same length (flush with the margins). Instead, use the flush-left
style, and leave the right margin uneven, or *ragged.* Do not divide words
at the end of a line, and do not use the hyphenation function to break
words at the ends of lines. Let a line run short rather than break a word
at the end of a line.

Number of lines. Type no more than 27 lines of text (not counting the
manuscript page header and the page number) on an $8\frac{1}{2} \times 11$ in. (22
$\times$ 28 cm) page with 1-in. (2.54-cm) margins.

5.05 *Order of the Manuscript Pages*

Number all pages except the artwork for figures consecutively. Arrange
the pages of the manuscript as follows:

- title page with running head for publication, title, and byline and
  institutional affiliation (separate page, numbered page 1)
- abstract (separate page, numbered page 2)
- text (start on a separate page, numbered page 3)
- references (start on a separate page)
- appendixes (start each on a separate page)
- author note (start on a separate page)
- footnotes (list together, starting on a separate page)
- tables (start each on a separate page)
- figure captions (list together, starting on a separate page)
- figures (place each on a separate page).

These elements will be rearranged to compose the printed article, but
the order listed above is critical for the processing and typesetting of the
accepted manuscript.

Exception: If you are preparing a thesis or dissertation, your university's guidelines may require footnotes, tables, and figures to be placed within the text (near the callout) instead of at the end (see chapter 6).

5.06 *Page Numbers and Manuscript Page Headers*

Page numbers. After the manuscript pages are arranged in the correct order, number them consecutively, beginning with the title page. Number all pages, except artwork for figures, in arabic numerals in the upper right-hand corner. The number should appear at least 1 in. (2.54 cm) from the right-hand edge of the page, in the space between the top edge of the paper and the first line of text. (The default setting in most word-processing software is $\frac{1}{2}$ in. from the top of the page, which is acceptable.) If a page must be inserted or removed after numbering is completed, renumber the pages; do not number inserted pages with, for example, "6a" or make other repairs.

Manuscript page headers. Pages occasionally are separated during the editorial process, so identify each manuscript page (except artwork for figures) with the first two or three words from the title in the upper right-hand corner above or five spaces to the left of the page number. (Do not use your name to identify each page, because the name will have to be removed if the manuscript receives masked review.)

Use the automatic functions of your word-processing program to cause the headers and page numbers to print out on your paper manuscript. (Do not type these manuscript page headers repeatedly in your word-processing file.) The manuscript page headers should not be confused with the running head for publication (see section 5.15), which goes only on the title page and appears on the published article.

5.07 *Corrections*

If you are using a computer, make all corrections in your word-processing file, and make a fresh printout of any corrected pages. Do not write corrections on the paper manuscript (the only handwriting that is acceptable is to note special characters and special instructions; see section 5.24). For typewritten manuscripts, keep corrections to a minimum, and make them neatly. Use correction paper, fluid, or tape to cover an error and type over it, but retype the page if it has many corrections. Do not type vertically in the margin, strike over a letter, type inserts on slips and attach them to pages, or write by hand on the manuscript.

5.08 *Paragraphs and Indentation*

Indent the first line of every paragraph and the first line of every footnote. For consistency, use the tab key, which should be set at five to seven spaces or $\frac{1}{2}$ in. The default settings in most word-processing programs are acceptable. Type the remaining lines of the manuscript to a uniform left-hand margin. The only exceptions to these requirements are (a) the abstract (see section 5.16), (b) block quotations (see section 5.13), (c) titles and headings (see sections 5.10 and 5.15), (d) table titles and notes (see section 5.21), and (e) figure captions (see section 5.22).

5.09 *Uppercase and Lowercase Letters*

The instruction "type in uppercase and lowercase letters" means to capitalize the first letter of important words (see section 3.13). The parts of a manuscript typed in uppercase and lowercase letters are

- most elements on the title page (i.e., the title and the byline, but not the running head for publication; see section 5.15),
- page labels (Abstract, Footnotes, etc.),
- most headings (see section 5.10),
- table titles (see section 5.21), and
- some elements of the reference list (see the examples in chapter 4).

5.10 *Headings*

Articles in APA journals use from one to five levels of headings. For most articles, three or four levels of heading are sufficient.

Three levels:

Centered Uppercase and Lowercase Heading

Flush Left, Italicized, Uppercase and Lowercase Side Heading

Indented, italicized, lowercase paragraph heading ending with a period.

Four levels:

Centered Uppercase and Lowercase Heading

Centered, Italicized, Uppercase and Lowercase Heading

Flush Left, Italicized, Uppercase and Lowercase Side Heading

Indented, italicized, lowercase paragraph heading ending with a period.

Some short articles may require only one or two levels of headings:

Centered Uppercase and Lowercase Heading

Flush Left, Italicized, Uppercase and Lowercase Side Heading

Five levels of heading may be required for some long articles. Subordinate the four levels previously described by introducing a CENTERED UPPERCASE HEADING as the first level of heading. (For more on headings, see section 3.31.)

5.11 *Spacing and Punctuation*

Space once after all punctuation as follows:

- after commas, colons, and semicolons;
- after punctuation marks at the ends of sentences;

- after periods that separate parts of a reference citation; and
- after the periods of the initials in personal names (e.g., J. R. Zhang).

Exception: Do not space after internal periods in abbreviations (e.g., a.m., i.e., U.S.) or around colons in ratios.

Hyphens, dashes, and minus signs are each typed differently.

- **hyphen:** Use no space before or after (e.g., trial-by-trial analysis).
- **em dash:** Type as an em dash or as two hyphens with no space before or after to set off an element added to amplify or to digress from the main clause (e.g., Studies--published and unpublished--are included).
- **en dash:** Type as an en dash or single hyphen with no space before or after. En dashes are used between words of equal weight in a compound adjective (e.g., Chicago–London flight).
- **minus:** The typeset minus sign is halfway between an en dash and a hyphen and is usually slightly higher than a hyphen or en dash. Use a hyphen with a space on both sides (e.g., a - b).
- **negative value:** Type as a hyphen with a space before but no space after (e.g., -5.25).

Placement of punctuation with parentheses depends on the context. If the context requires a comma (as this sentence does), the comma follows the closing parenthesis. If a complete sentence ends with a parenthesis, the period follows the closing parenthesis (as in this sentence). (If a complete sentence, like this one, is enclosed in parentheses, the period is placed inside the closing parenthesis.) See section 5.13 for use of punctuation with quotations.

Sections 3.01–3.09 provide more detail on punctuation.

5.12 *Seriation*

To show seriation within a paragraph or sentence, use lowercase letters (not italicized) in parentheses:

> Participants considered (a) some alternative courses of action, (b) the factors influencing the decision, and (c) the probability of success.

To indicate seriation of separate paragraphs (e.g., itemized conclusions or successive steps in a procedure), number each paragraph with an arabic numeral, followed by a period but not enclosed in or followed by parentheses:

> 1. Begin with paragraph indent. Type second and succeeding lines flush left.
> 2. The second item begins a new paragraph.

See section 3.33, also on seriation.

5.13 *Quotations*

Short quotations. Quotations of fewer than 40 words should be incorporated into the text and enclosed by double quotation marks (" ").

Long quotations. Display quotations of 40 or more words in a double-spaced block of typewritten lines with no quotation marks. Do not single-space. Indent five to seven spaces or $\frac{1}{2}$ in. from the left margin without the usual opening paragraph indent. If the quotation is more than one paragraph, indent the first line of second and additional paragraphs five to seven spaces or $\frac{1}{2}$ in. from the new margin. (See section 3.34 for examples of quotations in text and of block quotations.)

Quoted material within quotations. Enclose direct quotations within a block quotation in double quotation marks. In a quotation in running text that is already enclosed in double quotation marks, use single quotation marks to enclose quoted material. (See section 3.34 for examples.)

Ellipsis points. Use ellipses to indicate that you have omitted material from a quotation. Type three periods with a space before and after each period to indicate an omission within a sentence. Type four periods to indicate an omission between two sentences (a period for the sentence followed by three spaced periods. . . .). (See also section 3.38.)

Brackets. Use brackets, not parentheses, to enclose material inserted in a quotation by some person other than the original writer (see section 3.38). Hand-drawn brackets are acceptable in typewritten manuscripts.

Quotation marks and other punctuation. When a period or comma occurs with closing quotation marks, place the period or comma before rather than after the quotation marks. Put other punctuation (e.g., colon, semicolon) outside quotation marks unless it is part of the quoted material.

> At the beginning of each trial, the experimenter said, "This is a new trial."
>
> After the experimenter said, "This is a new trial," a new trial began.
>
> Did the experimenter forget to say, "This is a new trial"?

See sections 3.34–3.41 for additional information on quotations.

5.14 *Statistical and Mathematical Copy*

Type all signs and symbols in mathematical copy that you can. If your typewriter or computer does not have special mathematical characters, type a character that resembles the symbol or draw in the symbol by hand. Type fences (i.e., parentheses, brackets, and braces), uppercase and lowercase letters, punctuation, and all other elements exactly as you want them to appear in the published article. Identify symbols, whether hand-written, typewritten, or printed from a computer, that may be hard to read or ambiguous to the typesetter. The first time the ambiguous symbol appears in the paper manuscript, spell out and circle the name right next to the symbol. Symbols that may be misread include 1 (one or the letter *l*), 0 (zero or the letter *o*), $\times$ (multiplication sign or the letter *x*), and Greek letters (beta or the letter *B* and chi or the letter *x*). Some letters (e.g., *c*, *s*, and *x*) have lowercase forms that are similar to their uppercase forms and, especially in subscripts and superscripts, might be misread. Labeling such letters as uppercase and lowercase will help the typesetter distinguish them.

Space mathematical copy as you would space words: $a+b=c$ is as difficult to read as wordswithoutspacing. Instead, type $a + b = c$.

Align signs and symbols carefully. Type subscripts half a line below the symbol and superscripts half a line above the symbol, or use the subscript and superscript features in your word-processing software. In most cases, type subscripts first and then superscripts (x_a^2). However, place a superscript such as the symbol for prime right next to its letter or symbol (x'_a). Because APA prefers to align subscripts and superscripts one under the other (stacking) for ease of reading instead of setting one to the right of the other (staggering), the copy editor will mark these characters for alignment in typesetting. If subscripts and superscripts should not be stacked, this must be indicated in a cover letter or on the manuscript.

The following examples show how symbols in mathematical copy are aligned and spaced and how symbols are identified:

$$F(2, 78) = 7.12, \quad p < .01$$

$$\text{(chi)} \rightarrow \chi^2(4, \quad N = 90) = 10.51, \quad p < .05$$

$$t(49) = 2.11, \quad p < .05$$

$$(z = 1.92, \quad p < .05, \quad \text{one-tailed})$$

Girls scored significantly higher on the
first three dimensions: $F(1, 751) = 52.84$,
$p < .01$; $F(1, 751) = 61.00$, $p < .01$;
and $F(1, 751) = 34.24$, $p < .01$.

$\boxed{\text{mult}}$
a 3 x 2 x 3 (Age x Sex x Weight) analysis

$(r = -.24)$

$\boxed{\text{lc kappa}}$ $\boxed{\text{lc alpha}}$
$\kappa\alpha = E[MS(A)]/E[MS(AB)]$

$\boxed{\text{lc omega}}$
$(\omega^2 = 0)$

Display a mathematical expression, that is, set it off from the text, by double-spacing twice (typing two returns) above and below the expression. If the expression is identified by a number, type the number in parentheses flush against the right margin. Pay particular attention to the spacing and alignment of elements in a displayed expression. If the expression is too long to fit on one line, break before signs of operation (e.g., plus, minus, or equal signs). The following are examples of expressions that may be displayed:

$\boxed{\text{mu}}$
$\boxed{\text{delta}}$ $\delta i = \dfrac{\mu_i E - \mu_i C}{\sigma i}$. $\boxed{\text{sigma}}$

(1)

$\boxed{\text{summation}}$ $\boxed{\text{beta}}$

(2)

$Y_i = \sum\limits_{j=1}^{p} x_{ij} \beta_j + e_i$,

$\boxed{\text{one}}$ $\boxed{\text{beta}}$

$Y = X\beta + E.$

$\boxed{\text{vertical bar}}$
$Pr\left[H_{t+k} = 1 \,\middle|\, W_t = 1 \right]$
$\boxed{\text{brackets}}$

$- Pr\left[H_{t+k} = 1 \,\middle|\, W_t = 0 \right],$

$z_1 = \dfrac{z_S}{\sqrt{1 - p_W}}$ $\boxed{\text{lc s}}$ $\boxed{\text{cap W}}$

Ms Prep

Instructions for Typing the Parts of a Manuscript

5.15 *Title Page*

The title page includes three elements: running head for publication, title, and byline and institutional affiliation. (If the paper is to receive masked review, also place the author note on the title page, following the bylines and affiliations. The journal editor will remove the title page before sending the manuscript out to reviewers.) Identify the title page with a manuscript page header and the page number 1, placed in the upper right-hand corner of the page (see section 5.06).

Running head for publication. An abbreviated title will be used as a running head for the published article. Type the running head flush left at the top of the title page (but below the manuscript page header) in all uppercase letters. Do not exceed 50 characters, including punctuation and spaces. (See section 1.06 for a description of running heads.)

Title. Type the title in uppercase and lowercase letters, centered between the left and right margins and positioned in the upper half of the page. If the title is two or more lines, double-space between the lines.

Byline and institutional affiliation. Type the names of the authors in the order of their contributions using uppercase and lowercase letters, centered between the side margins, one double-spaced line below the title. For names with suffixes (e.g., Jr. and III), separate the suffix from the rest of the name with a space instead of a comma. Type the institutional affiliation, centered under the author's name, on the next double-spaced line.

John Q. Foster II and Roy R. Davis Jr.

Educational Testing Service, Princeton, New Jersey

If two or more authors who follow each other in the order are at the same institution, type the authors' names on one line if space permits. Separate the names of two authors with the word *and*; separate the names of three or more authors with commas, and insert the word *and* before the name of the last author. The institutional affiliation appears on the next double-spaced line, just as it would for one author:

Juanita Fuentes, Paul Dykes, and Susan Watanabe
University of Colorado at Boulder

If several authors are from different institutions, type the names on separate lines. Double-space between lines. Examples of such settings follow:

Two authors, two affiliations:

David Wolf
University of California, Berkeley

Amanda Blue
Brandon University

Three authors, two affiliations:

Mariah Meade and Sylvia Earleywine
Georgetown University

Jeffrey Coffee
Dartmouth College

Three authors, two affiliations, affiliation shared by first and third authors:

David A. Rosenbaum
University of Massachusetts, Amherst

Ms Prep

Jonathan Vaughan
Hamilton College

Heather Jane Barnes
University of Massachusetts, Amherst

Three authors, three affiliations:

Hannah Mindware
Catholic University of America

Dieter Zilbergeld
Max Planck Institute

Joshua Singer
University of Nevada, Las Vegas

5.16 *Abstract*

Begin the abstract on a new page, and identify the abstract page with the manuscript page header and the page number 2 in the upper right-hand corner of the page. (See section 5.06 for more information on page number placement and manuscript page headers.) Type the label Abstract in uppercase and lowercase letters, centered, at the top of the page. Type the abstract itself as a single paragraph in block format (i.e., without paragraph indentation), and do not exceed 120 words. Type all numbers —except those that begin a sentence—as arabic numerals. (See section 1.07 for advice on writing abstracts.)

5.17 *Text*

Begin the text on a new page, and identify the first text page with the manuscript page header and the page number 3 in the upper right-hand corner of the page. (See section 5.06 for more information on page number placement and manuscript page headers.) Type the title of the paper centered at the top of the page, double-space, and then type the text. The sections of the text follow each other without a break; do not start a new page when a new heading occurs. Each remaining manuscript page should also carry the manuscript page header and the page number.

5.18 *References*

Start the reference list on a new page. Type the word References (Reference, if there is only one) in uppercase and lowercase letters, centered, at the top of the page.

Double-space all reference entries. (Although some theses and dissertations use single-spaced reference lists, single-spacing is not acceptable for manuscripts submitted to journals or books because it does not allow space for copyediting and typesetter's marks.) APA publishes references in a *hanging indent* format, meaning that the first line of each reference is set flush left and subsequent lines are indented. If a hanging indent is difficult to accomplish with your word-processing program, it is permissible to indent your references with paragraph indents. The chosen format should be consistent throughout the references.

5.19 *Appendixes*

Double-space the appendixes and begin each one on a separate page. Type the word Appendix and the identifying capital letters (A, B, etc., in the order in which they are mentioned in text) centered at the top of the page. If there is only one appendix, do not use an identifying letter; the word Appendix is sufficient. Double-space and type the title of the appendix, centered, in uppercase and lowercase letters. Double-space, indent the first line five to seven spaces or $\frac{1}{2}$ in., and begin the text of the appendix.

If tables are to be included in an appendix, precede each appendix table number with a capital *A* (starting with Table A1) or, if the paper includes more than one appendix with tables, the capital letter of the appendix in which it belongs. Format the table as described in section 5.21. If an appendix consists of only one table and no introductory text, the centered appendix label and title serve as the table title. In the case of multiple tables but no text, each table should be set up as a separate appendix.

If figures are to be included in an appendix, number them separately from any text figures, beginning with 1 and preceding the numeral with the letter of the appendix in which the figure belongs. List appendix figure captions after those of figures included in the main text, following the guidelines in section 5.22.

5.20 *Footnotes and Notes*

Four types of notes appear in APA journals: author, content, copyright permission, and table notes. Table notes are discussed in section 5.21.

The **author note** is not numbered or cited in the text. Type this note double-spaced on a separate page following the references or appendixes, if any, or, if the paper is to receive masked review, on the title page (see section 5.15). If this note is on a separate page, center the label Author Note in uppercase and lowercase letters at the top of the page. Start each paragraph of the note with an indent, and type separate paragraphs for the authors' names and current affiliations; changes in affiliations; acknowledgments and special circumstances, if any, regarding the study (e.g., dissertation, update to a longitudinal study; see section 3.89); and last, the author's address for correspondence (begin the sentence with Correspondence concerning this article should be addressed to).

Content footnotes and **copyright permission footnotes** that are mentioned in the text are numbered consecutively in the order in which they appear in the article. (Copyright permission footnotes to tables and figures are typed as part of the table note or figure caption; see section 3.73 for sample permission notes.) To indicate in text the material being footnoted, use superscript arabic numerals. Type the footnote numbers slightly above the line, like this,[1] *following* any punctuation mark except a dash. A footnote number that appears with a dash—like this[2]—always precedes the dash. (The number falls inside a closing parenthesis if it applies only to matter within the parentheses.[3]) Footnote numbers should not be placed in text headings.

Center the label Footnotes in uppercase and lowercase letters at the top of a separate page. Type all content and text copyright permission footnotes together, double-spaced. Do not use the footnote or endnote function of your word-processing program—the footnotes most likely will not print in the desired location (immediately after the author note) and could drop out of the file altogether during translation (at the production office or at the typesetter). Indent the first line of each footnote five to seven spaces or $\frac{1}{2}$ in., like the first line of a paragraph, and type the footnotes in the order in which they are mentioned in text. Number the footnotes to correspond to their numbers in text.

5.21 *Tables and Table Titles, Notes, and Rules*

Tables are numbered consecutively in the order in which they are first mentioned in the text and are identified by the word Table and an arabic numeral. Double-space each table, regardless of length, and begin each table on a separate page. Place the manuscript page header and the page number in the upper right-hand corner of every page of a table.

Table titles and headings. Type the word Table and its arabic numeral flush left at the top of the table. Double-space and begin the table title flush left, capitalizing the initial letters of the principal words (see section 3.13) and italicizing the title. If the title is longer than one line, double-space between lines, and begin subsequent lines flush left under the first line.

Center column heads and subheads over the appropriate columns within the table, capitalizing only the initial letter of the first word of each heading (do not capitalize the second part of a hyphenated word unless it is a proper noun). Allow at least three spaces between the longest word in one column head and the longest word in another, and align material in each column (e.g., align decimal points). Allow at least three spaces between columns. Center table spanner heads over the entire width of the table (see section 3.67 for more on table spanners). If a table is longer than a manuscript page, begin the second and subsequent pages by repeating the column heads.

Table notes. Double-space all notes at the end of the table flush left. (For more detailed information on table notes, see section 3.70.)

Table rules. Separate the table title from the headings, the headings from the body, and the body from the table notes using horizontal rules. Use the underline key or the table border function of your word-processing program. Place rules in the body of the table only if necessary to clarify divisions. Do not use vertical rules. (See Table Examples 1–12 in chapter 3 for examples of correctly typed tables.)

5.22 *Figures and Figure Captions*

Figures are also numbered consecutively in the order in which they are first mentioned in the text. Use the word *Figure* and an arabic numeral.

Make certain that each figure is labeled with (a) the manuscript page header (not the author's name) and the figure number outside the image area of the figure or on the back and (b) the word *TOP* to indicate how the figure should be placed on the printed page if its orientation is not obvious (e.g., as with photomicrogaphs or illustrations of shapes).

Each figure must have a caption that includes the figure number:

Figure 1. Time criteria in the naming task.

Do not put the captions for figures on the figures themselves. Type all figure captions together, including any for figures to be included in an appendix, starting on a separate sheet. Center the label Figure Captions, in uppercase and lowercase letters, at the top of the page. Begin each caption flush left, and type the word *Figure,* followed by the appropriate number (or letter and number for appendix figures) and a period, all in italics. In the text of the caption, which is not italicized, capitalize only the first word and any proper nouns. If the caption takes up more than one line, double-space between lines, and type the second and subsequent lines flush left.

5.23 *Spelling Check*

Most word-processing programs have a function that checks spelling. Use it. Although an electronic spelling check cannot take the place of proofreading the article, because words spelled correctly may be used incorrectly, it will at least ensure that there are no typographical errors in the manuscript that could make their way into print when your electronic file is used to publish the article.

5.24 *Special Instructions for Typesetting*

Please note on the manuscript or in a cover letter any special instructions for alignment, line endings, and so forth that need to be preserved when the manuscript is typeset. For example, line endings or capitalization may be important for duplicating text presented as stimuli to participants; subscripts and superscripts may need to be typeset one after another instead of in a stacked alignment.

5.25 *Number of Copies*

Each journal editor requires a specific number of copies (usually three or four), in English, of a submitted manuscript. Consult the journal's instructions to authors for specific submission requirements. One manuscript must be the original and must include the glossy or laser prints of any figures plus a set of photocopied figures. The additional copies should be sharp photocopies (including a full set of photocopied tables and figures) on paper of good quality.

The original manuscript is marked by the APA copy editor and used by the typesetter; it therefore must withstand repeated handling. The additional copies are for editorial review and for the editor's central file.

5.26 *Cover Letter*

Enclose a letter when submitting a manuscript to a journal editor. Include the following:

- specific details about the manuscript (title, length, number of tables and figures),
- a request for masked review, if that is an option for the journal and you choose to use it,
- information about any previous presentation of the data (e.g., at a scientific meeting),
- information about the existence of any closely related manuscripts that have been submitted for simultaneous consideration to the same or to another journal,
- notice of any interests that might be seen as influencing the research

(e.g., financial interests in a test or procedure, funding by pharmaceutical companies for drug research, etc.),

- verification that the treatment of subjects (human or animal) was in accordance with the ethical standards of APA (see Principles 6.1–6.20 in the "Ethical Principles of Psychologists and Code of Conduct," APA, 1992a), and
- a copy of the permission granted to reproduce or adapt any copyrighted material from another source or a notice that permissions are pending. (See sections 7.01, 8.07, and 8.08. The production office will need the granted request on receipt of your accepted manuscript.)

It is the responsibility of the corresponding author to make sure that all authors are in agreement with the content of the manuscript and with the order of authorship before submitting an original or revised submission. The cover letter should assure the editor that such agreements have been reached and that the corresponding author will take responsibility for informing coauthors in a timely manner of editorial decisions, reviews received, changes made in response to editorial review, and the content of revisions. If the manuscript is accepted, all the authors will need to certify authorship (see section 7.01).

Finally, include your telephone number, fax number, e-mail address, and mailing address for future correspondence. (See Appendix E for a sample submission letter.)

5.27 *Contents of Package*

After you have proofread the typed manuscript (and have made any necessary corrections) and written the cover letter, the manuscript is ready for mailing. The package should contain

- your cover letter, including all numbers and addresses for future correspondence (see Appendix E);
- the original manuscript, including all tables and the glossy or laser prints of all figures;

- the number of additional photocopies of the manuscript required by the journal to which the manuscript is being submitted; and
- letters of permission to reproduce or adapt any copyrighted material (text, figures, or tables) that appears in the manuscript.

Be sure to keep a copy of the entire manuscript, including figures and tables, in case the package is lost in the mail.

Do not bind or staple the manuscript pages. Editors and printers prefer to work with loose sheets held together by a paper clip. To protect the manuscript from rough handling in the mail, use a strong or padded envelope.

Send the manuscript electronically or by first-class mail to the journal editor, not to APA's central office. Check the most recent issue of the journal or the journal's Web site to ascertain the current editor's name and address and for specific instructions on submission.

5.28 *Editor Acknowledgment of Manuscript Submission*

When a manuscript is received in the editor's office, the editor assigns the manuscript a number and, usually within 48 hours, sends an acknowledgment of receipt to the author. (See chapter 8 for information about the APA publication process.)

5.29 *Interim Correspondence*

While a manuscript is under consideration, be sure to inform the editor of any substantive corrections needed, any change in address, and so forth. In all correspondence, include the complete manuscript title, the authors' names, and the manuscript number.

Sample Paper and Outlines

The sample paper and sample paper outlines in Figures 5.1, 5.2, and 5.3 were prepared especially for the *Publication Manual* to illustrate some applications of APA style in typed form. These are not actual manuscripts, and they have not been reviewed for content. Numbers and captions refer to sections of the *Publication Manual*.

Figure 5.1. Sample one-experiment paper. The circled numbers refer to numbered sections in the *Publication Manual.*

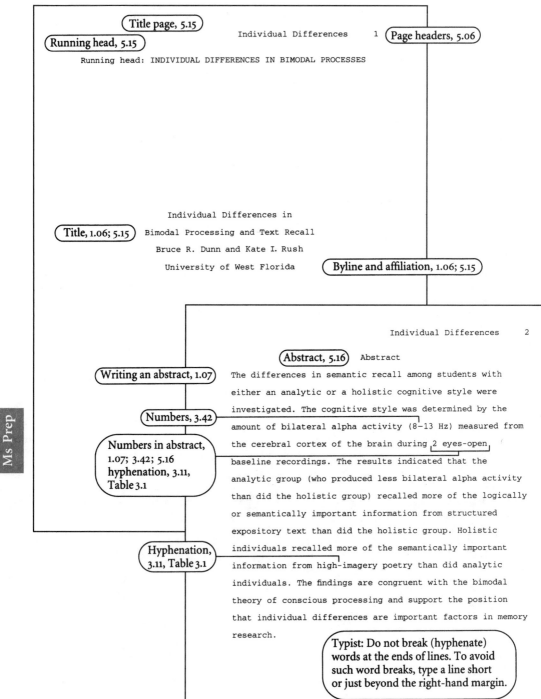

5.29 MANUSCRIPT PREPARATION

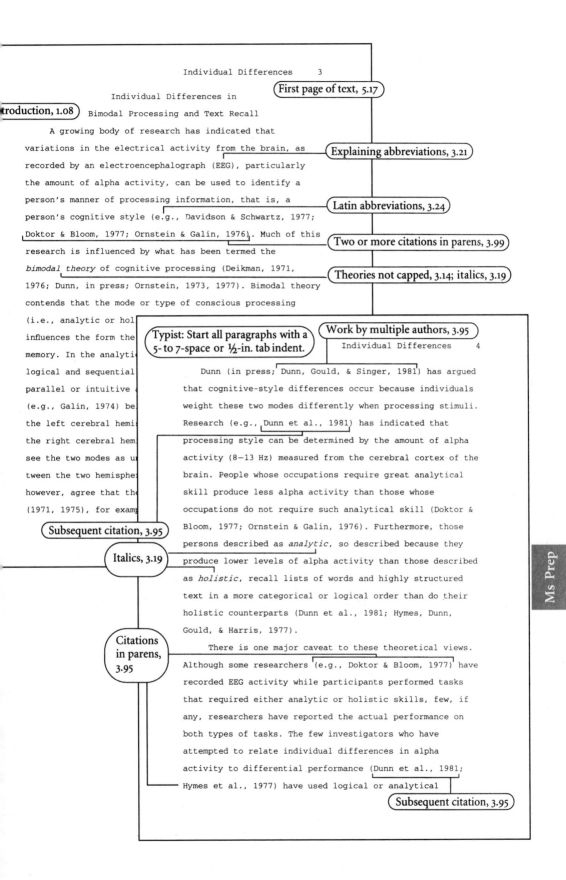

Individual Differences   3

Individual Differences in

Bimodal Processing and Text Recall

A growing body of research has indicated that variations in the electrical activity from the brain, as recorded by an electroencephalograph (EEG), particularly the amount of alpha activity, can be used to identify a person's manner of processing information, that is, a person's cognitive style (e.g., Davidson & Schwartz, 1977; Doktor & Bloom, 1977; Ornstein & Galin, 1976). Much of this research is influenced by what has been termed the *bimodal theory* of cognitive processing (Deikman, 1971, 1976; Dunn, in press; Ornstein, 1973, 1977). Bimodal theory contends that the mode or type of conscious processing (i.e., analytic or hol... influences the form the... memory. In the analyti... logical and sequential... parallel or intuitive... (e.g., Galin, 1974) be... the left cerebral hemi... the right cerebral hem... see the two modes as u... tween the two hemisphe... however, agree that th... (1971, 1975), for examp...

First page of text, 5.17

Introduction, 1.08

Explaining abbreviations, 3.21

Latin abbreviations, 3.24

Two or more citations in parens, 3.99

Theories not capped, 3.14; italics, 3.19

Typist: Start all paragraphs with a 5- to 7-space or ½-in. tab indent.

Work by multiple authors, 3.95

Individual Differences   4

Dunn (in press; Dunn, Gould, & Singer, 1981) has argued that cognitive-style differences occur because individuals weight these two modes differently when processing stimuli. Research (e.g., Dunn et al., 1981) has indicated that processing style can be determined by the amount of alpha activity (8–13 Hz) measured from the cerebral cortex of the brain. People whose occupations require great analytical skill produce less alpha activity than those whose occupations do not require such analytical skill (Doktor & Bloom, 1977; Ornstein & Galin, 1976). Furthermore, those persons described as *analytic*, so described because they produce lower levels of alpha activity than those described as *holistic*, recall lists of words and highly structured text in a more categorical or logical order than do their holistic counterparts (Dunn et al., 1981; Hymes, Dunn, Gould, & Harris, 1977).

There is one major caveat to these theoretical views. Although some researchers (e.g., Doktor & Bloom, 1977) have recorded EEG activity while participants performed tasks that required either analytic or holistic skills, few, if any, researchers have reported the actual performance on both types of tasks. The few investigators who have attempted to relate individual differences in alpha activity to differential performance (Dunn et al., 1981; Hymes et al., 1977) have used logical or analytical

Subsequent citation, 3.95

Italics, 3.19

Citations in parens, 3.95

Subsequent citation, 3.95

Ms Prep

Figure 5.1. (continued)

Individual Differences   5

verbal materials and tasks; no researcher has reported

performance on a holistic task. Thus, research to this time

has measured only quantitative differences in analytical

processing and has not identified the two qualitatively

distinct styles implied by the terms *analytic* and *holistic*.

In this study we attempted to identify the qualitative

differences between styles by having participants recall a

high-imagery poetry passage with little logical or

analytical content. It was assumed that encoding and

recalling material consisting of images would require more

holistic processing than would encoding highly logical

expository text. Our ba

by experts on the struc

1968; Whalley, 1967), w

metaphor, is an irreduc

If it is assumed t

tightly structured expo

of a hypothetical logic

high-imagery poetry is

persons shoul

readily than expository

the opposite pattern.

test these

(Precise wording, 2.04)

(Acknowledging participation, Bias Guideline 3 (chapter 2))

Individual Differences   6

Method (Headings, 3.31, 5.10)

Participants   (Age, 2.17)

Sixty upper division university students (30 women and

30 men, mean age = 21.6 years) volunteered to participate.

All participants were strongly right-handed, as determined

by the Laterality Assessment Inventory (Sherman & Kulhavy,

1976). Volunteers were paid for their participation and

were treated in accordance with the "Ethical Principles of

Psychologists and Code of Conduct" (American Psychological

Association, 1992).

Materials

Two passages with approximately the same number

of words were used. The first passage, "Chemical

Pesticides," was a 155-word expository passage developed by

Howell (1980) and based on the work of Meyer and Freedle

(1979). We chose this particular passage because the

highest level of its semantic structure was defined by a

logical cause-and-effect relation. All items directly

related to this level were considered to be the most

important points of the passage, and all items indirectly

related were considered to be less important (see Howell,

1980; Meyer, 1975). The second passage was a 161-word poem

by Richard Eberhart titled "Seals, Terns, Time" (cited in

Brown & Milstead, 1968). We chose the poem after consulting

with three poetry specialists, who agreed that the poem was

(Numbers, 3.43)

(Hyphenation, Table 3.1)

(Hyphenation, Table 3.1)

(Quotation marks, 3.06; capitalization, 3.13)

(Citations, 3.95)

(Numbers, 3.42; hyphenation, Table 3.1)

(Citation to secondary source, Example 22 (chapter 4))

M 1.0

Ms Prep

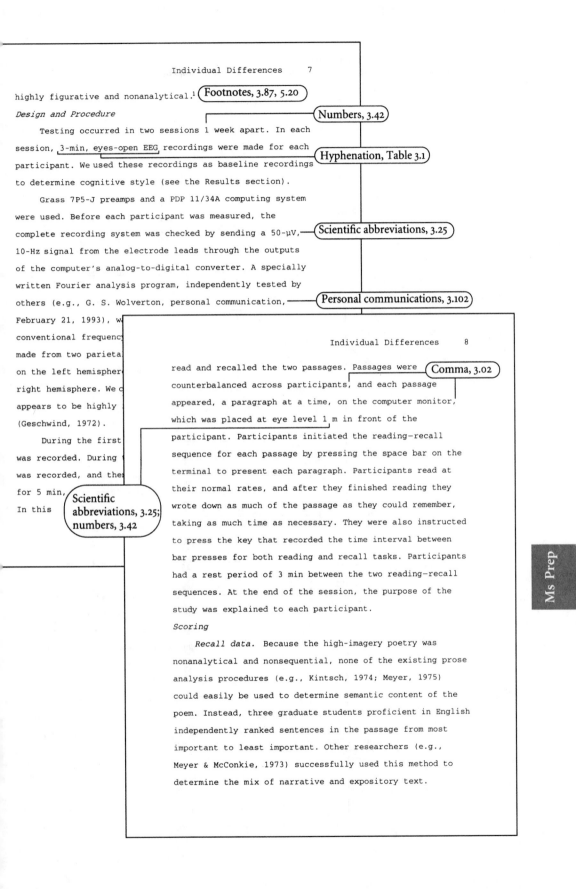

highly figurative and nonanalytical.[1] **Footnotes, 3.87, 5.20**

Design and Procedure   **Numbers, 3.42**

Testing occurred in two sessions 1 week apart. In each
session, 3-min, eyes-open EEG recordings were made for each
participant. We used these recordings as baseline recordings   **Hyphenation, Table 3.1**
to determine cognitive style (see the Results section).

Grass 7P5-J preamps and a PDP 11/34A computing system
were used. Before each participant was measured, the
complete recording system was checked by sending a 50-µV,—   **Scientific abbreviations, 3.25**
10-Hz signal from the electrode leads through the outputs
of the computer's analog-to-digital converter. A specially
written Fourier analysis program, independently tested by
others (e.g., G. S. Wolverton, personal communication,—   **Personal communications, 3.102**
February 21, 1993), w
conventional frequency   **Individual Differences   8**
made from two parieta
on the left hemispher   read and recalled the two passages. Passages were   **Comma, 3.02**
right hemisphere. We   counterbalanced across participants, and each passage
appears to be highly   appeared, a paragraph at a time, on the computer monitor,
(Geschwind, 1972).   which was placed at eye level 1 m in front of the
                        participant. Participants initiated the reading—recall
During the first   sequence for each passage by pressing the space bar on the
was recorded. During   terminal to present each paragraph. Participants read at
was recorded, and the   their normal rates, and after they finished reading they
for 5 min,   wrote down as much of the passage as they could remember,
In this   **Scientific**   taking as much time as necessary. They were also instructed
           abbreviations, 3.25;   to press the key that recorded the time interval between
           numbers, 3.42   bar presses for both reading and recall tasks. Participants
                        had a rest period of 3 min between the two reading—recall
                        sequences. At the end of the session, the purpose of the
                        study was explained to each participant.

Scoring

Recall data. Because the high-imagery poetry was
nonanalytical and nonsequential, none of the existing prose
analysis procedures (e.g., Kintsch, 1974; Meyer, 1975)
could easily be used to determine semantic content of the
poem. Instead, three graduate students proficient in English
independently ranked sentences in the passage from most
important to least important. Other researchers (e.g.,
Meyer & McConkie, 1973) successfully used this method to
determine the mix of narrative and expository text.

Ms Prep

Figure 5.1. *(continued)*

Individual Differences 9

The expository "Chemical Pesticides" passage was analyzed in an identical manner, even though established analysis procedures like Meyer's (1975) could have been used to make the resultant semantic hierarchies as equal as possible. Two independent raters judged participants' recall protocols and then determined which recalled sentences were contained in the formerly described semantic hierarchies. The scoring method was determined, and paraphrased versions of the sentences were scored as well. The reliability of the ratings was acceptable (93%) by a reverse-scoring procedure. Because the resultant hierarchies had unequal levels
10 sentences of each hierarchy information, and the last 15 se subordinate i
scores were used.

EEG data. Each second of E muscle artifacts. If any artifa EEG data was deleted. Fourier t vert the remaining EEG data int bandwidths within the range of

Resul

A Pearson product–momen substantial relation power scores, which were taken

(Symbols, 3.58; numbers, 3.42)

(Statistics, 3.57, 5.14)

(Decimal fractions, 3.46)

(Comma, 3.02)

(Math copy, 5.14)

(Variables, 3.18)

(Back-to-back numbers, 3.44)

Individual Differences 10

$r(59) = .87$, $p < .01$. (The probability of a Type I error was maintained at .05 for all subsequent analyses.) Therefore, the alpha power scores were averaged for each participant and served as the basis for dichotomizing participants into analytic and holistic groups. Those participants whose scores were below the median were classified as analytic; those whose scores were above the median were classified as holistic. This procedure has been used to classify analytic and holistic persons in past research (e.g., Hymes et al., 1977), which has demonstrated that alpha power scores are highly reliable.

Recall Data

The proportional recall data were analyzed with a 2 × 2 × 2 (Type of Processor × Passage × Level of Subordination) mixed analysis of covariance, with average reading time serving as the covariate and with passage and level serving as repeated measures. Although several main effects and two-way interactions reached statistical significance, they were of little interest because a significant three-way (Type of Processor × Passage × Level of Subordination) interaction was obtained, $F(1, 58) = 29.93$, $p < .01$. For ease of interpretation, Figure 1 shows this interaction as 2 two-way (Passage × Level of Subordination) interactions, one for each processing style. The three-way interaction indicates that analytic

(Citing fig 3.83)

Ms Prep

persons recalled proportionally more superordinate
information from the logically structured expository text
than from the high-imagery poetry. In contrast, the
holistic group recalled more of the important information
from the poem than from the expository passage.
Simple-effects tests of the interaction showed that the
analytic group's mean recall of important information from
the expository text (.70) was greater than the holistic
group's mean recall (.52). Furthermore, the holistic group
recalled more important information from the poem than the
analytic group did (.72 vs. .55).

EEG data

   Reading data. The bilateral alpha power scores
recorded during reading
and subjected to a 2 ×
mixed analysis of varia
passage.[2] The main eff
significant: The holist
score (3.35) was greate
(1.35), $F(1, 28) = 14.8$
More important, the two
interaction also yielde
.005. The data in the t
Table 1 show that the a
activity when they read

Descriptive statistics appear in the figure (see section 3.57)

Decimal fractions, 3.46

Latin abbreviations, 3.24

Special characters, 5.02

lon, 04, 5.11

tistical py, 3.57

Adverbs, .09

Discussing tables, 3.63

Descriptive statistics appear in the table (see section 3.57)

occurred for the holistic group. In addition, the holistic
group generally appeared to produce more alpha activity
than did the analytic group, regardless of the type of
passage. This finding was confirmed with Scheffé's post hoc
tests ($p < .05$).

   Recall data. The recall alpha data were analyzed in
the same way the reading alpha data were analyzed. Type of
processor was again found to be significant, $F(1, 28) =$
5.70, $p < .03$, with the holistic group's mean alpha score
(2.30) being greater than the analytic group's (1.12). The
two-way interaction was also significant, $F(1, 168) = 6.23$,
$p < .03$, and followed a pattern similar to that found with
the reading alpha data (see the bottom half of Table 1).

Discussion

   The present data are congruent with the bimodal theory
of processing (Deikman, 1971; Dunn, in press; Ornstein,
1977; Paivio, 1975) from which the analytic—holistic
dimension was derived. As we hypothesized, the analytic
group recalled more of the important information from
logically structured text (cause followed by effect) than
the holistic group did. On the other hand, holistic
participants recalled more important information from the
less structured and more metaphorical text (poetry) than
analytic participants did. This finding is clearly indicated
by the relatively poor superordinate recall of the poetry

Ms Prep

Figure 5.1. (*continued*)

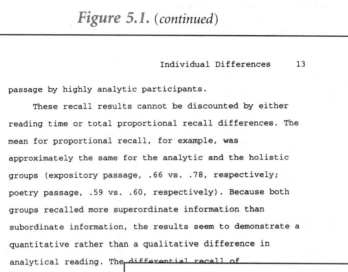

Individual Differences   13

passage by highly analytic participants.

These recall results cannot be discounted by either reading time or total proportional recall differences. The mean for proportional recall, for example, was approximately the same for the analytic and the holistic groups (expository passage, .66 vs. .78, respectively; poetry passage, .59 vs. .60, respectively). Because both groups recalled more superordinate information than subordinate information, the results seem to demonstrate a quantitative rather than a qualitative difference in analytical reading. The differential recall of superordinate informati the poem by the two gro tative explanation. As et al., 1981), holistic tivity than did analyti call tasks. Furthermore more alpha activity whi tory text than while re activity showed the opp qualitatively distinct

Admittedly, the e structure across the pa Future rese analytic-holistic cogn

Same surname, 3.98

Typist: Indent block quotations 5 spaces from left margin.

Quotations, 3.34, 5.13

Individual Differences   14

variables and by varying visuospatial tasks in order to determine their effects on the recall and perceptual performance of analytic and holistic individuals. Also, other promising individual-difference constructs, such as extraversion (H. J. Eysenck, 1967; M. W. Eysenck, 1976, 1977) and field dependency (Witkin, Dyk, Faterson, Goodenough, & Karp, 1962), should be compared with the analytic—holistic dimension in terms of success in predicting differential recall.

The results have a more indirect implication, which is reflected in the following statement by M. W. Eysenck (1976):

In spite of the obvious importance of individual differences in human learning and memory, relatively few investigators incorporate any measure of intelligence, personality, or motivation into their studies. Instead, they prefer to relegate individual differences to the error term in their analyses of variance. (p. 75)

Given the robustness of these results and the results of others (for reviews, see M. W. Eysenck, 1977, and Goodenough, 1976), it may behoove memory researchers to pay closer attention to individual differences.

Ms Prep

References (Typing references, 5.18)

(Constructing references in APA style, chapter 4)

American Psychological Association. (1992). Ethical principles
of psychologists and code of conduct. *American
Psychologist, 47,* 1597-1611.

Brown, H., & Milstead, J. (1968). *Patterns in poetry: An
introductory anthology.* Glenview, IL: Scott, Foresman.

Cohen, G. (1975). Hemisphere differences in the effects
of cuing in visual recognition tasks. *Journal of
Experimental Psychology: Human Perception and
Performance, 1,* 366-373.

Davidson, R. J., & Schwartz, G. E. (1977). The influence of
musical training on patterns of EEG asymmetry during
musical and non-musical self-generation tasks.
Psychophysiolog

Deikman, A. J. (1974
of General Psych

Deikman, A. J. (1976
mystic experien
A. J. Deikman, &
ness (pp. 67-88]

Doktor, R., & Bloom,
lateralization c
determined by EE
385-387.

Dunn, E. R. (in pres

memory from text. In V. M. Rentel, S. Corson, &
B. R. Dunn (Eds.), *Psychophysiological aspects of
reading.* Elmsford, NY: Pergamon Press.

Dunn, B. R., Gould, J. E., & Singer, M. (1981). *Cognitive
style differences in expository prose recall* (Tech.
Rep. No. 210). Urbana-Champaign: University of
Illinois, Center for the Study of Language Processing.
(ERIC Document Reproduction Service No. ED 205 922)

Eysenck, H. J. (1967). *The biological basis of personality.*
Springfield, IL: Charles C Thomas.

Eysenck, M. W. (1976). Extraversion, verbal learning, and
memory. *Psychological Bulletin, 83,* 75-90.

Eysenck, M. W. (1977). *Human memory: Theory, research,
and individual differences.* Elmsford, NY: Pergamon
Press.

Galin, D. (1974). Implications for psychiatry of left and
right cerebral specialization. *Archives of General
Psychiatry, 31,* 572-583.

Geschwind, H. N. (1972). Language and the brain. *Scientific
American, 105*(2), 76-83.

Goodenough, D. R. (1976). The role of individual differences
in field dependence as a factor in learning and memory.
Psychological Bulletin, 83, 675-694.

Howell, W. L. (1980). Expository prose recall by young,
hospitalized schizophrenics (Doctoral dissertation,

Ms Prep

Figure 5.1. (*continued*)

Individual Differences   17

Florida State University, 1989). *Dissertation Abstracts*

International, 41, 1011B.

Hymes, J. T., Dunn, B. R., Gould, J. E., & Harris, W. (1977,

February). *Effects of mode of conscious processing on*

recall and clustering. Paper presented at the meeting of

the Southeastern Psychological Association, Hollywood, FL.

Kintsch, W. (1974). *The representation of meaning in memory.*

Hillsdale, NJ: Erlbaum.

Meyer, B. J. F. (1975). *The organization of prose and its*

effects on memory. Amsterdam: North-Holland.

Meyer, B. J. F., & Freedle, R. O. (1978). *Effects of*

discourse type on

State University,

Meyer, B. J. F., & Simp

recalled after hea

Pyschology, 65, 10

Ornstein, R. E. (Ed.).

consciousness: A b

Ornstein, R. E. (1982).

consciousness (2nd

Jovanovich.

Ornstein, R. E., & Simp

studies of conscio

Gray, A. J. Deikma

consciousness (pp.

Individual Differences   18

Paivio, A. (1971). *Imagery and verbal processing.* New York:

Holt, Rinehart & Winston.

Paivio, A. (1975). Imagery and synchronic thinking.

Psychological Review, 16, 147–163.

Sherman, L. G., & Kulhavy, R. W. (1976). *The assessment of*

personality: The Sherman-Kulhavy Laterality Inventory

(Tech. Rep. No. 4). Tempe: Arizona State University,

Center for the Study of Human Intellectual Processes.

Whalley, T. R. (1967). *Poetic process: An essay in poetics.*

Lancaster, PA: Old World Publishing.

Witkin, H., Dyk, R. B., Faterson, H. F., Goodenough, D. R.,

& Karp, M. R. (1962). *Psychological differentiation:*

Studies of field dependency. New York: Wiley.

Author Note   (Author note, 3.89, 5.20)

Bruce R. Dunn and Kate I. Rush, Department of Psychology, University of West Florida.

Kate I. Rush is now at the Department of Psychology and Human Behavior, Brown University.

We fabricated these experiments for the *Publication Manual*, although we assumed, on the basis of past research, that the hypotheses we examined had face validity.

We thank Donna B. Oberholtzer, Claire J. Reinburg, and Frances Y. Dunham, who ranked the sentences, and those who kindly volunteered to participate in the study. We also thank Linda S. Garlet for preparing the artwork.

Correspondence con
addressed to the author
obtained from the autho
not exist. In submitted
address of the author t

(Semicolon, 3.03)

Footnotes   (Footnotes, 3.87, 5.20)

[1]If poetry specialists had been consulted, we would have expressed appreciation here to our colleagues Ronald V. Evans, University of West Florida; Harold Pepinsky, Ohio State University; and Bonnie J. F. Meyer, Arizona State University, for their assistance in choosing a poem.

[2]For the sake of brevity, we have reported only a
f we had actually
e treated hemisphere
e introduction, would
the cerebral
ry.

Table 1   (Tables, 3.62–3.74)

Mean Alpha Power Scores as a Function of Type of Processor and Passage

Type of processor	Passage	
	Exposition	Poetry
Reading alpha data		
Analytic	0.93	1.76
Holistic	3.96	1.98
Recall alpha data		
Analytic	0.71	1.93
Holistic	2.64	0.82

Ms Prep

Figure 5.1. (*continued*)

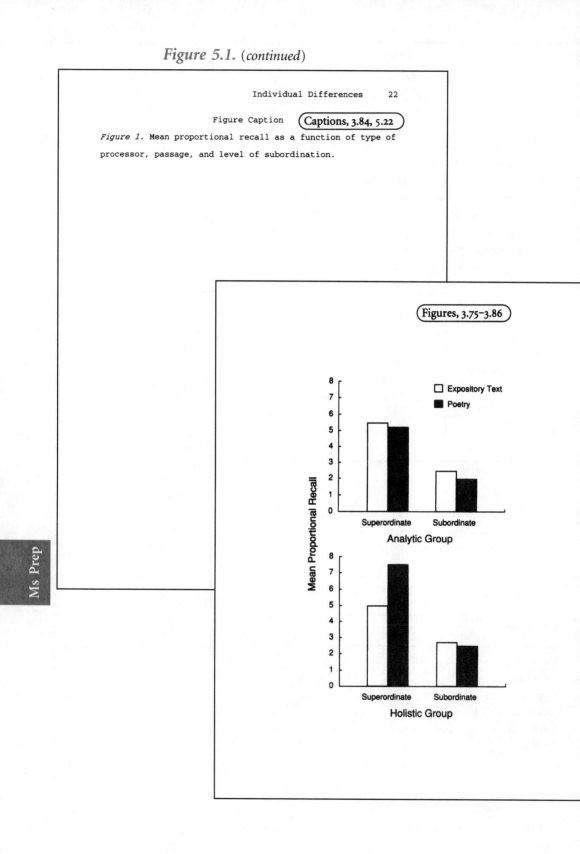

Individual Differences   22

Figure Caption   ⬭ Captions, 3.84, 5.22 ⬭

Figure 1. Mean proportional recall as a function of type of
processor, passage, and level of subordination.

⬭ Figures, 3.75–3.86 ⬭

Ms Prep

Figure 5.2. Outline of the text of a sample two-experiment paper. The circled numbers refer to numbered sections in the *Publication Manual.* This abridged manuscript illustrates the organizational structure characteristic of multiple-experiment papers. Of course, a complete multiple-experiment paper would include a title page, an abstract page, and so on.

```
                              Prose Recall      3

             Effect on Prose Recall of
         Individual Differences in Cognitive Style   (Types of articles, 1.04)
      Recently researchers have shown increased interest in
   the relation between cognitive style differences and
   comprehension of text. Several researchers in this area
   have attempted to show
   (Wolk & DuCette, 1974)                              Prose Recall      4
   Spiro & Tirre, 1980) to
   together, these constru          electroencephalic (EEG) baseline recordings were made.
   the cognitive-style dim             . . . [section continues].
   by Dunn (in press). . .          Results
                       Expe               All data were converted to z scores, and with Pearson
   Method                          product-moment correlations, a correlation matrix was
        Participants. Sixt          generated (see Table 1). Because the multiple independent
   (32 men and 28 women, n          and dependent variables were related, I analyzed the data
   for the study. . . . [se         using the Statistical Analysis System canonical correlation
        Materials. Four ex          routine (Barr, Goodnight, Sall, & Helwig, 1976). . . . .
   [section continues].             [section continues].
        Personality and co         Discussion
   description of the thr                The results of Experiment 1 indicate that although
   measured for each is gi          locus of control and field dependency correlated with the
   of individual differen           set of dependent variables, they did so only through their
   formation from text tha          correlation with the alpha activity index of analytical
   locus of control and fie         processing.
   [section continues].                  Because only highly logical verbal materials were used
                                    in Experiment 1, it could be argued that this study
   (Headings, 3.32, 5.10;           measured only quantitative differences in analytical
   multiple experiments, 1.12)      processing. Experiment 2 was designed to identify
                                    qualitative differences between styles. . . . [section
                                    continues].

   (Multiple experiments, 1.12) ———————— Experiment 2
                                    Method
                                         Participants. Forty upper division, right-handed
```

Ms Prep

Figure 5.2. (continued)

college students (20 women and 20 men, mean age = 21.7 years) volunteered to participate. . . . [section continues].

Materials. A 205-word poem by Fyodor Sologue (cited in Markov & Sparks, 1966) titled "The Devil's Swing" was selected because three poetry specialists who were consulted agreed that the poem was full of imagery and nonanalytical content. . . . [section continues].

Design and Procedure. The design and procedure were identical to those of Experiment 1, except that the students read only one passage. . . . [section continues].

Data scoring. Two independent raters judged participants' recall protocols and determined which recalled sentences were contained in the previously described semantic hierarchy. . . . [section continues].

Results

A correlation matrix on the *z*-transformed data again showed that the predictor variables—analytical processing, locus of control, and field dependency—were significantly intercorrelated (*ps* < .01). . . . [section continues].

General Discussion

The results of both experiments strongly suggest that the analytical processing dimension is a better predictor

(Typing dashes, 5.11)

of individual differences in the recall of higher order information from text than are the personality constructs of locus of control and field dependency. . . . [section continues].

[Follow the form of the one-experiment sample paper to type references, the author note, footnotes, tables, and figure captions.]

Ms Prep

Figure 5.3. Outline of the text of a sample review paper. This abridged manuscript illustrates the organizational structure characteristic of review or theoretical papers. Of course, a complete review or theoretical paper would include a title page, an abstract page, and so on.

Analytical Cognitive Style   3

Analytical Cognitive Style as a Factor

in Memory for Text

Cognitive or personality style differences traditionally have been ignored in the field of human learning and memory (Eysenck, 1977). This situation is surprising, given the growing body of literature showing that individuals differ in how they encode and retrieve simple and complex verbal information (for summaries, see Eysenck, 1977, and Goodenough, 1976). The present review has two purposes: (a) to demonstrate that when the popular personality and cognitive co[...] (Rotter, 1966) and field depe[...] Goodenough, & Karp, 1962)—are[...] recall studies, similar resu[...] (b) to suggest that this sim[...] constructs overlap with the [...] style dimension.

(Types of articles, 1.04)
(Seriation, 3.33, 5.12)

———— Locus o[...]

Rotter (1966) suggested[...] as opposed to external, locu[...] events are contingent on the[...] rather than on chance or on [...] continues].

Research on Learning Word Li[...]

A widely held belief in[...]

(Headings, 3.32, 5.10)

Analytical Cognitive Style   4

create cognitive categories while learning lists of words and then use those categories as the basis for retrieval (Bousfield & Tulving, 1966). The results of Bartel, DuCette, and Wolk (1972) indicate that only those with an internal locus of control use this strategy. . . . [section continues].

Research on Recall

The argument that people with an external locus of control and those with an internal locus of control use different strategies to encode and retrieve simple word lists can be made when complex material serves as the stimulus. . . . [section continues].

————Field Dependency

A field-independent person, in contrast to a field-dependent person, can overcome an embedding context and can deal with a perceptual field analytically. . . . [section continues].

Research on Learning Word Lists

Researchers obtain results similar to those found in the locus-of-control literature when they use field dependency as the individual-difference construct in studies done with simple verbal materials. . . . [section continues].

Research on Text Recall

Annis (1979) has found individual differences in field dependency and text recall that parallel those found in a

Ms Prep

Figure 5.3. (*continued*)

study of locus of control by Wolk and DuCette (1974). . . . [section continues].

Relationship of Locus of Control and Field

Dependency With Analytic Processing

The constructs of locus of control, field dependency, and analytic processing style are related to a certain extent because the definitions of the constructs overlap. The overlap in the constructs occurs because of shared behavior referents. . . . [section continues].

Conclusions

Although the constructs of locus of control and field dependency generally measure different aspects of personality and cognitive functioning, they appear to measure the same degree of text encoding. That factor appears to be individual differences in analytic and holistic processing. . . . [section continues].

[Follow the form of the one-experiment sample paper to type references, the author note, footnotes, tables, and figure captions.]

CHAPTER SIX

Material Other Than Journal Articles

The APA *Publication Manual* is intended primarily as a guide to preparing manuscripts for journal publication. Authors also use the *Publication Manual* to prepare theses, dissertations, and student papers; papers for oral presentation; and papers published in abbreviated form. This chapter briefly explains some of the differences between these materials and journal articles.

Theses, Dissertations, and Student Papers

6.01 *Final Manuscript*

The author of a thesis, dissertation, or student paper produces a "final" manuscript; the author of a journal article produces a "copy" manuscript (which will become a typeset article). The differences between these two kinds of manuscripts help explain why the requirements for theses, dissertations, and student papers are not necessarily identical to those for the manuscripts submitted for publication in a journal.

Copy manuscripts have been described throughout the *Publication Manual.* Their life span is short; they are normally read by editors, reviewers, and typesetters only and are no longer usable after they have been typeset. Copy manuscripts must conform to the format and other policies of the journal to which they are submitted.

Final manuscripts, however, reach their audiences in the exact form in which they are prepared. Final manuscripts have a long life span; they may be read by many people over a long time. The difference between how copy manuscripts and final manuscripts are used is one reason for the differences between the preparation of journal articles and the preparation of theses, dissertations, and student papers. A number of variations from the requirements described in the *Publication Manual* are not only permissible but also desirable in the preparation of final manuscripts.

Many psychology departments require that theses and dissertations be prepared according to the *Publication Manual*. Use of the *Publication Manual* in the production of these papers is excellent preparation for a research-productive career, but theses and dissertations are submitted to the student's graduate school, not to a journal. Therefore, they must satisfy the graduate school's specific requirements, even if these requirements depart from the style outlined in the *Publication Manual*. Graduate schools should provide students (and typists) with written guidelines that explain all modifications to APA style. (*Note:* A thesis or dissertation in its original form is not acceptable for submission to APA journals.)

Many departments have also adopted the *Publication Manual* for undergraduate senior theses, term papers, laboratory reports, and the like. The *Publication Manual* is not intended to cover scientific writing at an undergraduate level, because preferences for style at that level are diverse. Instructions to students to "use the *Publication Manual*" should be accompanied by specific guidelines for its use.

6.02 *Content Requirements*

The purpose of theses, dissertations, and student papers and the nature of the reading audience (professor or committee members) may dictate variations from the requirements for manuscripts submitted for publication. The following discussion describes the sections of a typical thesis, dissertation, or student paper and touches on some of the common variations among psychology departments. Psychology departments should inform students of any special requirements. For practical guidance on planning for and completing dissertations and theses, see Cone and Foster's (1993) *Dissertations and Theses From Start to Finish: Psychology and Related Fields.*

Preliminary pages. Introductory material for a thesis or dissertation usually includes a title page, an approval page, an acknowledgment page, a table of contents, a list of tables and figures, and an abstract. Requirements for these items vary among institutions. Because requirements for the length of abstracts often vary the most, some common guidelines on length are given here.

Many institutions require that abstracts be prepared according to the requirements of *Dissertation Abstracts International.* The maximum length for a dissertation abstract submitted to *Dissertation Abstracts International* is 350 words, far longer than the maximum of 120 words for most abstracts in APA journals.

In psychology dissertations, the abstract is now often substituted for the summary, but the author and the dissertation committee usually make the choice. In general, standards for theses and dissertations are similar. Abstracts for student laboratory reports are more often expected to follow APA limits on length.

Introduction. The introduction in a thesis or dissertation is similar to that in a journal article (see section 1.08), except that the author of a thesis or dissertation may be expected to demonstrate familiarity with the literature by developing the background more comprehensively. The decision about length is usually delegated to the chair of the department or dissertation committee; thus, requirements vary widely.

Students writing laboratory reports are often permitted to cite material from secondary sources with appropriate referencing. This practice is not encouraged in journal articles, theses, or dissertations.

Method, Results, and Discussion. The content of these sections in undergraduate and graduate papers is similar to that in journal articles (see sections 1.09, 1.10, and 1.11, respectively).

Summary. As noted, the trend is to substitute the abstract for the summary.

References. Generally, only references cited in the text are included in the reference list; however, an occasional exception can be found to this rule. For example, committees or departments may require evidence that students are familiar with a broader spectrum of literature than that immediately relevant to their research. In such instances, the reference list may be called a bibliography.

Appendixes. Although space and content requirements may limit the use of appendixes in journal articles, the need for complete documentation often dictates their inclusion in undergraduate and graduate papers. The following materials are appropriate for an appendix: verbatim instructions to participants, original scales or questionnaires, and raw data. In addition, psychology departments may require sign-up sheets or informed consent forms and statistical calculations in appendixes to laboratory reports. It may be appropriate to include a copy of the instrument you used for data collection in an appendix to your thesis or dissertation if the instrument is not well known (consult with your advisor if you are unsure) or has not been published. For reasons of test security and copyright protection, request permission in writing from the copyright holder (usually the publisher) to reproduce the instrument.

6.03 *Manuscript Preparation Requirements*

Each university has requirements for the format of theses, dissertations, and student papers, which may differ from those in the *Publication Manual.* The purpose of these requirements is to impose consistency in manuscripts by individuals from various disciplines.

The following are guidelines for preparing a typical undergraduate or graduate paper. These guidelines may not be applicable to laboratory reports, because in laboratory courses students are often expected to prepare reports in the style required for actual submission to an appropriate journal. The student should find out whether (or in what respects) the university's or department's requirements for theses, dissertations, and student papers take precedence over those of the *Publication Manual.*

Writers are reminded that they are preparing the "final" copy. Because the manuscript will not be set in type, the manuscript must be as readable as possible. Many of APA's format requirements aid production for publication. Reasonable exceptions to APA style for theses and dissertations often make sense and are encouraged to better serve communication and improve the appearance of the final document. For example, tables may be more readable if single-spaced, and justified margins may substitute for ragged right margins (in this case, end-of-line hyphens are acceptable).

Paper, corrections, copies, and margins. Most requirements for rag content and weight of paper are established to provide durable copies of theses and dissertations for the library. Only corrections that do not mar the appearance or lessen the durability of the manuscript are permitted. Most universities permit photocopies. The left-hand margin must be wide enough for binding, usually 1½ in. (4 cm). The top margin on the first page of a new chapter (section) may be wider than other margins. Typists should observe requirements carefully, because some of each margin is trimmed in the binding process.

Chapters. The sections of a research report (Introduction, Method, Results, and Discussion) are frequently regarded as chapters; each begins on a new page. They may or may not include a chapter number.

In APA style, the introduction is not labeled. However, the arrangement of pages or sections in most theses and dissertations may require that the introduction be labeled because no other heading appears on that page.

Figures, tables, and footnotes. In a manuscript submitted for publication, figures, tables, and footnotes are placed at the end of the manuscript; in theses and dissertations, such material is frequently incorporated at the appropriate point in text as a convenience to readers. Short tables may appear on a page with some text. Each long table and each figure is placed on a separate page immediately after the page on which the table or figure is first mentioned. Figure captions are typed below the figure or, in some cases, on the preceding or facing page. Footnotes to the text are typed at the bottom of the page on which they are referenced.

Pagination. Preliminary pages usually carry lowercase roman numerals. Throughout the manuscript, certain pages may be counted in the numbering sequence without actually carrying a number. The position of numbers on the first pages of chapters or on full-page tables and figures may differ from the position of numbers on other pages. Page numbers continue throughout the appendix.

Spacing. Double-spacing is required throughout most of the manuscript. When single-spacing would improve readability, however, it is usually encouraged. Single-spacing can be used for table titles and headings, figure captions, references (but double-spacing is required *between* references), footnotes, and long quotations. Long quotations may also be indented five spaces or $\frac{1}{2}$ in.

Judicious triple- or quadruple-spacing can improve appearance and readability. Such spacing is appropriate after chapter titles, before major subheadings, before footnotes, and before and after tables in the text.

Converting the Dissertation Into a Journal Article

Students who want to get started on publishing their research may find the guidelines that follow to be helpful. They were adapted with permission from Calfee and Valencia's (2001) *APA Guide to Preparing Manuscripts for Journal Publication.*

A logical place for the beginning scholar to commence the task of publishing is with the dissertation. Turning a thesis into a publishable manuscript requires work on length, selectivity, writing style (editorial and expository), and interpretation of data. By giving attention to these features, you will increase the chance of having your manuscript accepted for publication. Reviewers and editors easily recognize a dissertation conversion. On the one hand, the distinctive features can mean a headache —lots of work for the reviewer. On the other hand, most reviewers are generous with their contribution of time and patience in guiding a new colleague through the publication maze. The harder a new member of the profession works to alleviate some of the more obvious and fixable problems separating a thesis from a publishable article, the easier the path will be.

6.04 *Trimming the Length*

Articles derived from dissertations typically are longer than other manuscripts. This is understandable. To reduce a 200-plus page document to a compact, 25- to 30-page article is no easy task. Yet, this paring must be done, and done with extreme care. The substance must be preserved while cutting the extraneous detail that is important for the dissertation but irrelevant for the journal article. How does an author approach the chore of turning a lengthy thesis into an article of the appropriate size for a journal? It is not a matter of "cutting and pasting," but one of selecting and rewriting.

In dissertations there is a tendency to say everything about the research problem under investigation. Again, this is understandable in that a doctoral thesis serves as a rite of academic passage. The completion of the thesis signifies that you have extensive knowledge about the topic under study and the requisite skills to pursue research on the problem. The following approaches often help with selectivity and brevity:

- If the dissertation covers several distinct research dimensions, you may want to narrow the focus to a specific topic—be selective in presenting the problem.
- Try to bring the results under control. Often the dissertation reports everything, including "almost significant" results.
- Try to avoid the common presentation pitfalls of many novice writers (e.g., reporting that the data were analyzed with a certain computer package or presenting significant findings in the Discussion section). For an excellent discussion on pitfalls and problems, see Carver (1984).
- There are certain conventions in dissertations that do not lend

themselves to presentation format for journal articles. For example, as Carver (1984) advised, "do not include a 'Definitions' section. ... This section is popular in doctoral dissertations but it is often a sign of naivete in research reports" (pp. 22–23).

■ Be selective in the references that are reported in the literature review. Dissertations often have an exhaustive number of citations—choose the most salient.

6.05 *Writing Style*

Many theses do not follow APA style (e.g., for tables, figures, references, and organization of sections). Failure to attend to APA style often signals stylistic problems throughout the manuscript—take special care to find out how your university's requirements depart from APA style, and then revise accordingly when editing your manuscript for publication.

What about the quality of expository writing? Armstrong's (1972) treatise on "The Dissertation's Deadly Sins" is helpful in addressing this issue. Among other problems, Armstrong argued that most theses suffer from overuse of the passive voice, pedantry, artificiality (e.g., overuse of the conditional), and redundancy. Such writing "sins" often create obstacles in setting forth ideas effectively.

In a similar vein, Holmes (1974–1975) spoke to other problems associated with dissertation writing, focusing on the need for modification or excision of content. He advised, "Cutting a manuscript is not simply a way of reducing length; it is also a way of strengthening communication. ... By eliminating the unnecessary, communication may be improved" (p. 40). Strive for clarity; get rid of extraneous words; avoid excessive reporting and repetition; be explicit, but not overly detailed; use the active voice; and, of course, use correct grammar.

6.06 *Interpretation of Data*

A common problem in a poorly prepared manuscript derived from a dissertation study is overinterpretation of the data. Inexperienced researchers tend to have unbridled faith in the strength of their results. Carver (1984) identified two examples of the overstatement of results, seen in the Discussion section: "'The results of this research *should generalize . . .*' is used, but the correct wording should be, 'The results of this research *are probably* generalizable.' '*Would be* well advised . . .' is written, but the phrase should be, '*might consider . . .*'" (p. 42).

Problems of overinterpretation in dissertations are not unexpected, given that the candidate has invested much time and energy in an academic undertaking. Thus, going beyond the results may come out of a sense of ownership and pride. Nevertheless, show restraint in forming your conclusions.

In summary, compared with a dissertation, a journal paper requires a tighter theoretical framework, a more succinct review of the literature, a more controlled presentation of methodology, and a more restrained discussion of results.

Material for Oral Presentation

If you are active in research, you will probably have occasion to present a paper at a convention, symposium, workshop, seminar, or other gathering of professionals. The following hints for preparing a paper for oral presentation are derived from McCall (1981) and Schlosberg (1965).

Material delivered verbally should differ from written material in its level of detail, organization, and presentation. Therefore, prepare an oral presentation differently from the way you would prepare a manuscript. Concentrate on only one or two main points, and keep reminding the audience what the central theme is by relating each major section of the presentation to the theme. The speaker's traditional strategy is still valid: Tell the audience what you are going to say, say it, and then tell them what you have said.

Omit most of the details of scientific procedures, because a listener cannot follow the same level of detail as a reader. The audience wants to know (a) what you studied and why, (b) how you went about the research (give a general orientation), (c) what you discovered, and (d) the implications of your results. A verbal presentation should create awareness about a topic and stimulate interest in it; colleagues can retrieve the details from a written paper, copies of which you may want to have available.

Do not read your presentation. Reading a paper usually induces boredom and can make even the best research sound second-rate. Instead, tell your audience what you have to say, just as you would in conversation. Having written notes in front of you while speaking will help you keep your focus, but use an outline of topic sentences rather than a complete manuscript so that you are not tempted to begin reading the paper.

Finally, rehearse your presentation until you can speak comfortably and look at your notes only occasionally. If your presentation includes slides, posters, or other visuals, be sure that they are readable and comprehensible from a distance and that their timing is appropriate. The best rehearsal is under conditions similar to the actual presentation. You are prepared for the oral presentation when you can succinctly tell your audience, eye to eye, what you want them to know.

Material Published in Abbreviated Form

Studies of specialized interest or limited importance are published as Brief Reports in some of the APA journals. A Brief Report, usually one to three typeset journal pages, summarizes the procedure and results of a study. Letters to the editor and comments on published articles also are published in some journals. Refer to the appropriate journals for details.

CHAPTER SEVEN

Manuscript Acceptance and Production

The efficient handling of a manuscript is a responsibility that the author, editor, typesetter, printer, and publisher share. This chapter describes procedures for submitting the manuscript and, if the manuscript is accepted, for handling the edited manuscript and typeset article.[1] You, the author, can contribute to the efficient processing and publication of articles by following the guidelines provided in this chapter.

The specific requirements for submitting a manuscript differ among journals. Therefore, before submitting a manuscript, refer to the most recent issue of the appropriate journal or to the journal's Web site. The journal's inside front cover and Instructions to Authors will tell you (a) the journal's area of coverage, that is, what kinds of manuscripts are appropriate for that journal; (b) the current editor's name and address; and (c) instructions for manuscript preparation and submission specific to that journal, including the number of copies you need to submit and whether the journal routinely uses masked review (see section 8.13).

---

[1] This chapter gives instructions to authors of journal articles. Authors and editors of book manuscripts should follow instructions given by the publisher's book production department.

Transmitting the Accepted Manuscript for Production

7.01 *Copyright Transfer, Certification of Authorship, Disclosure of Interests, and Permissions*

When a manuscript is accepted for publication (see chapter 8 on APA's publication policies and process), the journal editor sends to the author a Publication Rights form regarding copyright and authorship. (If not already dealt with at an earlier stage, the author will also need to provide a statement concerning any conflicts of interest.)

Copyright transfer. The corresponding author (a) transfers the copyright on the published article to APA or (b) certifies that the majority of the authors or the primary authors are employees of the U.S. government and that the work was performed as part of their employment and is not protected by U.S. copyright law (therefore, it is in the public domain). In the case of work performed under U.S. government contract, APA retains the copyright but grants the U.S. government royalty-free permission to reproduce all or portions of the article and authorizes others to do so for U.S. government purposes. APA owns the copyright on APA journal articles for 75 years from the time of publication. The copyright transfer to APA includes both print and electronic rights to the article. This permits APA to (a) more widely distribute the work, (b) control reuse by others, and (c) handle the paperwork involved in copyright registration and administration. APA permits authors to reuse their work in several ways, which are outlined on the Publication Rights form.

Certification of authorship. By signing this part of the Publication Rights form, each author (a) accepts responsibility for the contents of the published article and (b) agrees on the order of authorship. Each author to be named in the byline must sign the certification of authorship. Photocopied or faxed signatures are acceptable for all but the corresponding author, whose signature must be an original one.

Disclosure of interests. Authors are required to sign a form that presents the APA policy on full disclosure of interests and asks authors to indicate financial agreements or affiliations with any product or services used or discussed in their papers, as well as any potential bias against another product or service.

Permission. It is the author's responsibility to (a) obtain letters of permission from copyright holders to reproduce copyrighted material and (b) enclose copies of these letters with the accepted manuscript. The author must acknowledge the copyright holder in a note that accompanies the reproduced material (see section 3.73 for format).

The author needs to allow ample time (several weeks) to secure permission. The main task is to identify the copyright holder at the time of submission and write for permission to reprint or adapt the material in both print and electronic form. Depending on the permissions policies of the copyright holder, permission may be required from both the copyright holder and the author of the requested material. Determining who holds the copyright can be a challenge, particularly for older works, because publishers may merge and copyrights may change hands. The permissions request should specify the source material (title of work, year of publication, page number, etc.) and the nature of the reuse (e.g., reprinting in a journal). Once permissions are granted, the author needs to include a permissions notice in the manuscript, following the wording and format shown in section 3.73 or specific wording at the copyright holder's request, and to send a copy of the copyright holder's permission letter with the accepted manuscript. If there are several permissions for an article, the author should identify on the copy of each permission letter the number of the new table or figure for which the reprinted or adapted work is being used. (See also section 3.41.)

7.02 *Preparing the Word-Processing File for Editing and Typesetting*

APA and many other publishers request that authors who prepare their manuscripts on a computer provide the electronic word-processing file of their manuscripts to the production office for editing and production. When the electronic manuscript file is used in the publication of your article, your original keystrokes are preserved, eliminating the costly and error-prone process of rekeying your article from the paper manuscript during typesetting. You may be asked to provide the electronic manuscript files on disks or by e-mail.

The APA Journals office asks for a copy of the word-processing file that you used to print out the paper manuscript in its final, accepted form, with the following changes:

- Any figures that are embedded in the file should be printed out in final form (see the subsection in section 3.80 on preparing the final print) and then deleted.
- If you used bibliographic software to create your references, please make sure the references are "unlinked" from the text.
- If you used the footnote or endnote function of your word-processing software, move the footnote text to the appropriate spot in the manuscript (following the author note; see sections 5.05 and 5.20) and replace the footnote references with superscript numbers.

The Journals office may also request electronic copies of your figures. TIFF is the preferred file format (either grayscale or black and white, depending on the type of figure (see the subsection in section 3.80 on submitting an electronic version of a figure), as it is most likely to be used successfully by our printers.

> Word processors and graphics software are always changing—go to www.apastyle.org for the latest information on file preparation.

7.03 *Future Correspondence*

The journal editor sends manuscripts accepted for publication to the APA Journals office for copyediting and production. Correspondence about copyediting of the manuscript, proofs, and other production matters should be sent to the Production Editor, in care of the particular journal, American Psychological Association, 750 First Street, NE, Washington, DC 20002-4242. Send correspondence concerning necessary substantive changes to the journal editor. Send address changes to both the journal editor and the APA Journals office. In all correspondence, include the complete article title, authors' names, journal name, and manuscript number.

Reviewing the Copyedited Manuscript

Both journal editors and copy editors introduce changes in manuscripts to correct errors of form, to achieve consistency with APA style, or to clarify expression. After copyediting, APA usually sends the manuscript back to the corresponding author for a review of the editing. The corresponding author needs to review the edited manuscript carefully, being alert for changes in meaning and being attentive to levels of heading and to markup of statistics, equations, and tables. This is also the time to finalize word preferences free of charge. If coauthors participate in the review of the copyedited manuscript, the corresponding author is responsible for consolidating necessary changes into the manuscript and returning it to the production editor and for keeping in touch with the production office. The cover letter from the production office includes instructions for marking changes to the edited manuscript, which differ according to whether the manuscript is edited electronically or on paper.

It is important to keep a copy of the manuscript with your changes marked and to return the copyedited manuscript to the APA Journals office within 48 hours so that the manuscript can be sent to the typesetter on schedule. Delays in returning the manuscript can result in delayed publication.

7.04 *Paper Manuscript*

You should answer the copy editor's queries or indicate changes to the manuscript neatly in the margins of the manuscript or on the tags attached to the manuscript, using *a lead pencil only*; if more detailed responses or changes are necessary, describe them in a cover letter. Substantive changes must be approved by the journal editor. Do not mark changes within the manuscript text, and *do not erase* the copy editor's marks, because such changes often result in typesetting errors. Instead, the copy editor will transfer your changes from the margins, tags, or cover letter to the manuscript text.

7.05 *Electronic Manuscript*

If the electronic version of your manuscript is being used for the editing and production of your article, you will receive either a printout of the text showing the editing changes (by regular mail) or a word-processing file in which the changes have been highlighted (by e-mail). You will also receive queries from the copy editor (these will be embedded in the word-processing file).

If you receive a printout, respond to each query (a) on the query sheet, (b) on the marked-up printout, or (c) in a cover letter. Make any additions or changes to the text in brightly colored ink or colored pencil on the marked-up printout. Keep a copy of the printout for your records, and return the original to the APA Journals office within 48 hours of receipt.

If you receive a word-processing file, respond to each query (a) within the "comments" section of the file or (b) in a return e-mail. Indicate any additions or changes in an e-mail—the copy editor will incorporate them into the master copy of the file in the production office. Respond by fax or e-mail within 48 hours of receipt, and keep a copy of the file and any changes or additions you request.

Proofreading

7.06 *Reading Proofs*

After a manuscript is set in type, the typesetter will send you the manuscript and two sets of typeset proofs (an original proof to read, correct, and return to APA and a duplicate for your files).

First, familiarize yourself with the proofreader's marks in Table 7.1,

Table 7.1. Proofreader's Marks

Margin mark	Mark in typeset text
ℒ	delete; take it out
◡	close up; print as one word
ℛ	delete and close up
a word	caret; insert here
#	insert a space
(eq. #)	space evenly where indicated
(stet)	let marked text stand as set
(tr)	transpose; change order the
/	used to separate two or more marginal marks and often as a concluding stroke after the final of several marginal marks
⌐	☞ set farther to the left
⌐	set farther to the right ⌐
//	// align on margin
☐	☐ indent
¶	¶ begin a new paragraph
(sp)	spell out (set 2 as two)
(OK/?)	the printer will underline or circle a typeset word (or words) to alert the author that the copy may be incorrect but has been set as typed on the manuscript
(cap)	set in capitals (CAPITALS)
(lc)	set in lowercase (lowercase)
(ital)	set in italic (*italic*)
(rom)	set in roman (roman)
(bf)	set in boldface (**boldface**)

Table 7.1. (*continued*)

Margin mark	Mark in typeset text
$\lvert = \rvert$	insert hyphen (self‿imposed)
$\vee$	superscript ($\vee$as in χ^2)
$\wedge$	subscript ($\wedge$as in H_2O)
$\diamondsuit$	centered ($\diamondsuit$for a centered dot in $p \cdot q$)
$\wedge,$	insert comma (yes‿whereas)
$\overset{\cdot}{\vee}$	insert apostrophe (editors‿)
$\odot$	insert period (end‿Then)
;	insert semicolon (this‿in)
:	insert colon (Tests‿Part 1)
$\vee/\vee$	insert quotation marks (‿less than‿comparative)
$(\,\vert\,)$	insert parentheses ‿only two‿
$[\,\vert\,]$	insert brackets (these‿12‿subjects)

Note. Authors, editors, and printers use proofreader's marks to indicate changes on printed proofs. These standard marks are used in pairs, one in the text where the change is to be made and one in the margin closest to the change. Adapted from *Merriam-Webster's Collegiate® Dictionary*, Tenth Edition © 1993 by Merriam-Webster, Inc. Adapted with permission.

and use them when marking corrections (using ink or colored pencil) on the page proofs of your article (see Figure 7.1).

Second, check the typeset proofs word for word against the manuscript to catch typographical errors. Another person (a copyholder) should read the manuscript aloud slowly while you read the proof; this technique is especially useful for proofreading tables. The copyholder should spell out complicated terms letter by letter and call out punctuation to catch all deviations from the manuscript. If there is no copyholder, proofread by reading word for word from the manuscript to the proof. Third, give the proof a literal read to catch any remaining errors.

Limit changes on these printed proofs to corrections of production errors and to updates of reference citations or addresses. This is not the time to rewrite the text. Changes that reflect preferences in wording should have been made at the time the edited manuscript was reviewed.

Third, check specific points:

- Are all queries fully answered?
- Is the hierarchy of headings and subheadings correct?
- Are all numbers and symbols in text, tables, and mathematical and statistical copy correct?
- Are tables correct? Do they show correct alignment? Are table notes, superscripts, and footnotes correct?
- Are figures correct? Do they carry correct captions and numbers? Are all labels properly spelled? Do symbols in the legends match those in the figure? Are halftones an acceptable reproduction of your photographs?

7.07 *Author's Alterations*

The purpose of proofreading is to ensure that the typeset page matches the edited manuscript. A change made on the proof for a reason other than achieving agreement with the edited manuscript is an author's alteration. All changes at the proof stage that result from your own error, omission, or failure to review the edited manuscript are charged to you as author's alterations; such charges include changing the edited version at the proofreading stage to reinstate the wording before editing.

The cost of author's alterations is computed according to the number of printed lines and pages affected by a change, and such alterations are costly. For example, the insertion or deletion of a single word may involve resetting several lines and remaking several pages. When a change on the proofs is essential, you should plan the alteration to minimize cost and

Figure 7.1. Marking proofs. (See section 7.06.)

Sample of a Proof Marked for Correction

(ital)/in   Make all marks in <u>colored pencil</u> or ink. Mark all corrections on the proofs; never alter the manuscript when correcting proofs. Because the original proofs are used by the Typesetter, mark neatly (lc)/#♯ using conventional proofreader's marks (see Table 7.1). When you find an error, make two marks, one in the text in the exact place where the correction is to be made and one in the margin next to the line in which the error occurs. Together the marks show exactly what is to be done. In the margin, circle words or abbreviations that are instructions. Do not circle words that new copy, and do not are circle symbols. For more than one correction in a single line, mark the corrections from left to right in the nearest margin, and separate them by a slanted line (/) for clarity. do not try to (cap) squeeze corrections between the printed lines. Include any special
an/(lc)/(ital)   instructions or questions in accompanying letter; do <u>Not</u> write them on the proofs.

Sample of a Corrected Proof

Make all marks in *colored pencil* or in ink. Mark all corrections on the proofs; never alter the manuscript when correcting proofs. Because the original proofs are used by the typesetter, mark them neatly using conventional proofreader's marks (see Table 7.1). When you find an error, make two marks, one in the text in the exact place where the correction is to be made and one in the margin next to the line in which the error occurs. Together the marks show exactly what is to be done. In the margin, circle words or abbreviations that are instructions. Do not circle words that are new copy, and do not circle symbols. For more than one correction in a single line, mark the corrections from left to right in the nearest margin, and separate them by a slanted line (/) for clarity. Do not try to squeeze corrections between the printed lines. Include any special instructions or questions in an accompanying letter; do *not* write them on the proofs.

confusion. For example, count the number of characters and spaces to be removed, and make an insertion that will use as nearly as possible the same number of characters and spaces. Print all changes clearly in the margin of the proof, or, if the changes are long, type them on a separate sheet attached to the proof. Indicate clearly on the proof where the correction is to be inserted. Any change in a figure means that you need to submit a revised, new print of the figure. Because the printer must rescan the figure, corrections to figures are especially costly. Alterations to columns and rows in tables and alterations to page layout are also expensive. In addition to the expense, numerous author's alterations can cause delays in publication and often lead to new errors. You can avoid alteration charges if you carefully review the edited manuscript before it is typeset. If you make extensive additions or deletions on the proof, the journal editor must approve the changes.

7.08 *Returning Proofs and Manuscript*

Copy all corrections on the original proofs onto your duplicate proofs (or make a photocopy of the corrected proofs), and retain the duplicate proofs for reference. Mail the original proofs and the manuscript within 48 hours of receipt to the Production Editor, in care of the particular journal, American Psychological Association, 750 First Street, NE, Washington, DC 20002-4242. If you do not return proofs promptly, publication may be delayed.

7.09 *Ordering Reprints*

You may order reprints of your article from the printer. You will receive a reprint order form and pricing information with your proofs. To obtain reprints, you must return the completed form to the printer at the time you are expected to return the proofs and the original manuscript to APA. Reprint rates vary according to the length of the article and the number of copies ordered. Reprints are usually delivered 6 to 8 weeks after publication of the article. Problems with reprint orders should be referred to a production manager in APA's Journals office.

Authors who publish articles in APA journals are permitted to reproduce their own articles for personal use without obtaining permission from APA as long as the material incorporates the copyright notice that appears on the original publication. Reproduction of your own articles for other than personal use requires written permission from APA. (See section 8.07 for more information on permission to reproduce APA-copyrighted material.)

After the Article Is Published

7.10 *Retaining Raw Data*

It is traditional in scientific publishing to retain data, instructions, coding systems, details of procedure, and analyses so that copies may be made available in response to inquiries from interested readers (see section 8.05). Therefore, you are expected to retain these materials for a minimum of 5 years after your article has been published.

Initial observations may take many forms, including, for example, participant responses to individual test or survey items, videotapes of participant performances, interviewer or observer notes, and physiological recordings. They need to be retained in a form that to the extent possible ensures that the information available to the original researcher is also available to the researcher seeking to confirm the original findings. For example, retaining only an electronic data file containing scale scores derived from a questionnaire is insufficient. A scoring or coding system for the logging or transformation of data should also be retained. The author's main concern when choosing the archival form for retaining data is to ensure that no information is lost and not to choose simply the most expedient means of archiving (e.g., using optical scanners to record response sheets may be problematic; Sackett, 2000).

7.11 *Correction Notices*

From time to time, errors occur in published journal articles. APA is not obligated to publish corrections for minor errors, but it will publish a correction promptly when an important piece of information in a journal article is incorrect, misleading, incomprehensible, or omitted. The decision to publish a correction rests with the journal editor unless the error is typographical, in which case the APA Journals office and the journal editor determine whether a published correction is warranted.

If you detect an error in your published article and think that a correction notice is warranted, submit a proposed correction notice to the journal editor. The notice should contain the following elements: (a) full journal title and year, volume number, issue number, and inclusive page numbers of the article being corrected; (b) complete article title and names of all authors, exactly as they appear in the published article; (c) precise location of the error (e.g., page, column, line); (d) exact quotation of the error or, in the case of lengthy errors or an error in a table or figure, an accurate paraphrasing of the error; and (e) concise, unambiguous wording of the correction. Because it is not the purpose of corrections to place blame for mistakes, correction notices do not identify the source of the error.

The cost of typesetting a notice to correct your own error is charged to you as an author's alteration. Such a notice can be expensive, particularly if the correction requires the resetting of tables or the reshooting of figures. You are more likely to avoid the kinds of errors requiring a correction notice if you carefully prepare the manuscript, carefully review the copyedited manuscript, and carefully review the typeset proofs.

CHAPTER EIGHT

Journals Program of the American Psychological Association

The American Psychological Association, founded in 1892 and incorporated in 1925, is the major organization of psychologists in the United States and includes more than 155,000 members. The mission of APA is to advance psychology as a science, as a profession, and as a means of promoting human welfare. One way APA accomplishes this mission is by disseminating psychological information through its publication program, of which scholarly journals are a major component.

Policies Governing the Journals

The policies and practices of the APA journals are based on formal actions of APA's governing bodies and on informal consensus and tradition. The association's Bylaws and Rules of Council state general journal policies enacted by APA's Council of Representatives. The Publications and Communications Board is one of several boards reporting to the APA Board of Directors, which in turn reports to the Council of Representatives. The Publications and Communications Board regularly assesses trends in the major areas of psychology and in specific journals and recommends the establishment, modification, or discontinuation of journals. The Council of Editors, a permanent committee established under the Publications and Communications Board, includes the editors of all journals published by APA. It meets to discuss commonly shared editorial problems and to make recommendations about specific journal policies and practices.

Thus, the Publications and Communications Board and the Council of Editors together establish specific policies for the journals. Journal editors and APA staff concerned with the publication of the journals implement the policies. Editors, operating within the framework of the general policies and ethical principles described in this chapter, select the manuscripts to be published in the journals. The APA staff produces the journals. Authors should review the policies and ethical principles described here for general orientation and also should note specific instructions published in every journal and policies of style and manuscript preparation described in the preceding chapters of the *Publication Manual*.

8.01 *Selection of Editors*

The Publications and Communications Board appoints the editors of journals on the recommendation of search committees that actively seek nominations of persons who have attained recognition in a journal's special area and are members of APA. Editors normally serve terms of 6 years. The editor appoints the number of associate editors authorized for the journal and selects as many consulting or advisory reviewers and ad hoc reviewers as are needed for the effective functioning of the journal. As many as 7,500 persons may participate each year as editors, associate editors, consulting or advisory reviewers, and ad hoc reviewers. The Publications and Communications Board and the editors of APA journals make an effort to include women and members of underrepresented groups as participants in the review process.

8.02 *Page Allocations*

Each year the Publications and Communications Board provides an allotment of printed pages for each of the journals. In making such allocations, the Board considers the number of manuscripts submitted to a journal, the journal's acceptance rate and publication lag, the availability of other publication outlets, and the potential loss to psychology from delays in publication or from rejection of manuscripts caused by restrictions on the journal's page allocation. The Board requires each editor to adhere to the journal's page allocation and to keep the publication lag from being unduly long.

8.03 *Publication Lag*

The interval between the date a manuscript is accepted and the date the manuscript is published is the *publication lag*. The publication lag varies from journal to journal but normally is about 7 months. The publication lag of each of the journals is given in the Summary Report of Journal Operations, which appears each year in the archival issue of the *American Psychologist*.

8.04 *Primary Publication*

Members of the scientific community generally agree that the characteristics of primary, or original, publication are that (a) articles represent research not previously published (i.e., first disclosure; see section 8.05), (b) articles are reviewed by peers before being accepted or rejected by a journal, and (c) articles are archival (i.e., retrievable for future reference).

Like a wall that is built one brick at a time, the peer-reviewed literature in a field is built by single contributions that together represent the accumulated knowledge of a field. Each contribution must fill a place that before was empty, and each contribution must be sturdy enough to bear the weight of contributions to come. To ensure the quality of each contribution—that the work is original, valid, and significant—authorities in the subspecialties of a field carefully review submitted manuscripts. The peer-reviewed journals in which the literature is preserved thus serve as "journals of record, that is, authoritative sources of information in their field" (Orne, 1981, p. 3). In the APA primary journals, the standard of primary publication is supported by the peer-reviewed system and protected by policies that prohibit multiple submission and duplicate publication.

8.05 *Ethics of Scientific Publication*

Much of this *Publication Manual* addresses scientific writing style. Style involves no inherent right or wrong. It is merely a conventional way of presenting information that is designed to ease communication. Different scholarly disciplines have different publication styles.

In contrast, there are basic ethical principles that underlie all scholarly writing. These long-standing ethical principles are designed to achieve two goals:

1. to ensure the accuracy of scientific and scholarly knowledge, and
2. to protect intellectual property rights.

The "Ethical Principles of Psychologists and Code of Conduct" (APA, 1992a) contain a number of principles that address the reporting and publishing of scientific data. Principles 5.01–5.10 and 6.06–6.26 are listed in Appendix C, and some are described in this section in greater detail. Please note that the "Ethical Principles of Psychologists and Code of Conduct" is not a static document—it will be revised and updated over time.

> Consult the APA Web site for the latest information on the Ethical Principles relevant to publishing at www.apastyle.org

Reporting of results (Principle 6.21). The essence of the scientific method involves observations that can be repeated and verified by others. Hence, psychologists do not make up data or modify their results to support a hypothesis (Principle 6.21a). Errors of omission also are prohibited. Psychologists do not omit troublesome observations from their reports so as to present a more convincing story.

Careful preparation of manuscripts for publication is essential, but errors can still occur. It is the author's responsibility to make such errors public if they are discovered after publication (Principle 6.21b). The first step is to inform the editor and the publisher so that a correction notice can be published (see section 7.11 on wording). The goal of such a correction is to correct the knowledge base so that the error is brought to the attention of future users of the information. Corrections published in APA journals are connected with the original article in the PsycARTICLES database so that the correction will be retrieved whenever the original article is retrieved.

Plagiarism (Principle 6.22). Psychologists do not claim the words and ideas of another as their own; they give credit where credit is due. Quotation marks should be used to indicate the exact words of another. *Each time* you paraphrase another author (i.e., summarize a passage or rearrange the order of a sentence and change some of the words), you will need to credit the source in the text. The following paragraph is an example of how one might appropriately paraphrase some of the foregoing material in this section:

> As stated in the fifth edition of the *Publication Manual of the American Psychological Association*, the ethical principles of scientific publication are designed to ensure the integrity of scientific knowledge and to protect the intellectual property rights of others. As the *Publication Manual* explains, authors are expected to correct the record if they discover errors in their publications; they are also expected to give credit to others for their prior work when it is quoted or paraphrased.

The key element of this principle is that an author does not present the work of another as if it were his or her own work. This can extend to ideas as well as written words. If an author models a study after one done by someone else, the originating author should be given credit. If the rationale for a study was suggested in the Discussion section of someone else's article, that person should be given credit. Given the free exchange of ideas, which is very important to the health of psychology, an author may not know where an idea for a study originated. If the author does know, however, the author should acknowledge the source;

Ethics

this includes personal communications. (For additional information on quotations and paraphrasing, see sections 3.34–3.41; for instructions on referencing publications and personal communications, see sections 3.94–3.103.)

Publication credit (authorship; Principle 6.23, a–c). Authorship is reserved for persons who receive primary credit and hold primary responsibility for a published work.

Authorship encompasses, therefore, not only those who do the actual writing but also those who have made substantial scientific contributions to a study. Substantial professional contributions may include formulating the problem or hypothesis, structuring the experimental design, organizing and conducting the statistical analysis, interpreting the results, or writing a major portion of the paper. Those who so contribute are listed in the byline. Lesser contributions, which do not constitute authorship, may be acknowledged in a note (see section 3.89). These contributions may include such supportive functions as designing or building the apparatus, suggesting or advising about the statistical analysis, collecting or entering the data, modifying or structuring a computer program, and recruiting participants or obtaining animals. Conducting routine observations or diagnoses for use in studies does not constitute authorship. Combinations of these (and other) tasks, however, may justify authorship. As early as practicable in a research project, the collaborators should decide on which tasks are necessary for the project's completion, how the work will be divided, which tasks or combination of tasks merits authorship credit, and on what level credit should be given (first author, second author, etc.; Fine & Kurdek, 1993). This is especially appropriate if one of the collaborators is new to the publishing process.

Collaborators may need to reassess authorship credit and order if major changes are necessary in the course of the project (and its publication). This is especially true in faculty–student collaborations, when students may need intensive supervision or additional analyses are required beyond the scope of a student's thesis or dissertation (Fine & Kurdek, 1993).

Ethics

The corresponding author (the author who serves as the main contact) should always obtain a person's consent before including that person's name in a byline or in a note. Each author listed in the byline of an article should review the entire manuscript before it is submitted.

Authors are responsible for determining authorship and for specifying the order in which two or more authors' names appear in the byline. The general rule is that the name of the principal contributor should appear first, with subsequent names in order of decreasing contribution. If authors played equal roles in the research and publication of their study, they may wish to note this in the second paragraph of the author note (see section 3.89).

Authors are also responsible for the factual accuracy of their contributions. The opinions and statements published are the responsibility of the authors, and such opinions and statements do not necessarily represent the policies of APA or the views of the editors.

When a paper is accepted by an editor, each person listed in the byline must verify in writing that he or she agrees to serve as an author and accepts the responsibilities of authorship (see the section on authors' responsibilities at the beginning of chapter 5).

Duplicate publication of data (Principle 6.24). Duplicate publication distorts the knowledge base by making it appear there is more information available than really exists. It also wastes scarce resources (journal pages and the time and efforts of editors and reviewers). Duplicate publication can also lead to copyright violations; an author cannot assign the copyright to more than one publisher.

An author must not submit to an APA journal a manuscript describing work that has been published in whole or in substantial part elsewhere. This policy does not necessarily exclude from consideration manuscripts previously published in abstracted form (e.g., in the proceedings of an annual meeting) or in a periodical with limited circulation or availability (e.g., in a report by a university department or by a government agency). This policy does exclude the same or overlapping material that has appeared in a publication that has been offered for public sale, such as conference proceedings or a book chapter; such a publication does not meet the criterion of "limited circulation." Publication of a Brief Report in an APA journal is with the understanding that an extended report will not be published elsewhere; the Brief Report is the archival record for the work. Problems of duplicate publication may also arise if material is first published through the mass media.

The same manuscript must not be submitted to more than one publisher at the same time. Submission of a manuscript implies commitment to publish in the journal if the article is accepted for publication. Authors submitting manuscripts to a journal should not simultaneously submit them to another journal, nor should they submit manuscripts that have been published elsewhere in substantially similar form or with substantially similar content. Authors in doubt about what constitutes prior publication should consult with the editor. If a manuscript is rejected by one journal, an author may then submit it to another.

Whether the publication of two or more reports based on the same or on closely related research constitutes duplicate publication is a matter of editorial judgment. Any prior publication should be noted (see section 3.89) and referenced in the manuscript, and the author must inform the journal editor of the existence of any similar manuscripts that have already been published or accepted for publication or that may be submitted for concurrent consideration to the same journal or elsewhere. The editor can then make an informed judgment as to whether the submitted manuscript includes sufficient new information to warrant consideration. If, during the review or production process, a manuscript is discovered to be in violation of duplicate publication policies and the author has failed to inform the editor of the possible violation, then the manuscript is rejected without further consideration. If such a violation is discovered after publication in an APA journal, appropriate action will be taken.

The author is obligated to present work parsimoniously and as completely as possible within the space constraints of journal publications. Data that can be meaningfully combined within a single publication should be presented together to enhance effective communication. Piecemeal, or fragmented, publication of several reports of the results from a single study is undesirable unless there is a clear benefit to scientific communication. An author who wishes to divide the report of a study into more than one article should inform the editor and provide such information as the editor requests. Whether the publication of two or more reports based on the same or on closely related research constitutes fragmented publication is a matter of editorial judgment.

The prohibition of piecemeal publication does not preclude subsequent reanalysis of published data in light of new theories or methodologies if the reanalysis is clearly labeled as such. There may be times, especially in the instances of large-scale or multidisciplinary projects, when it is both necessary and appropriate to publish multiple reports. Multidisciplinary projects often address diverse topics, and publishing in a single journal may be inappropriate. Repeated publication from a longitudinal study is often appropriate because the data from different times make unique scientific contributions; useful knowledge should be made available to others as soon as possible.

As multiple reports from large-scale or longitudinal studies are made, the author is obligated to cite prior reports on the project to help the reader evaluate the work accurately. For example, in the early years of a longitudinal study, one might cite all previous publications from it. For a well-known or very long-term longitudinal study, one might cite the original publication, a more recent summary, and earlier articles that focused on the same or related scientific questions addressed in the current report. Often it is not necessary to repeat the description of the design and methods of a longitudinal or large-scale project in its entirety. The author may refer the reader to an earlier publication for this detailed information. It is important, however, to provide sufficient information so that the reader can evaluate the current report. It is also important to make clear the degree of sample overlap in multiple reports from large studies. Again, authors should inform and consult with the editor.

Journal articles sometimes are revised for publication as book chapters. The author has a responsibility to reveal to the reader that portions of the new work were previously published and to cite and reference the

Ethics

source. If copyright is owned by a publisher or by another person, the author must acknowledge copyright and obtain permission to adapt or reproduce.

Data verification. Researchers must make their data available to the editor at any time during the review and production process if questions arise with respect to the accuracy of the report (see section 7.10). Otherwise, the submitted manuscript can be rejected.

To permit competent professionals to confirm the results and analyses, authors are expected to retain raw data for a minimum of 5 years after publication of the research. Other information related to the research (e.g., instructions, treatment manuals, software, details of procedures) should be kept for the same period. This information is necessary if others are to attempt replication. Authors are expected to comply promptly and in a spirit of cooperation with such requests (Principle 6.25). Sometimes special concerns must be addressed, such as confidentiality of the participants and proprietary or other concerns of the sponsor of the research (Frankel, 1993). Generally, the costs of complying with the request should be borne by the requester.

To avoid misunderstandings, it is important for the researcher requesting data and the researcher providing data to come to a written agreement about the conditions under which the data are to be shared. Such an agreement should include a statement about whether the data to be shared are for verification or for other purposes; a specific description of the analyses to be conducted by the requester and the limitations thereof; a statement about whether sharing the provided data with others is permissible; and an agreement about how the findings of the analysis are to be made public, especially how authorship will be decided.

Professional reviewers (Principle 6.26). Editorial review of a manuscript requires that the editors and reviewers circulate and discuss the manuscript. During the review process, the manuscript is a confidential and privileged document. Editors and reviewers may not, without the author's explicit permission, quote from a manuscript under review or circulate copies of it for any purpose other than that of editorial review (see section 8.06). If a reviewer consults with a colleague about some aspect of the manuscript, the reviewer should inform the editor. In addition, editors and reviewers may not use the material from an unpublished manuscript to advance their own or others' work without the author's consent.

Research participants. Principles 6.06–6.20 specify the standards psychologists are to follow in conducting research with humans and animals. Authors are required to certify (in the cover letter that accompanies a submission, in the description of participants in the text of the manuscript, or by signing a form sent by the editor) that they have followed these standards as a precondition of publishing their articles in APA journals. Failure to follow these standards can be grounds for rejecting a manuscript for publication or for retraction of a published article.

8.06 *Author's Copyright on an Unpublished Manuscript*

Authors are protected by federal statute against unauthorized use of their unpublished manuscripts. Under the Copyright Act of 1976 (title 17 of the *United States Code*), an unpublished work is copyrighted from the moment it is fixed in tangible form—for example, typed on a page. Copyright protection is "an incident of the process of authorship" (U.S. Copyright Office, 1981, p. 3). Until the author formally transfers copyright (see section 7.01), the author owns the copyright on an unpublished manuscript, and all exclusive rights due the owner of the copyright of a published work are also due the author of an unpublished work. To ensure copyright protection, include the copyright notice on all published works. The notice need not appear on unpublished works. Registration of copyright provides a public record and is usually a prerequisite for any legal action.

Suspected infringements of the author's copyright on a manuscript submitted to an APA journal should be referred to the Chair of the APA Publications and Communications Board.

8.07 *Copyright and Permission to Reproduce APA Material*

APA owns the copyright on material published in its journals (see section 7.01 on the author's transfer of copyright to APA). Therefore, authors who wish to reproduce an APA article in full, to quote text of more than 500 words, or to copy two or more tables or figures must secure written permission from APA and from the author of the reproduced material. APA normally grants permission contingent on permission by the author; inclusion of the APA copyright notice on the first page of reproduced material; and payment of a fee per table, figure, or page. Requests for permission to reproduce material should be directed to APA's Permissions Office.

APA requires no written permission or fees when

- authors of manuscripts being considered for publication reproduce or adapt a *single* table or figure from an article, provided that permission from the author of the original, published work is obtained and that full credit is given to that author and to APA as copyright holder through a complete and accurate citation;
- authors reproduce their own material for personal use (e.g., to prepare reprints)—however, if they use their own material commercially, authors must secure prior written permission from APA;
- instructors and educational institutions photocopy isolated articles for nonprofit classroom or library reserve use; and
- abstracting and indexing services use abstracts.

Libraries are permitted to photocopy beyond the limits of U.S. copyright law provided that the per-copy fee is paid through the Copyright Clearance Center, 222 Rosewood Drive, Danvers, Massachusetts 01923.

8.08 *Other Copyrighted Material*

Material copyrighted by sources other than APA. Copyright policies vary among publishers. Authors submitting manuscripts to APA who wish to reproduce material from non-APA-copyrighted sources must contact the copyright holders (usually the publishers) to determine their requirements (see section 7.01).

Editorial Management of Manuscripts

8.09 *Editorial Responsibilities*

The *editor* of each journal is responsible for the quality and content of the journal within the framework of the policies and rules of procedure established for the journals by APA. An *associate editor* of a journal assists the editor in the editorial management of the journal and usually has responsibility for a specific content area of the journal or for a portion of the manuscripts submitted to the journal. An associate editor may act as editor in all stages of the consideration of a manuscript, including communication with an author regarding acceptance, rejection, or required revision of a manuscript. *Consulting and advisory reviewers* and *ad hoc reviewers* review manuscripts and make recommendations to editors or to associate editors concerning the disposition of manuscripts.

The *production managers, supervisors, technical production editors* (also called *copy editors*), and *electronic publishing specialists* are on the staff of the APA central office. They copyedit, proofread, provide quality assurance, and manage the production of APA journals.

8.10 *Date of Receipt of Manuscripts*

When a manuscript is received in an editor's office, its date of receipt is noted, and, usually within 48 hours, the editor sends an acknowledgment of its receipt to the author. If the manuscript is accepted for publication, the printed version will show the date the manuscript was originally received in the editor's office, the date on which an acceptable revision was received (most articles carry this date, but a few manuscripts do not need revision), and the date the manuscript was accepted. The *American Psychologist* and *Contemporary Psychology: APA Review of Books* do not publish these dates.

8.11 *Order of Publication of Articles*

Most APA editors publish articles in the order of their receipt. Editors may (a) advance or delay publication of an article for the purpose of assembling issues on related topics or (b) advance publication of an article for reasons such as timeliness (e.g., brief articles of comment and reply) or importance of material. APA staff may, with the editor's knowledge, advance or delay publication of an article in the interest of creating an issue with the most economical number of pages as determined by printing requirements.

The order of publication of articles in the *American Psychologist* is determined by the requirements of official APA documents and by the necessity for timely publication of certain reports and articles.

8.12 *Procedures in Editorial Review*

After the editor has acknowledged the receipt of a manuscript, the manuscript is reviewed (see Figure 8.1 on the APA publication process). By submitting a manuscript to an APA journal, an author implicitly consents to the circulation of copies and to the discussion of the manuscript that are necessary for editorial review. The editor may accept or reject a manuscript outright, that is, before its review by an associate editor or by reviewers. Most of the time, however, the editor sends the manuscript to an associate editor or to reviewers. Editors and associate editors usually send manuscripts to two reviewers, and sometimes to more than two. Some editors routinely use a system of masked review; others use masked review at the author's request (see section 8.13).

The period of review can vary, depending both on the length and complexity of the manuscript and on the number of reviewers asked to evaluate it, but the review process typically takes 2 to 3 months. After 2 or 3 months, the author can expect to be notified either of the action taken on the manuscript or, if a delay occurs before or during the review process, of the status of the manuscript. If not notified in 3 months, the author may appropriately contact the editor for information.

Reviewers provide the editor with an evaluation of the manuscript's quality and appropriateness for the journal (see section 8.14). The de-

Figure 8.1. The APA Publication Process

Author submits manuscript to editor ◄─────────────────────┐
│   │
Editor acknowledges receipt   │
of manuscript   │
│   │
Reviewers and editors review   │
manuscript   │
│──────────────┬──────────────┬──────────────┐   │
│   Acceptance   │   │
│   conditional on   Rejection   │   │
│   satisfactory   encouraging   │   │
ACCEPTANCE   revision   revision   Rejection │
│   │   │   │   │
│   Author submits   Author may revise │   │
│   revised manuscript manuscript and   │   │
│   to editor   resubmit ─────────┴────────────┘
│
Author receives and signs Publication
Rights form, Disclosure of Interests
form, and, if needed, ethical compliance
form, and returns form(s) and any
needed letters of permission to reproduce
or adapt copyrighted material to editor
│
Editor sends manuscript and disk
(if available) to APA for editing
│
PRODUCTION
│
APA production editor usually sends
edited manuscript to author for review
│
Author reviews edited manuscript,
answers queries, and returns
manuscript to APA within 48 hours
│
APA sends manuscript and disk
(if available) to typesetter
│
Typesetter sends manuscript, proofs,
and reprint order form to author
│
Author proofreads and mails proofs   Author completes reprint order
and manuscript to APA within 48 hours   form and sends to printer
│   │
PUBLICATION   │
│   Printer sends reprints to author
│   │
APA sends bill for author   Printer sends bill for
alterations to author   reprints to author

cision to accept a manuscript, to reject it, or to ask for revision is the responsibility of the editor (or, in some cases, of an associate editor); the editor's decision may differ from the recommendation of any or all reviewers. The editor may accept a manuscript on the condition that the author make satisfactory revisions. Such conditional acceptances may involve, for example, reanalysis, reinterpretation, or correction of flaws in presentation and organization.

Most manuscripts need to be revised, and some manuscripts need to be revised more than once (revision does not guarantee acceptance). Initial revisions of a manuscript may reveal to the author or to the editor and reviewers deficiencies that were not apparent in the original manuscript, and the editor may request further revision to correct these deficiencies. During the review process, an editor may ask an author to supply material that supplements the manuscript (e.g., complex statistical tables, instructions to participants).

When necessary revisions involve correcting basic flaws in content, the editor may reject the manuscript but invite resubmission of a revised manuscript.

If the editor rejects a manuscript or returns it to the author for revision, the editor explains why the manuscript is rejected or why the revisions are required. The editor does not have to provide the reviewers' comments to the author but frequently chooses to do so. Editors do not undertake the major editorial revision of manuscripts. Authors are expected to follow editors' detailed recommendations for revising, condensing, or correcting and retyping to conform with the style specified by the *Publication Manual*. When resubmitting a revised manuscript, authors are encouraged to enclose a cover letter responding to all the reviewers' comments (whether authors agree or disagree with the comments). Should editors wish to undertake major changes themselves, they will consult with the author.

If a manuscript is rejected, the journal editor retains one copy, and other copies are destroyed. If the author believes a pertinent point was overlooked or misunderstood by the reviewers, the author may appeal the editor's decision by contacting the editor. If the author is not satisfied with the response, the next step is to contact the Chief Editorial Advisor. If a satisfactory resolution is still not achieved, the author may appeal to the Publications and Communications Board.

8.13 *Masked Review*

The APA journal editors, either routinely or at the author's request, use masked review. Masked review requires that the identity of the author of a manuscript be concealed from reviewers during the review process. Authors should read the Instructions to Authors, a statement published in every issue of every journal, to determine whether a journal routinely uses masked review or offers masked review to authors who request it. Authors are responsible for concealing their identities in manuscripts that are to receive masked review: For example, the author note must be typed on the manuscript's title page, which the editor removes before the manuscript is reviewed (see sections 5.06 and 5.15).

8.14 *Evaluation of Manuscripts*

The goal of the APA primary journals is to publish useful original information that is accurate and clear. For this reason, editors and reviewers look for a manuscript that

- makes an original, valid, and significant contribution to an area of psychology appropriate to the journal to which it is submitted;
- conveys its message clearly and as briefly as its content permits; and
- is in a form that follows the style described in the *Publication Manual.*

A manuscript that does not fully meet the second criterion but is otherwise acceptable is returned to the author for revision prior to further editorial consideration. A manuscript that does not meet the third criterion may be returned for revision prior to any editorial consideration. Some specific questions that may help the author assess the quality of a manuscript against these general criteria are given in the sections on quality of content and quality of presentation in chapter 1.

CHAPTER NINE

Bibliography

This bibliography is in three sections: The first section, which gives the historical background of the APA *Publication Manual*, lists the predecessors of this edition in chronological order. The second section is an alphabetical listing of all references cited in the *Publication Manual*. The third section, which is subdivided and annotated, suggests further reading.

9.01 *History of the* Publication Manual

Instructions in regard to preparation of manuscript. (1929). *Psychological Bulletin, 26,* 57–63.

Anderson, J. E., & Valentine, W. L. (1944). The preparation of articles for publication in the journals of the American Psychological Association. *Psychological Bulletin, 41,* 345–376.

American Psychological Association, Council of Editors. (1952). Publication manual of the American Psychological Association. *Psychological Bulletin, 49*(Suppl., Pt. 2), 389–449.

American Psychological Association, Council of Editors. (1957). *Publication manual of the American Psychological Association* (Rev. ed.). Washington, DC: Author.

American Psychological Association. (1967). *Publication manual of the American Psychological Association* (Rev. ed.). Washington, DC: Author.

American Psychological Association. (1974). *Publication manual of the American Psychological Association* (2nd ed.). Washington, DC: Author.

American Psychological Association. (1983). *Publication manual of the American Psychological Association* (3rd ed.). Washington, DC: Author.

American Psychological Association. (1994). *Publication manual of the American Psychological Association* (4th ed.). Washington, DC: Author.

9.02 *References Cited in This Edition*

American Psychological Association. (1984). *Preparing abstracts for journal articles and Psychological Abstracts* [Draft]. Washington, DC: Author.

American Psychological Association. (1992a). Ethical principles of psychologists and code of conduct. *American Psychologist, 47,* 1597–1611.

American Psychological Association. (1992b). *PsycINFO user manual.* Washington, DC: Author.

Armstrong, R. P. (1972). The dissertation's deadly sins. *Scholarly Publishing, 3,* 241–247.

Bartol, K. M. (1981, August). *Survey results from editorial board members: Lethal and nonlethal errors.* Paper presented at the meeting of the American Psychological Association, Los Angeles.

The bluebook: A uniform system of citation (17th ed.). (2000). Cambridge, MA: Harvard Law Review Association.

Boston, B. O. (1992, November). Portraying people with disabilities: Toward a new vocabulary. *The Editorial Eye, 15,* 1–3, 6–7.

Bruner, K. F. (1942). Of psychological writing: Being some valedictory remarks on style. *Journal of Abnormal and Social Psychology, 37,* 52–70.

Calfee, R. C., & Valencia, R. R. (2001). *APA guide to preparing manuscripts for journal publication.* Washington, DC: American Psychological Association.

Carver, R. P. (1984). *Writing a publishable research report in education, psychology, and related disciplines.* Springfield, IL: Charles C Thomas.

Cleveland, W. S. (1994). *Visualizing data.* Summit, NJ: Hobart Press.

Cohen, J. (1988). *Statistical power analysis for the behavioral sciences* (2nd ed.). Hillsdale, NJ: Erlbaum.

Cone, J. D., & Foster, S. L. (1993). *Dissertations and theses from start to finish: Psychology and related fields.* Washington, DC: American Psychological Association.

Ehrenberg, A. S. C. (1977). Rudiments of numeracy. *Journal of the Royal Statistical Society A, 140*(Pt. 3), 277–297.

Fine, M. A., & Kurdek, L. A. (1993). Reflections on determining authorship credit and authorship order on faculty–student collaborations. *American Psychologist, 48,* 1141–1147.

Frankel, M. S. (1993). Professional societies and responsible research conduct. In *Responsible science: Ensuring the integrity of the research process* (Vol. 2, pp. 26–49). Washington, DC: National Academy Press.

Holmes, O. (1974–1975). Thesis to book: What to get rid of. *Scholarly Publishing, 6,* 40–50.

Holt, R. R. (1959). Researchmanship or how to write a dissertation in clinical psychology without really trying. *American Psychologist, 14,* 151.

Huth, E. J. (1987). Prose style. In *Medical style and format* (pp. 260–287). Philadelphia: ISI Press.

Instructions in regard to preparation of manuscript. (1929). *Psychological Bulletin, 26,* 57–63.

Jacobson, N. S., & Truax, P. (1991). Clinical significance: A statistical approach to defining meaningful change in psychotherapy research. *Journal of Consulting and Clinical Psychology, 59,* 12–19.

Kendall, P. C. (Ed.). (1999). Clinical significance [Special section]. *Journal of Consulting and Clinical Psychology, 67,* 283–339.

Knatterud, M. E. (1991, February). Writing with the patient in mind: Don't add insult to injury. *American Medical Writers Association Journal, 6,* 10–17.

Lalumière, M. L. (1993). Increasing the precision of citations in scientific writing. *American Psychologist, 48*, 913.

Maggio, R. (1991). *The bias-free word finder: A dictionary of nondiscriminatory language.* Boston: Beacon Press.

Maher, B. A. (1974). Editorial. *Journal of Consulting and Clinical Psychology, 42*, 1–3.

McCall, R. B. (1981). *Writing strategy and style.* Unpublished manuscript.

Merriam-Webster's collegiate dictionary (10th ed.). (1993). Springfield, MA: Merriam-Webster.

Mullins, C. J. (1977). *A guide to writing and publishing in the social and behavioral sciences.* New York: Wiley.

National Bureau of Standards. (1979, December). Guidelines for use of the modernized metric system. *Dimensions/NBS*, pp. 13–19.

Nurnberg, M. (1972). Punctuation—Who needs it? In *Questions you always wanted to ask about English but were afraid to raise your hand* (pp. 168–241). New York: Washington Square Press.

Orne, M. T. (1981). The why and how of a contribution to the literature: A brief communication. *International Journal of Clinical and Experimental Hypnosis, 29*, 1–4.

Pfaffman, C., Young, P. T., Dethier, V. G., Richter, C. P., & Stellar, E. (1954). The preparation of solutions for research in chemoreception and food acceptance. *Journal of Comparative and Physiological Psychology, 47*, 93–96.

Raspberry, W. (1989, January 4). When "Black" becomes "African American." *The Washington Post*, p. A19.

Raykov, T., Tomer, A., & Nesselroade, J. R. (1991). Reporting structural equation modeling results in *Psychology and Aging:* Some proposed guidelines. *Psychology and Aging, 6*, 499–503.

Reisman, S. J. (Ed.). (1962). *A style manual for technical writers and editors.* New York: Macmillan.

Sackett, P. (2000, March 24–26). Some thoughts on data retention. In *American Psychological Association Board of Scientific Affairs Agenda*

(Item 8, Exhibit 1). (Unpublished letter, available from the American Psychological Association, Publications Office, 750 First Street, NE, Washington, DC 20002-4242)

Schaie, K. W. (1993). Ageist language in psychological research. *American Psychologist, 48,* 49–51.

Schlosberg, H. (1965). Hints on presenting a paper at an APA convention. *American Psychologist, 20,* 606–607.

Scientific Illustration Committee. (1988). *Illustrating science: Standards for publication.* Bethesda, MD: Council of Biology Editors.

Serlin, R. C., & Lapsley, D. K. (1985). Rationality in psychological research: The good-enough principle. *American Psychologist, 40,* 73–83.

Skillin, M. E., & Gay, R. M. (1974). *Words into type* (3rd ed.). Englewood Cliffs, NJ: Prentice-Hall.

University of Chicago Press. (1993). *The Chicago manual of style* (14th ed.). Chicago: Author.

U.S. Copyright Office. (1981). *Circular R1: Copyright basics* (Publication No. 341-279/106). Washington, DC: U.S. Government Printing Office.

VandenBos, G. R. (2001). *Disguising case material for publication.* (Unpublished manuscript, available from the American Psychological Association, Publications Office, 750 First Street, NE, Washington, DC 20002-4242)

Wainer, H. (1997). Improving tabular displays: With NAEP tables as examples and inspirations. *Journal of Educational and Behavioral Statistics, 22,* 1–30.

Walker, A., Jr. (Ed.). (2001). *Thesaurus of psychological index terms* (9th ed.). Washington, DC: American Psychological Association.

Webster's third new international dictionary, unabridged: The great library of the English language. (1993). Springfield, MA: Merriam-Webster.

Wilkinson, L., & the Task Force on Statistical Inference. (1999). Statistical methods in psychology journals: Guidelines and explanations. *American Psychologist, 54,* 594–604.

9.03 *Suggested Reading*

General

American National Standard for the preparation of scientific papers for written or oral presentation (ANSI Z39.16-1979). (1979). New York: American National Standards Institute. (Available from American National Standards Institute, Inc., 11 West 42nd Street, New York, NY 10036)

> Official standard of the American National Standards Institute; outlines specific guidelines for the preparation of scientific articles for publication.

Day, R. A. (1979). *How to write and publish a scientific paper*. Philadelphia, PA: ISI Press.

> Provides complete instructions for the writing, preparation, and submission of manuscripts for publication.

E-what? A guide to the quirks of new media style and usage. (2000). Alexandria, VA: EEI Press.

> A useful guide to editing and writing about or for the Internet. Includes a list of trademarked names, a glossary, and recommendations for treatment of Internet addresses, spelling, and hyphenation.

Sabin, W. A. (1992). *The Gregg reference manual* (7th ed.). Lake Forest, IL: Glencoe.

> A general guide on punctuation, grammar, spelling, and other basics for writers and publishers in business and academic settings. Provides rationale to rules so the user can "manipulate the principles of style with intelligence and taste." Includes tips on editing, proofreading, and adjusting format at the computer.

Skillin, M. E., & Gay, R. M. (1974). *Words into type* (3rd ed.). Englewood Cliffs, NJ: Prentice-Hall.

> Detailed guide to the preparation of manuscripts, the handling of copy and proofs, copyediting style, typographical style, grammar and word usage, and typography and illustration.

University of Chicago Press. (1993). *The Chicago manual of style* (14th ed.). Chicago: Author.

> A standard reference for authors, editors, printers, and proofreaders that provides clear and simple guidelines for preparing and editing copy. Discusses the technicalities of preparing copy, such as mathematical material, for scientific publication.

Parts of a Manuscript

Cremmins, E. T. (1982). *The art of abstracting.* Philadelphia, PA: ISI Press.

> Describes in detail how to create an abstract; focuses on the cognitive skills used, that is, reading, thinking, writing, and editing.

Writing Style

Bates, J. D. (1980). *Writing with precision: How to write so that you cannot possibly be misunderstood* (3rd ed.). Washington, DC: Acropolis Books.

> Discusses the principles of clear, effective writing; offers help on preparing and writing specific kinds of material, such as letters, memoranda, and reports.

Bernstein, T. M. (1971). *Miss Thistlebottom's hobgoblins.* New York: Farrar, Straus & Giroux.

> Subtitled as *The careful writer's guide to the taboos, bugbears, and outmoded rules of English usage.*

Boring, E. G. (1957). *CP* speaks. . . . *Contemporary Psychology, 2,* 279.

> An editorial on psychologists and good writing by the first editor of *Contemporary Psychology.*

Copperud, R. H. (1980). *American usage and style: The consensus.* New York: Van Nostrand Reinhold.

> Compares the judgments of leading authorities and sources on points of usage and style.

Fowler, H. W. (1965). *A dictionary of modern English usage* (2nd ed.). New York: Oxford University Press.

> A classic dictionary of usage; offers detailed information on

grammar and style, on spelling and pronunciation, and on punctuation.

Harlow, H. F. (1962). Fundamental principles for preparing psychology journal articles. *Journal of Comparative and Physiological Psychology, 55*, 893–896.

An editor's humorous remarks on the content and style of scientific reporting.

Strunk, W., Jr., & White, E. B. (1979). *The elements of style* (3rd ed.). New York: Macmillan.

A classic that offers concise, clear advice on writing well.

Trimble, J. R. (1975). *Writing with style: Conversations on the art of writing.* Englewood Cliffs, NJ: Prentice-Hall.

Offers informal advice on the fundamentals of writing, on how to begin and how to proceed, and on the importance of clear thinking in achieving clear writing; also offers specific advice on punctuation, quotations, and general usage.

Woodford, F. P. (1967). Sounder thinking through clearer writing. *Science, 156*, 743–745.

Suggests that a graduate course on scientific writing can strengthen and clarify scientific thinking.

Zinsser, W. (1990). *On writing well: An informal guide to writing nonfiction* (4th ed.). New York: HarperCollins.

Informal discussion of principles that are basic to strong, uncluttered writing.

Nondiscriminatory Language

American Association of University Presses. (in press). *Guidelines for bias-free usage.* New York: Author.

A guide for scholarly writers and the people who edit their work; extensive sections on gender bias and on race, ethnicity, citizenship and nationality, and religion; smaller but substantive sections on sexual orientation, age, and disabilities; fine examples from university press manuscripts.

American Psychological Association. (1977, June). *Guidelines for nonsexist language in APA journals* [Reprint of section 2.12 of the 3rd ed. of the *Publication Manual of the American Psychological Association*]. Washington, DC: Author. (Available from the American Psychological Association, Publications Office, 750 First Street, NE, Washington, DC 20002-4242)

> More than 30 examples of problematic usage, grouped according to ambiguity, stereotyping, and evaluative language; several forms of alternative wording are provided.

American Psychological Association, Board of Ethnic and Minority Affairs & Publications and Communications Board. (1989). *Guidelines for avoiding racial/ethnic bias in language* [Draft]. Unpublished manuscript. (A current version of the guidelines is available from the American Psychological Association, Publications Office, 750 First Street, NE, Washington, DC 20002-4242)

> Discusses the importance of adequate description of research participants and the selection of appropriate terminology to describe racially and ethnically diverse people.

American Psychological Association, Committee on Disability Issues in Psychology. (1992). *Guidelines for nonhandicapping language in APA journals.* Unpublished manuscript. (A current version of the guidelines is available from the American Psychological Association, Publications Office, 750 First Street, NE, Washington, DC 20002-4242)

> Clarifies the distinction between *disability* and *handicap.* Explains how to avoid victimizing people with disabilities and ways to use language that focuses on the individual; offers many additional examples of positive language.

American Psychological Association, Committee on Lesbian and Gay Concerns. (1991). *Avoiding heterosexual bias in language.* Unpublished manuscript. (A current version of the guidelines is available from the American Psychological Association, Publications Office, 750 First Street, NE, Washington, DC 20002-4242)

> Discusses history of the term *homosexuality* and ways to increase

the visibility of lesbians, gay men, and bisexual people in writing; provides more than 15 examples of problematic and preferred language.

Boston, B. O. (1992, November). Portraying people with disabilities: Toward a new vocabulary. *The Editorial Eye, 15,* 1–3, 6–7.

Discusses ways to portray "people with disabilities in a sensitive, straightforward, and positive way without producing convoluted English in the process" (p. 1).

Gaw, A. C. (Ed.). (1993). *Culture, ethnicity, and mental illness.* Washington, DC: American Psychiatric Press.

Examines the expression and treatment of mental illness in the context of culture, with chapters on African Americans, American Indians, Asian Americans, Hispanic Americans, women, ethnic elders, and gay men and lesbians. Glossaries of ethnic terms are offered from Chinese, Japanese, Korean, Filipino, Mexican, and Puerto Rican cultures.

Guidelines for reporting and writing about people with disabilities (4th ed.) [Brochure]. (1994). Lawrence: University of Kansas, Media Project of the Center on Independent Living.

Offers several guidelines on portraying people with disabilities and provides a glossary of appropriate terminology for specific disabilities.

International Association of Business Communicators. (1982). *Without bias: A guidebook for nondiscriminatory communication* (2nd ed.). New York: Wiley.

Provides guidelines for language that is free of bias regarding ethnicity, sex, age, and disability.

Knatterud, M. E. (1991, February). Writing with the patient in mind: Don't add insult to injury. *American Medical Writers Association Journal, 6,* 10–17.

Drawing examples from medical manuscripts, the author discusses dehumanizing jargon and grammar and offers guidelines on "preserving patients' dignity on the printed page."

The language of homosexuality. (1993, April/May). *Copy Editor, 4,* 1–2.

> An interview with the editor of the *Encyclopedia of Homosexuality* and a discussion of word choices (*preference* vs. *orientation, gay* vs. *homosexual, lesbian* vs. *gay,* etc.).

Maggio, R. (1991). *The bias-free word finder: A dictionary of nondiscriminatory language.* Boston: Beacon Press.

> Alphabetical listing of word entries, with alternatives for the terms that connote bias and thoughtful explanations for why they do so. The Writing Guidelines that precede the listing are outstanding, discussing writers' natural frustration and resistance toward writing without bias, why naming is so important to people, and the "insider/outsider rule."

McGraw-Hill. (1983). *Guidelines for bias-free publishing.* New York: Author.

> Provides writing and illustration guidelines for equal treatment of the sexes and for fair representation of minority groups and people with disabilities.

Moulton, J., Robinson, G. M., & Elias, C. (1978). Sex bias in language use: "Neutral" pronouns that aren't. *American Psychologist, 33,* 1032–1036.

> Reports data demonstrating that even when used in a supposedly neutral context, "generic" male terms induce people to think of males.

National Committee on Women in Public Administration of the American Society for Public Administration. (1979). *The right word: Guidelines for avoiding a sex-biased language.* Washington, DC: American Society for Public Administration.

> Guidelines for the use of nonsexist language in administrative and legislative contexts.

Rush, W. L., & The League of Human Dignity. (n.d.). *Write with dignity: Reporting on people with disabilities.* Lincoln: University of Nebraska, Hitchcock Center.

> Dictionary-style listing of disabilities and related terminology, plus guidelines on interviewing people with disabilities.

Schaie, K. W. (1993). Ageist language in psychological research. *American Psychologist, 48*, 49–51.

> A general article on avoiding ageist bias in research, including discussion on objective research design and on reporting what the research actually demonstrates without adding value-laden assumptions.

Metrication

American national standard for metric practice (ANSI/ISEE 268-92). (1992). New York: American National Standards Institute. (Available from American National Standards Institute, Inc., 11 West 42nd Street, New York, NY 10036, or Institute of Electrical and Electronics Engineers, Inc., Standards Department, 445 Hoes Lane, Piscataway, NJ 08855)

> Includes sections on the International System of Units (SI) and symbols, rules for SI style and usage, rules for conversion and rounding, and an appendix of conversion factors.

Goldman, D. T. (1981). SI: Prognosis for the future. *Journal of College Science Teaching, 10*, 222–225.

> Outlines the history of the adoption of the SI and discusses potential modifications of the SI.

Page, C. H., & Vigoureux, P. (Eds.). (1972). *The International System of Units (SI)* (National Bureau of Standards Special Publication 330). Washington, DC: U.S. Government Printing Office.

> The approved translation of the French Système International d'Unités. Contains the resolutions and recommendations of the General Conference on Weights and Measures on the SI, as well as recommendations for the practical use of the SI.

Mathematics

American Institute of Physics. (1978). *Style manual* (3rd ed., rev.). New York: Author. Includes detailed instructions for the presentation of mathematical expressions, as well as an appendix of special characters and signs available for typesetting.

Swanson, E. (1979). *Mathematics into type* (Rev. ed.). Providence, RI: American Mathematical Society.

> Offers detailed, practical instructions on preparing mathematical copy.

University of Chicago Press. (1993). Mathematics in type. In *The Chicago manual of style* (14th ed., pp. 433–457). Chicago: Author.

> Discusses how to prepare mathematical copy.

Tables and Figures

Bertin, J. (1983). *Semiology of graphics* (W. Berg & H. Wainer, Trans.). Madison: University of Wisconsin Press. (Original work published 1973)

Cleveland, W. S. (1994a). *The elements of graphing data*. Summit, NJ: Hobart Press.

Cleveland, W. S. (1994b). *Visualizing data*. Summit, NJ: Hobart Press.

Cleveland, W. S., & McGill, R. (1984). Graphical perception: Theory, experimentation, and application to the development of graphical methods. *Journal of the American Statistical Association, 79*, 531–554.

Hill, M., & Cochran, W. (1977). *Into print: A practical guide to writing, illustrating, and publishing*. Los Altos, CA: William Kaufman.

> Includes general and technical information on the preparation of photographs, drawings, graphs, and charts.

Houp, K. W., & Pearsall, T. E. (1980). *Reporting technical information* (4th ed.). New York: Macmillan.

> Discusses kinds of illustrations (tables as well as figures) and the importance of selecting the appropriate type of illustration; provides guidelines for ensuring that the presentation of graphics is simple and clear.

Illustrations for publication and projections (ASA Y15.1–1959). (1959). New York: American National Standards Institute. (Available from American National Standards Institute, Inc., 11 West 42nd Street, New York, NY 10036)

> Explains and illustrates the preparation of legible and effective

diagrams and graphs for technical publications or with oral presentations.

Nicol, A. A. M., & Pexman, P. M. (1999). *Presenting your findings: A practical guide for creating tables.* Washington, DC: American Psychological Association.

Scientific Illustration Committee. (1988). *Illustrating science: Standards for publication.* Bethesda, MD: Council of Biology Editors.

> Defines standards for preparing all kinds of artwork, including computer graphics and color printing, to support the presentation of scientific data; provides outstanding examples and descriptions of what goes into quality graphics.

Tufte, E. R. (1983). *The visual display of quantitative information.* Cheshire, CT: Graphics Press.

Wainer, H. (2000). *Visual revelations: Graphical tales of fate and deception from Napoleon Bonaparte to Ross Perot* (2nd ed.). Hillsdale, NJ: Erlbaum.

Walker, H. M., & Durost, W. N. (1936). *Statistical tables: Their structure and use.* New York: Bureau of Publications, Teachers College, Columbia University.

Editorial Policies

Bishop, C. T. (1989). *How to edit a scientific journal.* Baltimore: Williams & Wilkins.

> Explains specific policies and procedures in the editing of a scientific journal.

DeBakey, L. (1976). *The scientific journal: Editorial policies and practices.* St. Louis, MO: Mosby.

> Offers guidelines for editors, reviewers, and authors in such areas as review of manuscripts, duplicate publication, and style and format.

Student Papers

Cone, J. D., & Foster, S. L. (1993). *Dissertations and theses from start to finish: Psychology and related fields.* Washington, DC: American Psychological Association.

>A practical guide for the graduate student, offering a step-by-step approach to initiate and complete a thesis or dissertation. Includes checklists for each stage of the project.

Maimon, P., Belcher, G. L., Hearn, G. W., Nodine, B. F., & O'Connor, F. W. (1981). *Writing in the arts and sciences.* Boston: Little, Brown.

>Introduces students to the processes of library and laboratory research in the sciences; provides step-by-step instructions on preparing the research paper from draft through final stages.

Turabian, K. L. (1987). *A manual for writers of term papers, theses, and dissertations* (5th ed.). Chicago: University of Chicago Press.

>Based on the University of Chicago Press's *Chicago Manual of Style,* provides style guidelines for the typewritten presentation of formal papers.

Woodford, F. P. (1967). Sounder thinking through clearer writing. *Science, 156,* 743–745.

>Argues that good scientific writing both reflects clear thinking and avoids condescension and pretentiousness.

APA Publications

For information on ordering APA publications and on information services, write the APA Order Department, 750 First Street, NE, Washington, DC 20002-4242, or visit our Web site, http://www.apa.org.

Checklist for Manuscript Submission

Listed in this appendix are questions concerning the most common oversights in manuscript preparation. Authors should review these items especially carefully before submitting their manuscripts to an editor. Numbers following entries refer to relevant section numbers in the *Publication Manual.*

Format

- Is the original manuscript typed or printed on 8½ × 11 in. (22 × 28 cm) white bond paper (5.01)?
- Is the entire manuscript—including quotations, references, author note, content footnotes, figure captions, and all parts of tables—double-spaced (5.03)? Is the manuscript neatly prepared (5.07)?
- Are the margins at least 1 in. (2.54 cm; 5.04)?
- Are the title page, abstract, references, appendixes, author note, content footnotes, tables, figure captions, and figures on separate pages (with only one table or figure per page)? Are they ordered in sequence, with the text pages between the abstract and the references (5.05)?
- If the manuscript is to receive masked review, is the author note typed on the title page, which is removed by the journal editor before review (5.15)?
- Are all pages (except figure pages) numbered in sequence, starting with the title page (5.06)?

Title Page and Abstract

- Is the title 10 to 12 words (1.06)?
- Does the byline reflect the institution or institutions where the work was conducted (1.06)?
- Is the abstract no longer than 120 words (1.07)?

Paragraphs and Headings

- Is each paragraph longer than a single sentence but not longer than one manuscript page (2.03)?
- Do the levels of headings accurately reflect the organization of the paper (1.05, 3.30)?
- Do all headings of the same level appear in the same format (3.30)?

Abbreviations

- Are any unnecessary abbreviations eliminated and any necessary ones explained (3.20, 3.21)?
- Are abbreviations in tables and figures explained in the table notes and figure captions or legends (3.21)?

Mathematics and Statistics

- Are Greek letters and all but the most common mathematical symbols identified on the manuscript (3.58, 5.14)?
- Are all non-Greek letters that are used as statistical symbols for algebraic variables in italics (3.58)?

Units of Measurement

- Are metric equivalents for all nonmetric units (except measurements of time, which have no metric equivalents) provided (3.50)?
- Are all metric and nonmetric units with numeric values (except some measurements of time) abbreviated (3.25, 3.51)?

References

- Are references cited both in text and in the references list (4.01)?
- Do the text citations and reference list entries agree both in spelling and in date (4.01)?
- Are text citations to nonempirical work distinguished from citations to empirical work (1.13)?
- Are journal titles in the reference list spelled out fully (4.11)?
- Are the references (both in the parenthetical text citations and in the reference list) ordered alphabetically by the authors' surnames (3.99, 4.04)?
- Are inclusive page numbers for all articles or chapters in books provided in the reference list (4.11, 4.13)?
- Are references to studies included in your meta-analysis preceded by an asterisk (4.05)?

Notes and Footnotes

- Is the departmental affiliation given for each author in the author note (3.89)?
- Does the author note include both the author's current affiliation if it is different from the byline affiliation and a current address for correspondence (3.89)?
- Does the author note disclose special circumstances about the article (portions presented at a meeting, student paper as basis for the article, report of a longitudinal study, relationship that may be perceived as a conflict of interest; 3.89)?
- In the text, are all footnotes indicated, and are footnote numbers correctly located (3.87)?

Tables and Figures

- Does every table column, including the stub column, have a heading (3.67)?
- Have all vertical table rules been omitted (3.71)?
- Are the elements in the figures large enough to remain legible after

the figure has been reduced to the width of a journal column or page (3.80)?

- Does lettering in a figure vary by no more than 4 point sizes of type (3.80)?
- Are glossy or high-quality laser prints of all figures included, and are the prints no larger than 8½ × 11 in. (22 × 28 cm; 3.80, 3.85)?
- Is each figure labeled with the correct figure number and short article title (3.83)?
- Are all figures and tables mentioned in the text and numbered in the order in which they are mentioned (3.63, 3.83)?

Copyright and Quotations

- Is written permission to use previously published text, tests or portions of tests, tables, or figures enclosed with the manuscript (8.08)?
- Are page or paragraph numbers provided in text for all quotations (3.39)?

Submitting the Manuscript

- Have you provided the required number of copies of the manuscript (in English), including the original (5.25)?
- Are the journal editor's name and address current (5.27)?
- Is a cover letter included with the manuscript? Does the letter (a) include the author's postal address, e-mail address, telephone number, and fax number for future correspondence and (b) state that the manuscript is original, not previously published, and not under concurrent consideration elsewhere? Does the letter inform the journal editor of the existence of any similar published manuscripts written by the author (5.26, Appendix E)?

Note to Students

Many psychology departments require that student papers, theses, and dissertations be prepared according to the *Publication Manual*. Of course, where departmental requirements differ from those in the *Publication Manual*, the departmental requirements take precedence. Familiarity with both departmental and *Publication Manual* requirements will enable students to prepare papers efficiently. The following sections of the *Publication Manual* are especially useful to students:

- Quotations (sections 3.34–3.41)
- Examples of Reference Citations (chap. 4)
- Manuscript Preparation Instructions (chap. 5)
- Sample Paper and Outlines (Figures 5.1–5.3, chap. 5)
- Bibliography (section 9.03, Student Papers)
- Theses, Dissertations, and Student Papers (chap. 6)
- Manuscript Checklists (Appendixes A and B)

Checklist for Transmitting Accepted Manuscripts for Electronic Production

Numbers following entries refer to relevant sections in the *Publication Manual.*

Preparing the Electronic File

- Are the following elements followed by a hard return?
  running head for publication
  title of article
  each byline
  each institutional affiliation
  abstract
  each paragraph
  each text heading
  each page label (e.g., Abstract, Author Note, Figure Captions)
  each reference
  each footnote
  each figure caption
- Does the text of the manuscript copy match the text of the electronic file? (7.02)
- Have all embedded figures been printed out and then deleted from the file? (7.02)

- If you used bibliographic software, are all references "unlinked" from the text? (7.02)
- Are footnotes or endnotes placed as text after the author note? In text, are footnote or endnote references superscript numbers? (7.02)
- If you are providing electronic copies of your figures, are they TIFF files in the appropriate format and resolution? (3.80, 7.02)

Ethical Standards for the Reporting and Publishing of Scientific Information

The following ethical standards are reprinted from the "Ethical Principles of Psychologists and Code of Conduct," which appeared in the December 1992 issue of the *American Psychologist* (Vol. 47, pp. 1597–1611). Standards 5.01–5.10 and 6.06–6.26 deal with the reporting and publishing of scientific information.

5.01 *Discussing the Limits of Confidentiality*

(a) Psychologists discuss with persons and organizations with whom they establish a scientific or professional relationship (including, to the extent feasible, minors and their legal representatives) (1) the relevant limitations on confidentiality, including limitations where applicable in group, marital, and family therapy or in organizational consulting, and (2) the foreseeable uses of the information generated through their services.

(b) Unless it is not feasible or is contraindicated, the discussion of confidentiality occurs at the outset of the relationship and thereafter as new circumstances may warrant.

(c) Permission for electronic recording of interviews is secured from clients and patients.

5.02 *Maintaining Confidentiality*

Psychologists have a primary obligation and take reasonable precautions to respect the confidentiality rights of those with whom they work or

Ethics

consult, recognizing that confidentiality may be established by law, institutional rules, or professional or scientific relationships. (See also Standard 6.26, Professional Reviewers.)

5.03 *Minimizing Intrusions on Privacy*

(a) In order to minimize intrusions on privacy, psychologists include in written and oral reports, consultations, and the like, only information germane to the purpose for which the communication is made.

(b) Psychologists discuss confidential information obtained in clinical or consulting relationships, or evaluative data concerning patients, individual or organizational clients, students, research participants, supervisees, and employees, only for appropriate scientific or professional purposes and only with persons clearly concerned with such matters.

5.04 *Maintenance of Records*

Psychologists maintain appropriate confidentiality in creating, storing, accessing, transferring, and disposing of records under their control, whether these are written, automated, or in any other medium. Psychologists maintain and dispose of records in accordance with law and in a manner that permits compliance with the requirements of this Ethics Code.

5.05 *Disclosures*

(a) Psychologists disclose confidential information without the consent of the individual only as mandated by law, or where permitted by law for a valid purpose, such as (1) to provide needed professional services to the patient or the individual or organizational client, (2) to obtain appropriate professional consultations, (3) to protect the patient or client or others from harm, or (4) to obtain payment for services, in which instance disclosure is limited to the minimum that is necessary to achieve the purpose.

(b) Psychologists also may disclose confidential information with the appropriate consent of the patient or the individual or organizational

Ethics

client (or of another legally authorized person on behalf of the patient or client), unless prohibited by law.

5.06 *Consultations*

When consulting with colleagues, (1) psychologists do not share confidential information that reasonably could lead to the identification of a patient, client, research participant, or other person or organization with whom they have a confidential relationship unless they have obtained the prior consent of the person or organization or the disclosure cannot be avoided, and (2) they share information only to the extent necessary to achieve the purposes of the consultation. (See also Standard 5.02, Maintaining Confidentiality.)

5.07 *Confidential Information in Databases*

(a) If confidential information concerning recipients of psychological services is to be entered into databases or systems of records available to persons whose access has not been consented to by the recipient, then psychologists use coding or other techniques to avoid the inclusion of personal identifiers.

(b) If a research protocol approved by an institutional review board or similar body requires the inclusion of personal identifiers, such identifiers are deleted before the information is made accessible to persons other than those of whom the subject was advised.

(c) If such deletion is not feasible, then before psychologists transfer such data to others or review such data collected by others, they take reasonable steps to determine that appropriate consent of personally identifiable individuals has been obtained.

5.08 *Use of Confidential Information for Didactic or Other Purposes*

(a) Psychologists do not disclose in their writings, lectures, or other public media, confidential, personally identifiable information concerning their patients, individual or organizational clients, students, research participants, or other recipients of their services that they obtained during the course of their work, unless the person or organization has consented in writing or unless there is other ethical or legal authorization for doing so.

(b) Ordinarily, in such scientific and professional presentations, psychologists disguise confidential information concerning such persons or organizations so that they are not individually identifiable to others and so that discussions do not cause harm to subjects who might identify themselves.

5.09 *Preserving Records and Data*

A psychologist makes plans in advance so that confidentiality of records and data is protected in the event of the psychologist's death, incapacity, or withdrawal from the position or practice.

5.10 *Ownership of Records and Data*

Recognizing that ownership of records and data is governed by legal principles, psychologists take reasonable and lawful steps so that records and data remain available to the extent needed to serve the best interests of patients, individual or organizational clients, research participants, or appropriate others.

6.06 *Planning Research*

(a) Psychologists design, conduct, and report research in accordance with recognized standards of scientific competence and ethical research.

(b) Psychologists plan their research so as to minimize the possibility that results will be misleading.

(c) In planning research, psychologists consider its ethical acceptability under the Ethics Code. If an ethical issue is unclear, psychologists seek to resolve the issue through consultation with institutional review boards, animal care and use committees, peer consultations, or other proper mechanisms.

(d) Psychologists take reasonable steps to implement appropriate protections for the rights and welfare of human participants, other persons affected by the research, and the welfare of animal subjects.

6.07 *Responsibility*

(a) Psychologists conduct research competently and with due concern for the dignity and welfare of the participants.

(b) Psychologists are responsible for the ethical conduct of research conducted by them or by others under their supervision or control.

(c) Researchers and assistants are permitted to perform only those tasks for which they are appropriately trained and prepared.

(d) As part of the process of development and implementation of research projects, psychologists consult those with expertise concerning any special population under investigation or most likely to be affected.

6.08 *Compliance With Law and Standards*

Psychologists plan and conduct research in a manner consistent with federal and state law and regulations, as well as professional standards governing the conduct of research, and particularly those standards governing research with human participants and animal subjects.

6.09 *Institutional Approval*

Psychologists obtain from host institutions or organizations appropriate approval prior to conducting research, and they provide accurate information about their research proposals. They conduct the research in accordance with the approved research protocol.

6.10 *Research Responsibilities*

Prior to conducting research (except research involving only anonymous surveys, naturalistic observations, or similar research), psychologists enter into an agreement with participants that clarifies the nature of the research and the responsibilities of each party.

6.11 *Informed Consent to Research*

(a) Psychologists use language that is reasonably understandable to research participants in obtaining their appropriate informed consent (except as provided in Standard 6.12, Dispensing With Informed Consent). Such informed consent is appropriately documented.

(b) Using language that is reasonably understandable to participants, psychologists inform participants of the nature of the research; they inform participants that they are free to participate or to decline to participate or to withdraw from the research; they explain the foreseeable consequences of declining or withdrawing; they inform participants of significant factors that may be expected to influence their willingness to participate (such as risks, discomfort, adverse effects, or limitations on confidentiality, except as provided in Standard 6.15, Deception in Research); and they explain other aspects about which the prospective participants inquire.

(c) When psychologists conduct research with individuals such as students or subordinates, psychologists take special care to protect the prospective participants from adverse consequences of declining or withdrawing from participation.

(d) When research participation is a course requirement or opportunity for extra credit, the prospective participant is given the choice of equitable alternative activities.

(e) For persons who are legally incapable of giving informed consent, psychologists nevertheless (1) provide an appropriate explanation, (2) obtain the participant's assent, and (3) obtain appropriate permission from a legally authorized person, if such substitute consent is permitted by law.

6.12 *Dispensing With Informed Consent*

Before determining that planned research (such as research involving only anonymous questionnaires, naturalistic observations, or certain kinds of archival research) does not require the informed consent of research participants, psychologists consider applicable regulations and institutional review board requirements, and they consult with colleagues as appropriate.

6.13 *Informed Consent in Research Filming or Recording*

Psychologists obtain informed consent from research participants prior to filming or recording them in any form, unless the research involves simply naturalistic observations in public places and it is not anticipated that the recording will be used in a manner that could cause personal identification or harm.

6.14 *Offering Inducements for Research Participants*

(a) In offering professional services as an inducement to obtain research participants, psychologists make clear the nature of the services, as well as the risks, obligations, and limitations. (See also Standard 1.18, Barter [With Patients or Clients]).

(b) Psychologists do not offer excessive or inappropriate financial or other inducements to obtain research participants, particularly when it might tend to coerce participation.

6.15 *Deception in Research*

(a) Psychologists do not conduct a study involving deception unless they have determined that the use of deceptive techniques is justified by the study's prospective scientific, educational, or applied value and that equally effective alternative procedures that do not use deception are not feasible.

(b) Psychologists never deceive research participants about significant aspects that would affect their willingness to participate, such as physical risks, discomfort, or unpleasant emotional experiences.

(c) Any other deception that is an integral feature of the design and conduct of an experiment must be explained to participants as early as is feasible, preferably at the conclusion of their participation, but no later than at the conclusion of the research. (See also Standard 6.18, Providing Participants With Information About the Study.)

6.16 *Sharing and Utilizing Data*

Psychologists inform research participants of their anticipated sharing or further use of personally identifiable research data and of the possibility of unanticipated future uses.

6.17 *Minimizing Invasiveness*

In conducting research, psychologists interfere with the participants or milieu from which data are collected only in a manner that is warranted by an appropriate research design and that is consistent with psychologists' roles as scientific investigators.

6.18 *Providing Participants With Information About the Study*

(a) Psychologists provide a prompt opportunity for participants to obtain appropriate information about the nature, results, and conclusions of the research, and psychologists attempt to correct any misconceptions that participants may have.

(b) If scientific or humane values justify delaying or withholding this information, psychologists take reasonable measures to reduce the risk of harm.

6.19 *Honoring Commitments*

Psychologists take reasonable measures to honor all commitments they have made to research participants.

6.20 *Care and Use of Animals in Research*

(a) Psychologists who conduct research involving animals treat them humanely.

(b) Psychologists acquire, care for, use, and dispose of animals in compliance with current federal, state, and local laws and regulations, and with professional standards.

(c) Psychologists trained in research methods and experienced in the care of laboratory animals supervise all procedures involving animals and are responsible for ensuring appropriate consideration of their comfort, health, and humane treatment.

(d) Psychologists ensure that all individuals using animals under their supervision have received instruction in research methods and in the care, maintenance, and handling of the species being used, to the extent appropriate to their role.

(e) Responsibilities and activities of individuals assisting in a research project are consistent with their respective competencies.

(f) Psychologists make reasonable efforts to minimize the discomfort, infection, illness, and pain of animal subjects.

(g) A procedure subjecting animals to pain, stress, or privation is used only when an alternative procedure is unavailable and the goal is justified by its prospective scientific, educational, or applied value.

(h) Surgical procedures are performed under appropriate anesthesia; techniques to avoid infection and minimize pain are followed during and after surgery.

(i) When it is appropriate that the animal's life be terminated, it is done rapidly, with an effort to minimize pain, and in accordance with accepted procedures.

6.21 *Reporting of Results*

(a) Psychologists do not fabricate data or falsify results in their publications.

(b) If psychologists discover significant errors in their published data, they take reasonable steps to correct such errors in a correction, retraction, erratum, or other appropriate publication means.

6.22 *Plagiarism*

Psychologists do not present substantial portions or elements of another's work or data as their own, even if the other work or data source is cited occasionally.

6.23 *Publication Credit*

(a) Psychologists take responsibility and credit, including authorship credit, only for work they have actually performed or to which they have contributed.

(b) Principal authorship and other publication credits accurately reflect the relative scientific or professional contributions of the individuals involved, regardless of their relative status. Mere possession of an institutional position, such as Department Chair, does not justify authorship credit. Minor contributions to the research or to the writing for publications are appropriately acknowledged, such as in footnotes or in an introductory statement.

(c) A student is usually listed as principal author on any multiple-authored article that is substantially based on the student's dissertation or thesis.

6.24 *Duplicate Publication of Data*
Psychologists do not publish, as original data, data that have been previously published. This does not preclude republishing data when they are accompanied by proper acknowledgment.

6.25 *Sharing Data*
After research results are published, psychologists do not withhold the data on which their conclusions are based from other competent professionals who seek to verify the substantive claims through reanalysis and who intend to use such data only for that purpose, provided that the confidentiality of the participants can be protected and unless legal rights concerning proprietary data preclude their release.

6.26 *Professional Reviewers*
Psychologists who review material submitted for publication, grant, or other research proposal review respect the confidentiality of and the proprietary rights in such information of those who submitted it.

References to Legal Materials

Legal periodicals and APA journals differ in the placement and format of references. The main difference is that legal periodicals cite references in footnotes, whereas APA journals locate all references, including references to legal materials, in the reference list. For most references, you should use APA format as described in chapter 4. References to legal materials, however, which include court decisions, statutes, and other legislative materials, and various secondary sources, will be more useful to the reader if they provide the information in the conventional format of legal citations. Some examples of references and citations to court cases, statutes, and other legislative materials appear in this appendix along with guidelines for their preparation. For more information on preparing these and other kinds of legal references, consult the latest edition of *The Bluebook: A Uniform System of Citation* (17th ed., 2000), which is the source for the legal citation style that follows.

Authors should ensure that their legal references are accurate and contain all of the information necessary to enable a reader to locate the material being referenced. Authors are encouraged to consult law librarians to verify that their legal references (a) contain the information necessary for retrieval and (b) reflect the current status of the legal authority cited, to avoid the possibility of relying on a case that has been overturned on appeal or on legislation that has been significantly amended or repealed.

D.01 *General Forms*

A reference form is provided in each of the following sections. For the most part, each reference form for statutes and other legislation includes

Legal

(a) a popular or formal title or name of the legislation and (b) the citation, either to the published compilation of legislative materials where the legislation is codified (e.g., a specific numbered section of a specific volume of the *United States Code*), including the statutory compilation's publication date in parentheses, or the identifying label for the legislation assigned by the enacting body during the particular legislative session (e.g., a specific section of an act identified by its public law number).

A typical reference form for court decisions includes (a) the title or name of the case (usually the one party versus another); (b) the citation, usually to a volume and page of one of the various sets of books (called *reporters,* which usually contain decisions of courts in particular political divisions, or *jurisdictions*) where published cases can be found (e.g., the *Federal Reporter, Second Series*); and finally (c) the precise jurisdiction of the court writing the decision (e.g., the New York Court of Appeals), in parentheses, including the date of the decision.

For both legislation and court decisions, certain additional descriptive information may follow the citation, which may pertain to the content of the legislation or court decision, the history of the legislation or court decision (e.g., later appeals of court decisions or later amendments to legislation), or other sources from which the legislation or court citation may be retrieved. Authors are encouraged to consult the *Bluebook* for the proper format for such additional information. Follow the *Bluebook* closely for correct abbreviation style. Some examples of the more common abbreviations that appear in APA journals are shown here.

Cong.	U.S. Congress
H.R.	House of Representatives
S.	Senate
Reg.	Regulation
Res.	Resolution
F.	*Federal Reporter*
F.2d	*Federal Reporter, Second Series*
F. Supp.	*Federal Supplement*
U.S.C.	*United States Code*

| Cong. Rec. | *Congressional Record* |
| Fed. Reg. | *Federal Register* |

D.02 *Text Citations of Legal Materials*

Although the reference format for legal materials differs from that of other kinds of works cited in APA publications, the text citations are formed in the same way and serve the same purpose. As with unauthored works (see section 3.97), give the first few words of the reference list entry and date; that is, give enough information in the text citation to enable the reader to locate the entry in the reference list quickly and easily. Examples of text citations and reference entries for specific kinds of legal materials are given in the following sections.

D.03 *Court Decisions (Bluebook Rule 10)*

In text, cite the name of the case (italicized) and the year of the decision. If 2 or more years are given, cite those years as well. Court cases often have several years, each of which reflects a specific stage in the case's history. Giving only one date could give the impression that only a single point in the case's history is being cited or might mislead a reader as to the timing of the case.

Reference form for cases:

Name v. Name, Volume Source Page (Court Date).

Abbreviate the published source (if any), court, and date as specified in the *Bluebook.*

1. Sample reference list entry to a case:

Lessard v. Schmidt, 349 F. Supp. 1078 (E.D. Wis. 1972).

Legal

Text citation:

> *Lessard v. Schmidt* (1972)
>
> (*Lessard v. Schmidt*, 1972)

Explanation: This decision was rendered by the federal district court for the Eastern District of Wisconsin in 1972. It appears in volume 349 of the *Federal Supplement* and starts on page 1078 of that volume.

2. Sample reference list entry to an appealed case:

> Durflinger v. Artiles, 563 F. Supp. 322 (D. Kan. 1981), *aff'd*, 727 F.2d 888 (10th Cir. 1984).

Text citation:

> *Durflinger v. Artiles* (1981/1984)

Explanation: This decision was rendered by the federal district court for the District of Kansas in 1981. On appeal, the decision was affirmed by the 10th Circuit Court of Appeals in 1984. Consult the *Bluebook* for the proper forms to signal the various stages in a case's history.

Unpublished cases
3. Sample reference to an unreported decision:

> Gilliard v. Oswald, No. 76-2109 (2d Cir. March 16, 1977).

Explanation: The docket number and the court are provided. The opinion was announced on March 16, 1977. To cite to a particular page of a slip opinion (opinion that is not published in a case reporter but is separately printed), use the form slip op. at [page number].

Alternative: You may cite unreported cases found on electronic databases, such as LEXIS or Westlaw (WL), instead of citing them to slip opinions. Give the name of the database, a record number if available, and enough information for the reader to find the case. Precede screen page numbers, if assigned, with an asterisk to distinguish them from the page number of the slip opinion; paragraph numbers, if assigned, should be preceded by a paragraph symbol.

With record number:

> Dougherty v. Royal Zenith Corp., No. 88-8666, 1991 U.S. Dist. LEXIS 10807, at *2 (E.D. Pa. July 31, 1991).

With no record number:

> Gustin v. Mathews, No. 76-7-C5 (D. Kan. Jan. 31, 1977) (LEXIS, Genfed library, Dist file).

Note: If the case is not available as a slip opinion or on-line, consult the *Bluebook* for other reference formats.

Court cases at the trial level
4. Sample reference to a state trial court opinion:

> Casey v. Pennsylvania-American Water Co., 12 Pa. D. & C.4th 168 (C.P. Washington County 1991).

Explanation: This decision was rendered by the Court of Common Pleas in Washington County, Pennsylvania, in 1991. (The Court of Common Pleas is the name of most of the trial-level courts in Pennsylvania. In other states, the trial-level courts are called *superior courts* or *supreme courts,* which can be confusing because one usually thinks of the supreme court as the highest court in any particular jurisdiction and not as the lowest. Authors should check the *Bluebook* for a listing of each jurisdiction's particular court structure.) The decision can be located in *Pennsylvania District and County Reports, Fourth Series,* beginning on page 168 of that volume.

5. Sample reference to a federal district court opinion:

Davis v. Monsanto Co., 627 F. Supp. 418 (S.D. W.Va. 1986).

Explanation: The opinion was rendered in the federal district court for the Southern District of West Virginia and was decided in 1986. It appears in volume 627 of the *Federal Supplement* and starts on page 418 of that volume.

Court cases at the appellate level
6. Sample reference to a case appealed to a state supreme court:

Compton v. Commonwealth, 239 Va. 312, 389 S.E.2d 460 (1990).

Explanation: This opinion was written by the Virginia Supreme Court in 1990. It can be found in volume 239 of the *Virginia Reports,* which publishes the state's supreme court decisions, starting on page 312. There is a parallel citation to volume 389 of the *South Eastern Reporter, Second Series,* starting on page 460. A reporter prints cases; the *South Eastern Reporter* is a regional reporter containing cases from several states in the southeastern section of the country.

7. Sample reference to a case appealed to a state court of appeals:

Texas v. Morales, 826 S.W.2d 201 (Tex. Ct. App. 1992).

Explanation: This opinion was rendered by the Texas Court of Appeals in 1992 and can be found in volume 826 of the *South Western Reporter, Second Series,* starting on page 201.

8. Sample references to cases decided by the U.S. Supreme Court:

Brown v. Board of Educ., 347 U.S. 483 (1954).

Maryland v. Craig, 110 S. Ct. 3160 (1990).

Explanation: Each of these cases was decided by the U.S. Supreme Court. The first citation is to the *United States Reports.* Such a citation is given when the appropriate volume of the *United States Reports* is available. The second citation is to the *Supreme Court Reporter.* Use this source when the volume of the *United States Reports* in which the case will appear has not yet been published.

D.04 *Statutes* (Bluebook *Rule 12)*

In text, give the popular or official name of the act (if any) and the year of the act. In the reference list entry, include the source and section number of the statute, and in parentheses give the publication date of the statutory compilation, which may be different from the year in the name of the act.

Reference form for statutes:

Name of Act, Volume Source § xxx (Year).

Abbreviate the source as specified in the *Bluebook.* A few states use chapter or article numbers instead of section numbers; use abbreviations or symbols as shown in the *Bluebook.*

9. Sample reference to a statute:

Mental Health Systems Act, 42 U.S.C. § 9401 (1988).

Text citation:

Mental Health Systems Act (1988)

Mental Health Systems Act of 1988

10. Sample reference to a statute in a state code:

> Mental Care and Treatment Act, 4 Kan. Stat. Ann. §§ 59-2901-2941 (1983 & Supp. 1992).

Explanation: This Kansas act can be found in codified version between sections 2901 and 2941 in chapter 59 of volume 4 of the 1983 edition of *Kansas Statutes Annotated.* Two amendments to the act and additional references are provided in the 1992 supplement for the *Kansas Statutes Annotated.* If you are discussing a particular provision of the law, cite the particular section in which the provision appeared (e.g., § 59-2903). *Ann.* stands for *Annotated,* which refers to the version of the Kansas statutory compilation containing summarized cases interpreting particular sections of the statute.

11. Sample reference to a statute in a federal code:

> Americans With Disabilities Act of 1990, 42 U.S.C.A. § 12101 *et seq.* (West 1993).

Explanation: This act can be located beginning at section 12101 of title 42 of the *United States Code Annotated,* which is the unofficial version of the *United States Code* (the official statutory compilation of the laws enacted by Congress). *Et seq.* is a Latin phrase meaning "and following" and is a shorthand way of showing that the act covers not just the initial section cited but also others that follow the initial section. In the parentheses is reflected that the *United States Code Annotated* is published by West Publishing and that 1993 is the publication date of the volume in which the cited sections can be found. Citing to U.S.C., U.S.C.A., or U.S.C.S. is the preferred method of citing legislation, because codified legislation is usually easier to work with and retrieve than are session laws, the form of legislation before it is codified. A session law citation is constructed as follows:

Americans With Disabilities Act of 1990, Pub. L. No. 101-336, § 2, 104 Stat. 328 (1991).

Explanation: The citation is to the version of the act in its uncodified form. The act was the 336th public law enacted by the 101st Congress. Section 2 is the particular section of the act cited (§ 2 happens to correspond to § 12101 of 42 U.S.C.A., which is where § 2 was ultimately codified). The text of the section cited can also be found in the official compilation of uncodified session laws, called *United States Statutes at Large* (abbreviated *Stat.*) at volume 104, p. 328. Volume 104 of the *United States Statutes at Large* was published in 1991.

D.05 *Legislative Materials (Bluebook Rule 13)*

For testimony and hearings, bills and resolutions, and reports and documents, provide in text the title or number (or other descriptive information) and the date.

Form for testimony at federal hearings and for full hearings:

Title, xxx Cong. (date).

12. Sample reference for federal testimony:

RU486: The import ban and its effect on medical research: Hearings before the Subcommittee on Regulation, Business Opportunities, and Energy, of the House Committee on Small Business, 101st Cong., 35 (1990) (testimony of Ronald Chesemore).

Text citation:

RU486: The Import Ban (1990)

(RU486: The Import Ban, 1990)

Explanation: This testimony was given before a subcommittee of the U.S. House of Representatives during the second session of the 101st Congress and can be located beginning on page 35 of the official pamphlet that documents the hearing. In the reference, always include the entire subject-matter title as it appears on the cover of the pamphlet, the bill number (if any), the subcommittee name (if any), and the committee name. To cite an entire hearing, certain adjustments to the citation should be made, as in Example 13.

13. Sample reference for a full federal hearing:

> *Urban America's need for social services to strengthen families: Hearing before the Subcommittee on Human Resources of the Committee on Ways and Means, House of Representatives,* 102d Cong., 1 (1992).

Text citation:

> *Urban America's Need* (1992)
>
> (*Urban America's Need,* 1992)

Explanation: This hearing was held in 1992 in the U.S. House of Representatives during the 102d Congress. The hearing begins on page 1 of the official pamphlet that was prepared after the hearing.

14. Form for unenacted federal bills and resolutions:

> Title [if relevant], bill or resolution number, xxx Cong., (Year).

The number should be preceded by *H.R.* (House of Representatives) or *S.* (Senate), depending on the source of the unenacted bill or resolution.

Reference list entry:

S. 5936, 102d Cong. § 4 (1992).

Text citation:

Senate Bill 5936 (1992)

(S. 5936, 1992)

15. Sample references to unenacted federal bills:

Equitable Health Care for Severe Mental Illnesses Act of 1993, H.R. 1563, 103d Cong. (1993).

Equitable Health Care for Severe Mental Illnesses Act of 1993, S. 671, 103d Cong. (1993).

Explanation: The first example is to a bill created in the U.S. House of Representatives during the 103d Congress; it was assigned the bill number 1563. The second example is the Senate's version of the same bill.

16. Form for enacted federal bills and resolutions:

xx. Res. xxx, xxx Cong., Volume Source Page (Year) (enacted).

Reference list entry:

S. Res. 107, 103d Cong., 139 Cong. Rec. 5826 (1993) (enacted).

Text citation:

Senate Resolution 107 (1993)

(S. Res. 107, 1993)

Explanation: This resolution by the Senate is numbered 107 and is reported in volume 139 of the *Congressional Record* on page 5826. Note that enacted bills and joint resolutions are laws and should be cited as statutes. Enacted simple or concurrent resolutions should follow this format.

17. Form for federal reports (Rep.) and documents (Doc.):

xx. Rep. No. xx-xxx (Year).

As with bills, report numbers should be preceded by *H.R.* or *S.* as appropriate. The report number is composed of the year of the Congress followed by a hyphen and the number of the report, and ending with the calendar year.

Reference list entry:

S. Rep. No. 102-114 at 7 (1991).

Text citation:

Senate Report No. 102-114 (1991)

(S. Rep. No. 102-114, 1991)

Explanation: This report was submitted to the Senate by the Senate Committee on Labor and Human Resources concerning the Protection and Advocacy for Mentally Ill Individuals Amendments Act of 1991. The reference is to material that starts on page 7 of that document.

D.06 *Administrative and Executive Materials (Bluebook Rule 14)*

For rules and regulations, advisory opinions, and executive orders, provide in text the title or number (or other descriptive information) and the date.

18. Form for federal regulation:

Title/Number, Volume Source § xxx (Year).

Reference list entries:

FTC Credit Practices Rule, 16 C.F.R. § 444 (1999).

Federal Acquisition Regulations for National Aeronautics and Space Administration, 55 Fed. Reg. 52,782 (Dec. 21, 1990) (to be codified at 48 C.F.R. pt. 1).

Text citations:

FTC Credit Practices Rule (1999)

(Federal Acquisition Regulations for National Aeronautics and Space Administration, 1990)

Explanation: The first rule was codified in 1999 in volume 16 of the *Code of Federal Regulations* (the official regulatory code) as section 444. The second rule was published in the *Federal Register* before being officially codified; the parenthetical information is a cross-reference (indicated in the entry in the *Register*) to the section of the *Code of Federal Regulations* where the rule will be codified.

19. Form for executive order:

Exec. Order No. xxxxx, 3 C.F.R. Page (Year).

Reference list entry:

Exec. Order No. 11,609, 3 C.F.R 586 (1971–1975), *reprinted as amended in* 3 U.S.C. 301 app. at 404-07 (1994).

Text citation:

Executive Order No. 11,609 (1994)

(Executive Order No. 11,609, 1994)

Explanation: Executive orders are reported in volume 3 of the *Code of Federal Regulations;* this one appears on page 586. Provide a parallel citation to the *United States Code* (U.S.C.) or, if U.S.C. is unavailable, to the *United States Code Service* (U.S.C.S.).

D.07 *Patents*

In text, give the patent number and the issue date (not application date) of the patent. In the reference list entry, include the inventor(s) to whom the patent is issued, and the official source from which the patent information can be retrieved.

20. Reference list entry:

Smith, I. M. (1988). *U.S. Patent No. 123,445.* Washington, DC: U.S. Patent and Trademark Office.

Text citation:

U.S. Patent No. 123,445 (1988)

(U.S. Patent No. 123,445, 1988)

Explanation: This patent was issued in 1988. I. M. Smith is the inventor who holds the patent right. The patent number is a unique identifying code given to every patent. In this reference example, the patent number represents a utility patent because there is no letter prefix. If this were a nonutility patent, such as a design patent (coded with a *D*), the patent number in the reference and citation would be D123,445.

Sample Cover Letter

February 2, 2001

Meredith S. Simpson, PhD
Editor, *Journal of Poetry and Psychology*
Department of Psychology
University of Xanadu
9 Prentic Hall
Xanadu, NY 10003-1212

Dear Dr. Simpson:

I am enclosing a submission to the *Journal of Poetry and Psychology* entitled, "Poetry and the Cognitive Psychology of Metrical Constructs." The manuscript is 40 pages long and includes 4 tables and 1 figure. I wish for the manuscript to be given a masked review and request that it not be sent to my ex-husband [name blocked out] for review. Although he is an expert in the area, I do not believe that he would be able to provide an unbiased review at this time.

Some of the data from this paper were previously presented at the annual meeting of the Poetry and Psychology Society in San Diego (March 1999). This is one of a series of papers examining cognition and creative writing (see references for a listing of those published and in press). There is some overlap in the content of the introduction sections, which we have noted in the text. We would be happy to provide copies of the other manuscripts if there should be any concern about duplicate or fragmented publication.

My coauthors and I do not have any interests that might be interpreted as influencing the research, and APA ethical standards were followed in the conduct of the study.

I have enclosed a copy of the permission granted us for the adaptation we made to the figure; permission is pending from the publisher for the poetry that is reproduced.

I will be serving as the corresponding author for this manuscript. All of the authors listed in the byline have agreed to the byline order and to submission of the manuscript in this form. I have assumed responsibility for keeping my coauthors informed of our progress through the editorial review process, the content of the reviews, and any revisions made. I understand that, if accepted for publication, a certification of authorship form will be required that all coauthors will sign.

Sincerely,

Janet Sestina, PhD
Associate Professor
University of Melville
112 Oceanside Drive
Quequeeg, ME 20031-2221

218-555-1212 (voice)
218-555-1213 (fax)
jsestina@melville.edu

Index

Controversial issues
   treatment in introductions,
      16–17, **1.08**
Coordinating conjunctions
   in parallel construction, 57–
      60, **2.11**
   used in pairs, 58–60, **2.11**
Copies
   number required, 303, **5.25**
   theses, dissertations, and
      student paper
      requirements, 325, **6.02**
Copy editors, 357, **8.09**
Copy manuscript, 321–322
Copyediting
   correspondence concerning,
      334–335, **7.03**
   electronic manuscripts, 336,
      7.05
   paper manuscripts, 335–336,
      7.04
   responding to queries, 335–
      336, **7.04**, 336, **7.05**
   reviewing manuscript, 335
Copyholders, 338, **7.06**
Copyright Act of 1976, 355, **8.05**
Copyright Clearance Center, 356,
      8.05
Copyrighted material
   author's copyright on
      unpublished
      manuscripts, 355–356,
      8.05
   checklist for submission, 382
   copyright permission
      footnotes, 202, **3.87**,
         300–301, **5.20**
   copyright transfer, 332, **7.01**
   figures, 199–200, **3.84**
   length of copyright, 332, **7.01**
   letters of permission, 333,
      7.01
   material copyrighted by
      sources other than APA,
         357, **8.08**

permission to quote, 122,
   3.41
permission to reproduce APA
   material, 356, **8.05**
photographs, 197, **3.82**
questionnaires, 206, **3.93**
tables, 174, **3.73**
tests, 206, **3.93**
Corporate documents, 259, **4.16**
Correction notices, 342–343,
   7.11, 348–349, **8.05**
Corrections
   manuscript preparation, 288–
      289, **5.07**
   theses, dissertations, and
      student paper
      requirements, 325, **6.02**
Correlational analyses
   sufficient statistics sets, 23,
      1.10
Correlations
   number of decimal places,
      129, **3.46**
   reporting, 22, 23, **1.10**
Correspondence
   concerning copyediting, 334–
      335, **7.03**
   interim, 305, **5.29**
Corresponding author, 351, **8.05**,
   335
Council of Editors, 345–346
Council of Representatives, 345
Courier typeface, 285, **5.02**
Court decisions
   reference citations, 399–403,
      D.03
Cover letters
   contents of, 303–304, **5.26**
   sample, 411–412
Critical reviews
   critiques from colleagues, 40,
      2.05, 204, **3.89**
Cropping photographs, 197–198,
   3.82

D

DAI. *See Dissertation Abstracts
   International*
Dangling modifiers, 52–53, **2.09**
Dash
   with footnote numbers, 300,
      5.20
   proper use of, 81–82, **3.05**
   spacing with, 291, **5.11**
Data. *See also* Statistics
   analytic approach,
      presentation in articles,
         8, **1.04**
   duplicate publication, 396,
      6.24, 351–354, **8.05**
   interpretation of data for
      dissertations, 328–329,
         6.06
   raw data, 264, 280–281, **4.16**,
      342, **7.10**
   retention of, 137, **3.53**
   verification of, 354, **8.05**
Databases
   aggregated, searchable, 278–
      279, **4.16**
   reference list style, 231, **4.15**
Date of receipt, 357–360, **8.10**
Dates
   expressed in numbers, 124,
      3.42
   of publication, 207–214,
      3.94–3.103
   punctuation of, 79, **3.02**
Decimal fractions, 128–129, **3.46**
Decimal quantities
   expressed in numbers, 124,
      3.42
   in tables, 157, **3.68**
Decimals, number of points,
   128–129, **3.46**
Decked heads, 158, **3.67**
Degrees of freedom
   punctuation of, 85, **3.07**
   reporting, 22, **1.10**
dementia, 69, **2.16**

Notes (*continued*)

    table material reprinted
        from a journal article or
        book, 175, **3.73**

Noun strings

    untangling, 33–34, **2.02**

Nouns

    collective, 45–46, **2.07**

    followed by numerals or
        letters, 97–98, **3.15**

    of foreign origin, plural form,
        44–45, **2.07**

    in phrases with present
        participles, 49–50, **2.08**

    proper, capitalization of, 96–
        98, **3.14**

    singular and plural joined by
        or or *nor,* 46, **2.07**

NTIS. *See* National Technical
    Information Service

Null hypothesis significance
    testing, 21, **1.10**

Numbers

    abstracts, 125, **3.42**

    ages, 124, **3.42**

    back-to-back modifiers, 127–
        128, **3.44**

    beginning a sentence, title, or
        text heading, 126, **3.43**

    below 10, 123, **3.42,** 125–126,
        3.43

    cardinal, 122–128, **3.42–3.45**

    combining figures and words
        to express, 127–128, **3.44**

    commas in numbers, 129–
        130, **3.48**

    common fractions, 126, **3.43**

    dates, 124, **3.42**

    decimal fractions, 128–129,
        3.46

    decimal quantities, 124, **3.42**

    determining number of
        decimal places, 129, **3.46**

    expressed in figures, 122–125,
        3.42

    expressed in words, 125–127,
        3.43

    fractions, 124, **3.42**

    general style rule, 122

    identifying displayed formulas
        and equations, 84, **3.07**

    lists of, 125, **3.42**

    money, 124, **3.42**

    numerals as numerals, 124,
        3.42

    one, 126, **3.43**

    ordinal, 128, **3.45**

    parts of books and tables,
        125, **3.42**

    percentages, 124, **3.42**

    percentiles and quartiles, 124,
        3.42

    plurals of, 130, **3.49**

    population size, 124, **3.42**

    preceding a unit of
        measurement, 123, **3.42**

    pronoun agreement with
        antecedent, 47, **2.08**

    punctuation of, 79, **3.02**

    ratios, 124, **3.42**

    reference list style, 216, 219,
        4.03

    roman numerals, 129, **3.47**

    rounded large numbers, 127,
        3.44

    samples and subsamples, 124,
        3.42

    scale scores and points, 124,
        3.42

    series, 125, **3.42**

    statistical or mathematical
        functions, 124, **3.42**

    subject-verb agreement, 44,
        2.07

    subjects in an experiment,
        124, **3.42**

    table numbers, 153, **3.65**

    10 and above, 122, **3.42**

    time, 124, **3.42**

    universally accepted usage,
        127, **3.43**

    zero, 126, **3.43**

Numbers, ranges of, 291, **5.11**

O

Observed cell means
    reporting, 23, **1.10**

Ohs, 285, **5.02**

older person, 69, **2.16**

Online documents. *See also*
    Electronic sources

    aggregated databases, 278–
        279, **4.16**

    electronic mailing list
        messages, 276, 278, **4.16**

    newsgroup messages, 276–
        277, **4.16**

    nonperiodical documents on
        the Internet, 273–274,
        4.16

    online forum and discussion
        group messages, 276–
        277, **4.16**

    periodicals, 271–273, **4.16**

    proceedings of meetings and
        symposia, 275–276, **4.16**

    reference list style, 223–224,
        4.07

    technical and research reports,
        274–275, **4.16**

Online forum messages
    reference list style, 276–277,
        4.16

one, 126, **3.43,** 294, **5.14**

100% graphs, 179, **3.77**

only
    as misplaced modifier, 51,
        2.09

or
    usage with *either,* 59–60, **2.11**

Oral presentations, 329–330

Order statistics
    sufficient statistics sets, 23,
        1.10

requirements, 325–326, **6.02**

types of tables, 160–169, **3.69**

use in Results section, 21, **1.10**

Technical and research reports

Internet documents, 274–275, **4.16**

reference list style, 234, 255–259, **4.16**

Technical production editors, 357, **8.09**

Technical terminology

italicizing, 101, **3.19**

use of, 35, **2.03**

Telephone conversations, 214, **3.102**

Television broadcasts and series, 267, **4.16**

Telnet, 270, **4.16**

Temporary compounds, 90, 92–93, **3.11**

Tenses. *See* Verbs

Test item materials

punctuation of, 82–83, **3.06**

Test scores

italicizing, 101, **3.19**

Test titles

capitalization of, 98–99, **3.16**

Tests

in appendixes, 206, **3.93**

Text

manuscript preparation, 298, **5.17**

that

gender agreement with antecedent, 48, **2.08**

versus *which*, 55, **2.10**

Theoretical articles

abstracts for, 14, **1.07**

description of, 8, **1.04**

Theoretical papers

sample, 319–320

Theories

analysis in articles, 8, **1.04**

Theses

content requirements, 322–324, **6.02**

final manuscript, 321–322

manuscript preparation requirements, 324–326, **6.02**

ordering manuscript pages, 288, **5.05**

reference list style, 235, **4.16**

submission of, 382–383

Third person usage, 37–38, **2.04**

in abstracts, 14, **1.07**

TIFF files, 195, **3.80**, 334, **7.02**

Time

expressed in numbers, 124, **3.42**

Time links

as transition devices, 32, **2.01**

Times Roman typeface, 285, **5.02**

Title page

byline, 296–298, **5.15**

checklist for submission, 379

institutional affiliation, 296–298, **5.15**

parts of, 10–12, **1.06**

running head for publication, 296, **5.15**

title, 296, **5.15**

Titles. *See also* Running heads

of articles or chapters

punctuation of, 82, **3.06**

reference list style, 226–227, **4.10**

book chapters, reference list style, 229–230, **4.13**

books, italicizing, 100, **3.19**

capitalization of major words, 95–96, **3.13**

function of, 10–11, **1.06**

microfilm publications, italicizing, 100, **3.19**

nonperiodicals, reference list style, 228, **4.12**

numbers at beginning, 126, **3.43**

periodicals

italicizing, 100, **3.19**

reference list style, 227–228, **4.11**

recommended length, 11, **1.06**

table titles, 155, **3.66**, 301, **5.21**

title page, 296, **5.15**

untitled work, 264, 265, **4.16**

words to avoid, 11, **1.06**

Tone of manuscript, 10, **1.05**

Trade names

capitalization of, 97, **3.14**

Transitional words

for continuity of thought, 32, **2.01**

misuse, 32, **2.01**

Transitions

use of adverbs, 53–54, **2.09**

Translated works

articles, 247, **4.16**

book chapters, 254–255, **4.16**

books, 251, **4.16**

Tukey test, 171, **3.70**

Type specifications

for figures, 188, **3.79**

Typeface

for manuscript preparation, 285–286, **5.02**

Typeset lettering, 190–191, **3.80**

Typesetting

preparing word-processing files, 333–334, **7.02**

special instructions, 303, **5.24**

Typewriters. *See* Manuscript preparation

Typographical errors, 332, **7.06**

U

UMI, 260–261, **4.16**

Undated works

reference citations, 213, **3.100**

reference list style, 225–226, **4.09**

Is Psychology Your Passion?

Become a Student Affiliate of the American Psychological Association

Enjoy the great benefits of student affiliation with the American Psychological Association—discounts on APA books and journals, monthly issues of *Monitor on Psychology* and *American Psychologist;* and much more. See all the Student Affiliate benefits at www.apa.org.

APA Student Affiliates: Please share these advantages with your fellow psychology students! Please photocopy the instructions on this page and the application on the next page and pass them along to a colleague.

Join the American Psychological Association

Please read these instructions, complete the application on the next page, and become a Student Affiliate of APA today!

To learn about student discounts on journals, books, and online PsycINFO and full-text article database, please visit www.apa.org.

To learn more about APAGS, please visit www.apa.org\apags

AMERICAN
PSYCHOLOGICAL
ASSOCIATION

Send your completed application *with payment* to the American Psychological Association, Membership Department, 750 First Street, NE, Washington, DC 20002-4242. Applications accompanied by credit card payments may be faxed to (202) 336-5568. For questions regarding this application, contact (202) 336-5580, (800) 374-2721, TDD/TTY (202) 336-6123, or membership@apa.org. Payments may be made by credit card, check, or money order (in U.S. dollars drawn on a U.S. bank) made payable to the American Psychological Association. Graduate student fee is just $40; undergraduate student fee is $27. Graduate students are automatically enrolled in the American Psychological Association of Graduate Students (APAGS). Undergraduate students may also join APAGS for an additional $13.

(over for application)

APA STUDENT AFFILIATE APPLICATION

(Please type or print clearly)

Full Name _____

First   Middle   Last

Mailing Address _____

_____

Phone _____ **Fax** _____ **Email** _____

- Have you at any time been convicted of a felony, sanctioned by any professional ethics body, licensing board, or other regulatory body or by any professional or scientific organization? ☐ Yes ☐ No *If yes, provide an explanation on a separate sheet.*

- *In making this application, I subscribe to and will support the objectives of the American Psychological Association as set forth in Article 1 of the Bylaws, and the Ethical Principles of Psychologists and Code of Conduct, as adopted by the Association, and I affirm that the statements made in this application correctly represent my qualifications, and understand that if they do not, my affiliation may be voided. The Ethical Principles of Psychologists and Code of Conduct is available on APA's Web site at www.apa.org/ethics. The Bylaws are available at www.apa.org/governance. Copies of these documents are also available to me upon request.*

_____

Applicant's Signature   Date

Please provide us with the following information: ☐ Female ☐ Male

- Mark *ONE* alternative that best describes your status for 2001 academic year:
  ☐ Freshman ☐ Sophomore ☐ Junior ☐ Senior ☐ Other Undergraduate
  ☐ Graduate Student ☐ Intern ☐ Postdoctorate ☐ Other Graduate

- What degree are you expecting to attain? (Mark *ONE* for highest degree for which you are currently enrolled.) | **Year you expect to receive (or have received) your degree:** _____
  ☐ B.A./B.S. or other undergraduate degree
  ☐ M.A. (*terminal*—not part of work toward a doctoral degree)
  ☐ M.S. (*terminal*—not part of work toward a doctoral degree)
  ☐ M.Ed. ☐ Education Specialist ☐ School Specialist
  ☐ Ph.D. ☐ Psy.D. ☐ Ed.D. Other (specify) _____

- Upon receipt of degree, will you pursue a license to practice as a psychologist? ☐ Yes ☐ No

---

PAYMENT INFORMATION

A. STUDENT AFFILIATE FEE (check one)
☐ Undergraduate ($27) .... _____
☐ Graduate ($40) .... _____

B. OPTIONAL APAGS MEMBERSHIP (UNDERGRADS ONLY: $13) _____

C. TOTAL AMOUNT .... _____

CREDIT CARD INFORMATION ☐ MasterCard ☐ VISA ☐ AMEX

Name _____

Billing Address _____

_____

Daytime Phone _____

Card No. _____ **Exp. Date** _____

Signature of Cardholder _____

PUBMANAD 01

Build Your Professional Library With These Best-Selling Resources

A-Style Helper™ 3.0

ware for new writers in the behavioral sciences.

ng term papers just got easier—thanks to the *APA-Style Helper 3.0,* the companion to the new *Publication Manual,* 5th Edition. The *APA-Style er 3.0* gives student writers clear and straight-ard help on formatting references, citations, ings, statistics, tables, and more. The *APA-Style er* will walk you through your paper as you e it. Step-by-step instructions indicate what ld be included in reports on empirical research, e reviews, and theoretical manuscripts. And the enient wizard feature tells you exactly where to t key sections for each type of paper or report. *APA-Style Helper* also offers assistance in locating reference formatting in the APA *Publication ual.* The convenient reference builder covers all s of references, including reviews, proceedings, s, periodicals, electronic media such as the d Wide Web, and more! esigned to save time for both students and

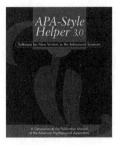

teachers, the *APA-Style Helper* conforms to the standards defined in the 2001 edition of the APA *Publication Manual* and is compatible with most standard PC-based word processing programs. *Available in a CD-ROM or download online.*

FOR CD-ROM: $39.95
PURCHASE AND DOWNLOAD ONLINE: PRICE: $34.95
ITEM # 4210502; ISBN 1-55978-830-7

SYSTEM REQUIREMENTS:
Windows: 95, 98, Me, NT 4.0, or 2000*; Pentium II 266; 64 MB RAM; 50 MB free hard disk space
Macintosh: OS 8.1*; PowerMac, PowerMacCube, iMac, or iBook; 40 MB RAM; 50 MB free disk space
*Help files for Windows 95, Windows NT 4.0, and Macintosh require Netscape Navigator 4.0+ or Internet Explorer 4.0+.

ading and Understanding ltivariate Statistics

Edited by Lawrence G. Grimm and Paul R. Yarnold

Reading and Understanding Multivariate Statistics helps researchers, students, and other readers of research to understand the purpose and significance of multivariate statistical techniques including multiple regression and corre-lation, path analysis, MANOVA, and many more. The editors

de a clear, conceptual understanding of what the stics mean in the research context, and they leave complexities of how to perform multivariate analysis her texts. *1995. 384 Pages. Softcover*

$29.95
4316510; ISBN 1-55798-273-2

rder today! Call 1-800-374-2721 or isit us online at www.apa.org/books.

Reading and Understanding MORE Multivariate Statistics

Edited by Laurence G. Grimm and Paul R. Yarnold

Since 1995, over 13,000 graduate students and researchers have relied on *Reading and Understanding Multivariate Statistics* for a basic understanding of the most commonly used multi-variate analyses in the research literature today. In *Reading and Understanding MORE Multivariate Statistics,* the editors provide the same accessible approach to a new group of multi-variate techniques and to related topics in measure-ment. Chapters demystify the use of cluster analysis, Q-technique factor analysis, structural equation mod-eling, canonical correlation analysis, and more. Whether you are a student, researcher, or consumer of research, this volume is guaranteed to increase your comfort level and confidence in reading and understanding multivariate statistics. *2000. 437 pages. Softcover.*

LIST: $29.95
ITEM # 431643A; ISBN 1-55798-698-3

Prices do not include shipping and applicable sales tax.

More Best-Selling APA Publications

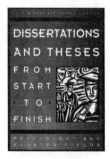